WE LIVED WITH A MOUNTAIN

WE LIVED WITH A MOUNTAIN

John McGourty

Flo' Publishing

Date of Publication:
2003

Published by:
Flo' Publishing
86 Park View
Wembley
Middlesex HA9 6JX

ISBN: 0-9544658-0-6

Printed by:
The Universities Press Ltd
Alanbrooke Road
Belfast BT6 9HF

CONTENTS

INTRODUCTION

The place that I and many others came from is today called 'The Mountain'. The area used to be known as Glenawley in the olden days, and lies in Fermanagh at the foot of Cuilcagh Mountain. From 1946, when the author arrived there, until the present day, 'The Mountain' has undergone tremendous change.

'We Lived With A Mountain' is one person's account of life there over a period of fifty years. It is not a work of art. It will have its errors and inadequacies. Neither is it a scholarly study. What it is I suppose is the melancholy ramblings of someone whose heart and spirit have never left 'The Mountain'.

ACKNOWLEDGEMENT

I would never have been able to produce this book but for the fact that I was given an immense amount of help by many people, many of whom have now sadly, gone to their eternal reward.

George Sheridan, who sadly passed away just before Christmas 1998, gave me unstinting help, advice and encouragement throughout the long period of this book's incubation. George's vast knowledge of the local history and lore of the 'mountain' was unreservedly left at my disposal, and he supplemented this information with copious letters about long forgotten individuals, stories and events. All this was further reinforced by his witty and humorous 'Reminiscences' in the 'Spark'. George also provided me with many photos.

John Thomas McGovern, for all his help, and his instantaneous reaction to my many diverse requests for help. Also to Jim Dolan and John James McNulty and Phil McCaffrey for similar help.

To Philip McGovern who kindly allowed me to use his account of building the road through Legnabrocky with his brothers Tommy and Eddie. R.I.P.

To the McCaffrey family, Monragh, who allowed me to use material from 'The Barrs of Poetry', by Phil McCaffrey.

To Nigel Haggan, for his account of life in the 'Mountain'.

The publishers of 'The Anglo Celt'.

The publishers of 'The Fermanagh Herald'.

The publishers of 'The Ulster Herald'.

The publishers of 'The Impartial Reporter'.

The publishers of 'The Belfast Newsletter'.

The publishers of 'Irelands Own', for permission to use many of their songs and poems.

John James McHugh, and his family, for allowing me to use extracts from John James's book, 'A Tale of Generations'.

The Appletree Press for permission to use material from Alan Warner's, 'Walking the Ulster Way'.

To the Dolan Family, Mrs Sheerin, Phillip and Mary Nolan, Phil and Agnes McCaffrey, Paschal and John Thomas McGovern, and Audrey Sheridan, for allowing me to use their precious family photos.

To Regina McGourty for photos.

To Terry McGovern, R.I.P. Francis Maguire, R.I.P. and my father R.I.P. whose tremendous regard for their fellow men, and their love of the 'Mountain' inspired me to write this book.

To Mrs 'Baby' 'Terry' McGovern, whose ready smile and cheeky greeting brought out hope and happiness on the harshest days, and who through bad times and good provided the heartbeat of the 'Mountain' for nearly three-quarters of a century.

And finally, to all the people who have ever lived in the 'Mountain' my hope is that this book has been able to catch a small glimpse of what it was like to live there when we were young, and that those who come after us, and are fortunate enough to roam about the hills, valleys, and streams of the 'Mountain' in time to come, have the opportunity to imagine and contemplate, in the long shadows of a slowly setting sun, what life was like when we were there.

CHAPTER 1

THE BEGINNING

As far as I can gather most of my family ancestors, at least back until the late nineteenth century, came from County Cavan. My Great-Grandfather, Farrell McGourty was born in 1841 and was a son of Thomas McGourty who lived at Teebawn (Teebane) which is about two miles North-West of Dowra, County Cavan. Thomas, along with other neighbouring McGourty families, was a tenant farmer, who farmed land owned by Harriet Parker and John N Stevenston. Harriet Parker may have married well because between 1874 and 1882 the landowners were named as Countess of Morley, and John N Stevenston.

Farrell, my Great-Grandfather took over the land worked by his father in 1881. He married Catherine McDermott from Leitrim and they had at least four children, Thomas, Farrell, Anne and Catherine. Thomas went to New York about 1900, where he had a market and grocery business at 917 Sixth Street. He wrote home to his parents on the 8th of April 1908. It is a very loving letter, and testifies to the fact that his parents are finding things hard economically, as is he. Nevertheless, he sends a Money Order for Twenty pounds, a huge sum in those days and promises to send more soon. Farrell, my Grandfather was born in Teebawn in 1881. He married Mary McLoughlin from County Leitrim and they had two sons, Thomas, born in 1914 and Farrell, my father, born in 1916. This family left Teebawn in 1926 and moved to a better farm of 87 acres at Gortnaleg, Blacklion.

My mother's family originated from James Maguire who was born at Dernaseer, Blacklion on 11 June 1870, and Bridget Leonard born at Drumelly, Holywell on June 1 1884. They were married at Arney on 19 July 1909 and had eight children. My mother, Bridget was born in 1918 at Roo, Blacklion, where my Grandfather had been given a farm of 27 acres by the Land Commission.

During the late 30s and 40s my father played gaelic football for the Blacklion team. This team won the North Leitrim Championship in 1938, 1941, '42, '44, '45, '46 and 1951. They won the Lundon Cup, often thought of as the 'Sam of the North' in 1939, but a dispute arose and it was taken off them. Then they won it in 1942, '43, '45, '46 and 1947. However by 1947 my father had given up playing.

My mother came from a musical family and she played the violin. She played with the Blacklion Ceili Band and was a wonderful fiddle player. She had to leave the band however soon after she got married when the infants would be coming along.

My father and mother were married on 27 January 1941 at St Patrick's Roman Catholic Church, Killinagh. At this time my father was working with farmers in counties Laois, Waterford and Wexford, digging potatoes or cutting and stooking wheat, or whatever work he could get. My mother used to get temporary work in farmers houses near to wherever my father was working. I was born in 1941 in Waterford, and when I was a few months old Aunt Annie and my mother took me back to Cavan, to Grahams's cottage at Cornagee, Blacklion.

When my father had no more work with farmers down south he returned home to Cornagee. He then began working with a farmer in Northern Ireland, and he slaughtered cattle and sheep and sold meat as well. In 1946 he began working piecework with Bord Na Mona in The Bog of Allen in Kildare, near Edenderry. He would cycle home once a fortnight, meet all the neighbours on the bridge at Cornagee, go to mass, play football on Sunday and start off on Sunday night for the return journey to Edenderry.

Life in Cornagee was idyllically pleasant. There were five houses close together at Grahams's. Fee's, Elliott's, Mason's and the Lee's lived there. Then there were other houses close by, like my McGourty Grandparents who only lived a quarter mile away. A lane, with a river alongside, ran past the gable-end of Grahams's house, where we lived. Farther on a stone bridge carried the lane across the river, and in the evenings the neighbours would congregate on the bridge to hear the latest gossip and discuss the war. The Elliott's had two sons in the Second World War, so the war took on a very real meaning in Cornagee. Peter (Petie) was born in 1943, and Kate in 1944. Kate died soon after birth. Rose and Ann, twins, were born in 1945.

I had a very happy time in Cornagee, playing about in the river with the ducks, or being mollycoddled by the neighbours. Most of my time was spent in Fee's, where there were three girls and four men, all grown up. At dinnertime Mrs Fee and all the girls would be flying about arranging the dinner. I remember that a lot of the time their dinner would be 'Culcannon' which I loved. This was made by boiling peeled potatoes and boiling onions and milk and adding both together when the potatoes were cooked. The potatoes were then pounded with a wooden pounder into 'Bruisee' and this 'Bruisee' was then arranged on each plate with a sunken valley in the middle which was filled with butter. When the dinner was ready the men would be called with a whistle, and they would arrive like giants, their great hobnail boots sending sparks all around me as I lay on my back on the stone floor. Often they would all carry me around the place while they checked their cattle or to watch them while they worked. The men took great delight in lifting me up on their shoulders and comparing our faces; their rough unshaven features with my young sensitive skin.

On the day that Rose and Ann were baptised I proved that I was not as innocent as I looked. After the baptism, all the neighbours congregated on the bridge on the lane, drinking and enjoying themselves. One of the neighbours had given me a slap a few days earlier for being naughty. Without anyone noticing I had got my hands on a hammer and given him a good clout on the head with it. Blood spurted everywhere but luckily he wasn't seriously injured. I got a good whacking for my dangerous initiative.

In the middle of 1946 a farm across the border in Fermanagh came up for sale. My father decided he wanted it and borrowed money from a farmer he used to work for and bought this farm. We all moved there in October 1946. On the day we were to leave for our new farm, Petie and I hid in a pine tree wood at Cornagee hoping the rest of the family would go on without us. We were found, and all the family's possessions were loaded onto a horse-trap. Our father had gone on a few days earlier, so Mammy,

Petie, Rose, Ann, I and the driver set off up into the mountain. We followed a rough, steeply upward road of deep ruts and strewn boulders as slowly and forlornly our beloved Cornagee receded into the distance. Eventually the little village disappeared for ever, and no one of us who left Cornagee that day has ever set foot in it since.

As we progressed along the road towards our new farm a massive black hulk of a mountain began to reveal itself in front of us. Our journey continued between high stone walls which were sometimes broken at the entrances to houses. After hours travelling we turned off the road onto a rutted track which twisted and meandered around small fields and rocky promontory's. As we went along this rutted track the wheel of the trap went up on a boulder and turned over. Rose and Ann who were on the trap were thrown off, and Ann was seriously injured. There was nothing to do but carry on, so our possessions were loaded once again and we proceeded on our journey as it began to get dark. After another mile or so the driver stopped and said he could go no farther. In the darkness he pointed the direction we should take, and leaving our possessions where they were we set off walking across the bog. As we started across the bog it was pitch dark, and we were all completely petrified. The ground was rough and slippery. There were great banks and boulders we walked straight into in the dark, which would nearly knock us out. Other times some of us became straddled on a hump, helpless to move. Eventually we crossed what we later found out to be the border into Northern Ireland, and into our own land, and if anything our passage became worse. First we were waylaid by knotted ferns which were over six feet high, and as we fought our way through the ferns we slipped and tripped on boulders underneath, destroying our shins. Sometimes as we fought our way through the ferns they would suddenly part and one of us would shoot forward landing on a slippery surface and our momentum would ricochet us into a deep hole, with fearful punishment in bumps and bruises and terrifying psychological battering which was enough to derange anyone in that horrid darkness. But as if it wasn't enough to be frightened alive by such a journey, we had another terror to contend with. The night was filled with a cacophony of scary noises. Suddenly, sometimes right at our feet, a big bird, a pheasant or something, would splutter out, creating pandemonium. As if in sympathy, foxes, other birds, sheep and rabbits pounding their feet, would all add to the noise, as if to denounce us. These noises are alright when one is used to them, but at that time the most frightening noise we would have known about would have been a cat, purring. At last we came to our new home, or at least we came to a light in the midst of blackness, and that is how I came to live in Glenawley, at the foot of the Cuilcagh Mountain.

The Mountain

Fermanagh in Northern Ireland is known by many people from all over Ireland as 'that poor county up in the wee north'. It is known by tourists from all over the world as 'The lakeland county' because of all the lakes and islands, big and small that are dotted around it. And Lough Erne completely bisects the county by running from Belturbet in Cavan through the middle of Fermanagh, entering Eire again at Belleek to continue towards the Atlantic Ocean. There is a saying that 'for one half of the year the lakes are in Fermanagh, and for the other half Fermanagh is in the lakes'. Even the county town of Enniskillen is built on an island in the Erne, though of course now it is urbanised far outside the island. Fermanagh is further distinguished by the rather bizarre or perverse nature of its terrain. For instance Knockninny Rock, near Derrylin, just rises up like a sentinel, from completely flat ground all around. Or take the Silles River, that flows close by, parallel to, and unexplainably in the opposite direction to the mighty Lough Erne, which it eventually enters near Enniskillen.

This north-western corner of Ireland, consisting of the mountains, lakes, rivers and glens of Cavan, Leitrim, Sligo, Donegal and Fermanagh is one of the most scenically beautiful places on earth. In the Ordinance Survey of Ireland in the 1830s, carried out by Royal Engineers, Lieutenant P Taylor says about Lough Erne - 'Lough Erne is navigable by barges and small craft throughout its whole extent, and presents by the magnitude of its waters, richly cultivated islands, sublime and diversified scenery; one of the most beautiful lakes in the world'. He says about Lough Melvin - 'Lough

Melvin presents, by the bold and lofty scenery of Sheanbrack, a portion of the Leitrim mountains, another of those very beautiful landscapes which so frequently embellish and adorn this supremely gifted country'.

The land of Fermanagh is almost totally unsuitable for arable farming, being so wet and boggy. Yet, the lowlands generate wonderfully moist and luscious grasses for the cattle, which allows farmers to produce excellent beef. But this restful and dreamy grassland forms only a part of Fermanagh, and when it meets the highlands it usually comes to a sudden and brutal end against the craggy, wooded and remote wildernesses, that form at least a third of the whole county. So if a visitor to this island town of Enniskillen, once a Maguire stronghold, looks to the south-west, they will see ranges of mountains far off in the distance. The greatest of these is the Cuilcagh Mountains, which nowadays provides a useful recreation area for hordes of adventurers and other visitors.

Cuilcagh is a strange mountain! It stands there full square in front of you. Some days it seems dour, brooding, as if it was holding up the whole world, often hidden and covered in mist. Other days it is breathtakingly clear, enigmatic, refreshing, its clearly defined lines challenging the sky. It is also a strange shape. From the distance it looks like an upturned bath, completely level across the top, with two equally sloping sides. Near the middle of the top there is a perfect gap, similar to cutting the shape of a matchbox out of the top edge of a sheet of paper. This mountain is further peculiarised in that its perimeter forms the border between Northern Ireland and Eire, and nowhere on Cuilcagh is there as much as a single bush or tree. On the far side of this mountain, in the Irish Republic, is the vast valley of Glangevlin, or 'Glan', an area that gradually ascends from the lowlands of Blacklion and Barran, and converges between the Ballinagleragh mountains and Cuilcagh in the boggy and remote wilderness of 'Glan Gap'. On the northern side of Cuilcagh there is a populated highland area which used to be known in the 1940s as Glenawley. It is now variously known as 'The mountain' or 'Marlbank Road' or 'Marlbank'. The natives of this mountain valley are often referred to, somewhat disparagingly, by the self perceived more cosmopolitan lowlanders as 'The mountaineers.'

Phil McCaffrey, the poet from Monragh in the Barrs, describes life in the 'mountain' in the early 1900s in his poem, 'Glenawley'.

Once in Glenawley we used to be merry,
Once in Glenawley we used to be gay,
Roving the brown hills with Tom, Biddy and Terry,
Or gay in the Curragh while making the hay.
Those were the days when White Murty Duffy
Excelled in the glory and health of his prime.
With scythe swinging freely he'd lash down an acre,
His three hour record is good for all time.

Though styled rough and ready, their friendship was steady,
There lived in Glenawley the best of good men.
Gave free of their labour to needy and neighbour,
And always stood ready to help out a friend.
Their wee mountain school was well put together,
With stones good and solid from Nolan's tight hill.
Half tons from a quarry were placed on the barrow,
When right in the handles was husky Pat Phil.

The valleys round Cuilcagh are fair to behold,
And lovely Legolagh is too,
When bountiful nature her riches unfold,
From Knockninny's Rock to Belcco.
Hear the song of the milk stream striking the pail,
Tunes in with the larks of the dawn.
This chorus rings early through Gola's sweet vale,
While the hay-making season is on.

Thrice blessed is the nation, 'twill ne'er defeat,
Her people shall never decay,
Where thousands of maidens, their housework complete,
Take the field with harvesting hay.
To save God's own bounty, they lead in the van,

Till the harvest is over and won
And they grace with beauty the fields of our land,
While the harvesting season is on.

A delight was to stroll by yon tumbling river,
That rips through the gorge and roars down the glen,
Sweeps round by the hill where the blue purple heather,
Makes lovely the home of the bonny moor-hen.
In young poaching days when we were caught taking,
A fine healthy trout on the end of the line,
We sneaked through the heather, all records there breaking,
The wild moor before us and Murty behind.

Yon pool dotted over through Tromogagh flowing,
A source of sweet pleasure in youth it was mine.
Oh merry the Maytime when south winds were blowing,
I tripped o'er the green banks with hook, rod and line.
Its course it is veiled in the mists of the mountain,
Enhancing the fame of the Marble Arch glen.

The hills of Glenawley, and her wide open spaces,
Get a wine laden tang in the health giving air,
Her lakes and her valleys of sweet sylvan beauty,
Are touched with a charm ne'er met with elsewhere.
The men of Glenawley are truly impatient,
To win for their homeland a place in the sun.
Their goal is a free and a unified nation,
They'll never cry halt till the battle is won.

In this modern transport age a nice tarred road zig-zags up the
Marlbank Braes carrying endless traffic into the 'mountain'. The
meandering of the road through the rocky and hazel-wooded
'mountain' acknowledges the relative luxury of modern living.
Telephone and electricity poles, water meters, new modern houses,
each adorned with the absolute minimum of two modern motor cars.
Not a sign of a horse, or even an ass in sight, but impatient tractors
clattering in all directions. Farther on, and then is discovered the
most potent status symbol of all, the transport of the 'mountain

yuppie', the all terrain three, or four wheeled motorbike. There are only nine families living in the 'mountain' now. It is a community predominated by old men, and old women, and only three families have young children. There is no 'ceihling' now. When the residents want to go for a night out, they usually go to the pubs in the 'Black' (Blacklion), or to dances further afield. The only communal building that there has ever been in the 'mountain' was the 'Marble Arches School, which is long since closed and abandoned. It was in this self same mountain that I was reared, and so I know that this is a very special place that has always been populated by a special breed of people, and I have never forgotten how I was brought up there.

Bailey's Folly (Bailey's Lodge)

Our new home was called Bailey's Folly, and was situated right at the beginning of the foothills of the Cuilcagh Mountain. Some Bailey man had given up building it because of the enormous cost of transporting stone from Cuilcagh. The Earl of Enniskillen then took it over and finished it as a hunting lodge. A temporary accommodation for him and his entourage as they hunted on the mountain. It was complete with kennels for the dogs, a stable for the horses, and a red roof made with tiles from the Florencecourt tilery. On our first night there, we had no beds, and had to huddle down as best we could around the great open fire. The moaning and whistling of the wind, and other strange eerie noises circulating about the large rooms, kept us frightened and awake all night. Our mother was absolutely terrified.

Bailey's Folly stood on the one green bit of land between the bogs and the mountain, and it was almost completely encircled by hills, for a long time preventing us children from having any idea of an outside world. The house was surrounded by many large ash trees, and up nearer the mountain, at the ruins of Hughie Macs house there were about fifty more large ash trees, and these trees were populated by thousands of crows that made a tremendous din. When we first came to Bailey's Folly, they seemed to be concentrating their whole effort in dive-bombing the house in order to drive us out. After a while our Grandfather, 'Ould Farrell', came and made an iron crane and a few crooks, so that mammy could hang the pots over the fire to do the cooking. We had no electric, no gas, no toilet, sink or bath. There was no road to the house, no street, no spring water, or any covering on the stone cold floor, or any light inside the house when it got dark except the light of the fire. Daddy would have to cadge milk from some far-off neighbour, but usually we had none. There might be tea or sugar but no milk. Or there could be milk but no tea. There would sometimes be bread, but nothing to put on it. our usual meal in the early days would be tea and fadge bread, and if some neighbour gave Daddy a piece of bacon we would have that. Sometimes, when a neighbour's cow calved they would give my father a bucket of beastings, which is rich yellow milk. I never liked it, but it is amazing what one will take when hungry. We ate tinned fish, because they were cheap, and sometimes Daddy would arrive with a few herrings. He also killed wild goats, we ate rabbits, and when we were really desperate my father would go and catch a salmon in the Marble Arches River despite the risk of being caught by the Water Bailiff. When Mammy baked bread she never had any milk to put in it, so there was always a blue streak around the crust. With the rationing there was a scarcity of white flour, and sometimes our bread had to be made with yellow Indian meal. We also used to eat rice, and Indian meal porridge.

My father gave up work in the Bog of Allen and concentrated on making up a stock of sheep, and he kept the rest of us busy gathering firewood for the winter. 'Ould Farrell' our grandfather, gave us a cow which at least gave us some milk.

The first time I saw my grandmother, Mrs Maguire, was when she came to stay for Christmas in 1946. My father and her weren't speaking then, but they maintained a sort of truce while she was there. One day I found her whispering to my mother, 'Jay-pee Bridget, this is an awful bloody hole.' Mammy agreed with her saying, 'Them rotten friggers of sheep make it far worse.' Mammy hated sheep. Granny taught us to play '25', 'Old Maid' and 'Patience'. Daddy looked on benevolently but never joined in, because a row would probably start as both he and Granny had wicked tempers.

The Big Snow

January 1947 was bitterly cold with a stiff wind. This is the month when Ann, who had lingered on for so long, at last sadly left us. Mammy was especially depressed, because another daughter, Kate, died earlier; and now Ann so soon afterwards was a terrible blow. Daddy got a tiny coffin made, and he and Mammy lined the inside with purple cloth, and Ann was laid gently into it. The lid was nailed down and a gold coloured nameplate fixed upon it. On what turned out to be one of the coldest days ever known, Daddy carried the little coffin out over the top of the hill at our house, on the way to Killinagh Cemetery, accompanied by a few strangers dressed in black. Two months later, Mammy's father, James, our grandfather, died.

January and February 1947 were bitterly cold with everything frozen. The ground was rock hard, and the sheep ran about in droves looking for something to eat. But there was nothing but the frozen heather. My father had to scramble about the rockfaces of Screg na Connell looking for ivy for them. It had been snowing for days and we were all wore out attending to the sheep, so one dark snowy night, Dad went off to Sheerins shop for flour or bread, telling us he wouldn't be long. There were always strange noises in our house, with the wind tearing through it, but this particular night there was an eerie total silence, and very soon we found out the reason. The snow was coming at such a rate that it blotted out all noise. Every crevice in window and door was blocked up with snow, and increasing mounds of snow were establishing themselves in front of our two fireplaces. There was nothing Mammy, Rose, Petie or I could do until it got bright in the morning. But it didn't get bright, and so we boiled kettlefulls of snow in an effort to melt our way out the door. But it was fruitless and then we ran out of firewood. The house is high, but it was completely covered with snow, and it is lucky it had a high chimney or we would have all been suffocated that day. We waited all day and eventually Daddy and a crowd of men dug a trench to the door and we were able to escape, to a degree. The snow was so high we were only able to travel in corridors cut in the snow to reach the turf-shed and water, and for a long time us young ones were unable to see above the rim of these claustrophobic snow corridors. Then my father had to try and find our sheep. It was impossible to know where one was going, because the contours of the land had all changed. Everything was white, bushes, trees, even Cuilcagh could not be distinguished in the white-out. The wind had blown the snow from the hard and frozen high ground, into the lower ground and depressions, levelling everything out. The wind and snow had driven the sheep to seek shelter in the low ground, and so they congregated in depressions which were quickly snowed in and frozen over, and then the sheep were trapped. Our father had little idea where they were, but Shep, our sheepdog, smelled about and located many. When Shep indicated a likely place, Daddy would push a long pole into the snow and when an eruption of steam hissed out of the hole, he knew he had found more sheep. Some of the sheep remained alive a tremendous length under the snow, as long as six weeks, but about half the flock were lost and the snow remained on the mountain until June. When the thaw came there was the most tremendous floods, with the water rushing down from the mountain. In some places where a torrent of water was rushing underground, it would suddenly erupt out of the ground like a volcano sending earth and stones in all directions. I have to admit that I secretly sardonically grin, when I hear townspeople and their children talk about snow. 'We might have some for Christmas.' 'I like a white Christmas,' or 'Christmas isn't the same without snow,' or 'Oh let me out to play in the lovely snow mummy.' In 1947 we all agreed that never were we more glad to see the end of snow, and didn't care if we never saw any more snow ever again.

Economic Situation

After the snow went in '47 the odd visitor started to come to our house. Hugh Melanophy from across the border, in the Barrs, was the first one who came. Visitors were so strange to Rose, Petie and I that we used to hide under the table or the beds in fear and refuse to come out until the strangers had gone. If we happened to be caught outside when the strangers came, we would stay outside until they were gone. Hugh was a particularly frightening character, because of his demeanour and the noise that accompanied him. He seemed to talk through his nose, and rather uncouthly at that. It seemed like a sort of a snarl to those that didn't know him. He wore a pair of heavy hobnail boots, which he had made himself. The noise he made, as he flittered and slithered across our stony floor was something like a bunch of shod runaway horses stampeding through a town. But Hugh played the button keyed accordion, and him and Mammy got on well as they swapped tunes and tried to play others together. Hugh would say, 'have ya iver heard this wan Bridget?', and he would play something, Mammy would present her technical criticism of the piece, like so, 'Well jasus Hugh that's not the way I'd play it. Listen to this,' and she would play the piece as it should be played, or at least as she thought it should be played. But Hugh would get a final 'dig' in by saying that, 'Well that's not the way that so and so plays it, and there's not much that he doesn't know about music.' But of course Hugh himself was no genius on the accordion, but what he lacked in talent he more than made up for in enthusiasm. The thought of this rough, artistically uncoordinated man, mesmerising us with his music is a bit far fetched, but he certainly entertained us. For when he started to play it was as if a demon had temporarily got a hold of him as he aimed kicks at the floor from all angles, knocking skelps off the stones with his hobnail boots. His whole body would explode with life, then contract, he would make horrible faces, as if he was about to die. He would elasticize himself into all sorts of excruciating positions, and then jerk violently as if in consummation with the crescendo. Eventually his passion would abate and he would finish playing, but he would never leave until Mammy played his favourite last tune. 'Pop goes the Weasel'. After a while we got used to Hugh coming to see us, and then we were always glad to see him come.

Another early visitor was Francie Maguire, or 'Connor' as we knew him. 'Connor' had a wickedly impish sense of humour which he used with relish. Daddy and him would discuss the weather, the price of sheep and cattle. Marshall aid, and why so and so got such a hammering in the 'Black' on Saturday night. Sometimes they would be wondering how the Marlbank-Greentown

Tug o War team would do in the next competition. Or at least 'Connor' would be wondering, because Daddy undermined his confidence in them by showing a lively scepticism of any tendency to bask in expectant glory. But nevertheless, 'Connor's' enthusiasm for 'Tug 'o War' hit some chord with me, and I have been interested in it ever since. But to Mammy these were mundane topics, of little interest really, and she could hardly wait to debate with 'Connor' the far more important bread and butter issues of the day, the state of Gaelic Football . . . 'Well Bridget, and what de ya think a yourr ould team now? Begod they're the worst iver I seen, and that's saying something.' 'Connor' knew well she idolised the Cavan team, and she would stingingly reply. 'Arragh what de yew know about football yomidan ya, an ya never kicked a ball in yer life?' 'Begod Bridget I'd do as well as some of thim omidans on the field the last day. There's ones on that Cavan team that need to be taken away to the sanatorium. Isn't that right Farrell?' My father would straighten himself up and say 'Arragh, the two of yis is ravin'. They'd be better taking them all away, and bringing out the ould codgers in the sanatorium, they'd do better. They couldn't do any worse.' In the face of this opposition Mammy would be speechless, and go off in a huff to rattle her pots, and make more bread. But 'Connor' was a very good-natured, and magnanimous debater, and so him and Mammy would always part on good terms, because in the end he would say, 'Ahhh . . . There's nothing like a good laff Missus, but by God woman, I'm telling you we'll get this team right yit.'

On the 3rd of August 1947 at Croke Park, Cavan defeated Roscommon 3-4 to 0-6 in the All Ireland semi final. The only one in the 'mountain' to have a radio at that time was Robert Sheridan, George Sheridan's father, and Mammy went off to see the match. She was like a bee buzzing, she was so excited when she returned. John Joe O'Reilly was the greatest captain of a team that was ever known. Simon Deignan, P J Duke, Tony Tighe, Mich Higgins, we knew everything about them, and God help anyone who made snide remarks about the Cavan team after that. On the 10th of August, Kerry beat Meath by nine points, so it was Kerry and Cavan in the 1947 All Ireland Final.

Daddy got an oil lamp and so we had light at last, that is when we had paraffin oil. Then we all helped to paint the inside of the house, though the colour scheme wouldn't have been all that harmonious. I remember the bottom half of the walls were painted bright blue and the top half green. Between these two Mammy used in ingenious template to paint in yellow running ducks. Sometimes there was a border underneath the ducks, giving the impression they were running along the top of a wall, and the green above seemed to be a field in the distance . . . 'Connor' arrived one day in a great state of excitement, and he could hardly wait to show us his new harmonica. For once Mammy and him didn't argue about Gaelic football, but instead played music for a couple of hours. 'Connor' said to me, 'Come here John till I show you how to play the 'French Fiddle'.' Sadly it takes longer than a few moments to learn to play, but yet even then I was inspired to some day master it, and thanks to 'Connor' I did master it, and it is the only musical instrument that I ever learned to play. But that day 'Connor' and Mammy played music instead of arguing was, one could say, the calm before the storm, for the All Ireland Final was fast approaching.

The big day came on the 14th September 1947 and the match was played in the Polo Grounds New York. The reason it was played there was to give a boost to the immigrant Irish after the Great War. Mammy and Daddy went off to hear it at Robert Sheridan's. (George's house). There was a crowd of people lined up around the door, and Mammy being tiny was hidden at the back. According to Daddy she was leppin' with the excitement of the occasion, and the fact that she couldn't hear Michael O'hEithir's commentary clearly. There was great excitement in New York too because the game started late and the allotted transmission time had run out, with the game still not finished. Michael O'hEithir had to plead for more transmission time in order to finish the commentary on the game. The game was played in stifling hot conditions, totally unsuitable for Irish Gaelic footballers. The laugh was that my father, and others, had their scepticism totally catered for as Cavan were almost annihilated by Kerry in the first half. Mammy had to stand there as her fellow listeners denounced the efforts of her heroes. Kerry players were sending in goals and points from all directions and at a critical period they were 8 points in front of Cavan. But this was no game or no day for the fainthearted, and Cavan organised themselves into a bewildering comeback as they fairly scorched across the field, destroying Kerry. By the end of the first half they had clawed their way back to lead by one point, 2-5 to 2-4. In the second half Kerry disintegrated, being no match for the now rampaging Cavan who won the only All Ireland Final ever to be played outside Ireland by 2-11 to 2-7. There is no doubt that this was probably the happiest and proudest day of my mother's life. Her prayers had been answered, her heroes had not let her down and from that day forward the players of that famous Cavan team were bestowed with an almost biblical reverence in our house and in our lives.

The Road, The Drain, The Radio, Reeds Rock

Nearly everything happened in 1948, but gratefully there was just a normal snow that year. In the spring Daddy had two almost laughable ideas, which he thought were necessary for the progress of the farm. First he decided we should make a road into the house, because everything that came to the house, like groceries, bags of flour or potatoes all had to be carried there by him over hedges and ditches, hills and hollows. And secondly he decided to make a drain through the bog to drain the land at the house. Completing these jobs with the machinery that there is today would be no small task, but in 1948 Daddy had only a turfspade, shovel and a crowbar, and Petie and I to help him. He started his road out at the Marlbank Road on what he thought was the best route to the house. The causeway he cut through the limestone rock there is still visible, but the route was impossible, up and down over hills and eventually he aborted the work. Instead he started on the drain, which was about three hundred metres long, two metres wide and two or three deep. This was a terrifying drain for me and Petie for five long years, as we worked through the day into the ink black night. Daddy skinned the scraws off the top of the ground and it was Petie's and my job to roll these up and then roll them to a depression in the ground to make it more level. The sharp heather used to take the skin off our arms and legs, and then the chemicals of the bog infected our injuries leaving us constantly burning and in terrible agony. We would be covered from head to foot in mud, and often barely able to move from tiredness. In the summer the midges would attack us, nipping every part of our bodies, and in the winter we would be criss-crossed with severe lacerations which we got from constantly falling on the slippery ice of the bog. The winter was by far the worst time on the drain as the elements seemed to conspire to punish us. It was nearly always pouring rain and our rags of clothes would be soaking. Violent squalls or hailstone storms would rage across the unsheltered bog. We would have to stand there helpless looking at the dreadful storm approaching. It was just as if a massive army was about to overrun and annihilate us. Our feet, hands and ears would become frozen, and then we had no option but go to the house and get some hot water to thaw out before carrying on again. The only weather that stopped work was the snow.

About the half of our sheep died in the spring, and a post-mortem showed they died from Anthrax, which is dangerous to humans, so we had to be careful. Daddy used to periodically go off to Mayo and Donegal buying and selling sheep, trying to make a few pounds. One day he sharpened up his old 'Macs Smile' razor blade on a jampot and shaved ready to go to Mayo. When he was ready he found all his money had disappeared. It was a real disaster, an awful thing to happen, and Daddy had a fearful temper. It was always shoot first and ask questions afterwards with him. But this day he was unbelievably quiet. It was a revelation, especially as he soon found out that his new sheepdog had chewed his money into chaff.

He started the road on a completely different route, and so then our work used to alternate between the road and the drain, as conditions or other things dictated. The road was about five hundred metres long and there was two main obstacles. One was that the track of the road had to be cut out of the side of a hill for two hundred and fifty metres, and the other was how to get the road across a swamp.

Also in the spring of '48, my father set potatoes in the garden at the back of the house and shortly afterwards for the first time since we came there people started coming to our bog to cut turf. Andy Reid from Rossa in the lowlands was the first who came. He looked a bit frightening at first, more like a soldier from the war than a turfcutter. He was dressed in Army khaki, and carried tin porringers and an army knapsack. On his head he wore a decorated hat similar to what the Union soldiers wore in the American Civil War. But his strange garb belied his ability to work hard in the bog, and he was the epitome of kindness itself. He always carried extra food in his knapsack, and never left the bog without giving us something to eat. He would bring us lovely wheaten meal bread, with proper butter and sometimes bits of jam for our own bread. He would also bring his saved up newspapers which Mammy enjoyed reading, and the rest of us liked looking at the pictures. Another popular turfcutter was Bertie Sheridan. If one could liken Andy Reid to the army, Bertie Sheridan's arrival in the bog could be likened to a concert at the Royal Albert Hall, with him as the leading comedian. Bertie was always accompanied by a huge entourage and he seemed to approach the job of saving turf less as a chore, more of an event. When he came to bring his turf home his retinue would consist of four or five dogs, about fourteen asses, hordes of children, and the mainspring of his outfit, cheeky youths. Like Wallis and the bouncing bomb, he was able to bounce his extremely immoral jokes off them, and enjoy himself as the effects reverberated among them. As the day went on, everyone else in the bog would be drawn in, and as eventually tempers flared, the crescendo of the evening would be reached with a dangerous free for all clod-fight, before the midges drove them all homeward.

As a result of not being able to hear the 1947 All Ireland Final properly, Mammy was determined to get her own wireless. She said to Daddy one day, after he sold sheep, 'I want money to get one of them yokes, wirelesses, or whatever you call them,' and off she went. She had to walk to Belcoo, and then catch a train from there to Enniskillen. Granny was put in charge of the house, and commenced to make currant and treacle bread. Petie and I were busy on the drain. What happened on the drain was that Daddy would cut a turf with the turfspade and then sling it with the same movement expecting me to catch it between ten and twenty metres away. I would then propel it farther on, where Petie would intercept it and throw it farther. But Petie and I would get tired, and it seemed that the tireder we became, the quicker Daddy slung out the turf. Consequently a great mound of turf soon appeared twenty yards away from the side of the drain, and when Daddy was away, as he was on this day, it was our job to move these turf and spread them out to dry. When evening came and Mammy still not home, we began to get restless and with Rose made our way to the top of the hill in front of the house. From the top of the hill there was a wonderful panoramic view of a world we did not yet know. Marlbank lay before us in restful splendour. We could see all the way to Belmore Mountain at Mullagdun, the rocky hills of burren, Ben Mountain at Doballey, and the mountains through Glenfarne and up to Sligo. When we turned around, the curvatures of the valleys on the approaches to Cuilcagh, made it seem as if, like a giant wave, it was about to engulf us. As we contemplated the view, Rose said 'I wonder where does Granny live?' Petie, the wise one said, 'That's where Mrs Dolan lives, over there.' And I said, 'Some day I'm going to find out what's out there.'

Mammy got her radio all right, but she had to leave it someplace, it was very heavy and Daddy collected it a few days later. Daddy was so busy now with roads, drains, sheep etc. that he made an arrangement with Charlie Cha (Maguire) to help him with the sheep. And so one day the two of them arrived with the radio, and Charlie knew how to make it work. He said 'Where de ya want it Missus?' 'Put it in that window Charlie, beside the bucket of water.' 'Jasus Christ woman, you're not putting it in the damp bloody window, of all places. Have you no bloody stand to perch it on?' 'I'll perch you on a stand in a minute Charlie. Take a look around. Can ya see a stand anywhere?' 'Right then Missus, if ya want it in the frigging wet window where it's going to be blown to bloody bits by lightning . . . There now Missus, isn't she the nice one.' A beech tree post the height of a telephone pole was set in the ground, about ten metres away from the house, with a bare wire running from the top of the post to the radio and insulated from the earth all the way. A steel bar was driven into the ground and another bare wire came from it to the wireless. Put a dry battery inside the radio and a wet battery outside and the 'yoke' was ready to go, though it took some courage for someone to switch it on. It was a beautiful radio no doubt. One half of its face was an intricate honeycomb of weaved gauze and the other half was covered with a lovely illuminated dial. Mammy had always believed that her violin was a Stradivanius, and it was strange that the name of this radio was a Strad. But the coming of this radio was certainly a momentous occasion for us all and a milestone in our lives. It was just as if we had got a new lodger and a very entertaining one at that.

Later on, one fine summer's evening in 1948, when I was still not seven, I seemed to have set off without any reason or idea where I was going. There were lots of people working in the bog and when Mammy missed me there was an awful panic. Everyone in the bog started looking for me through the holes and swamps of the bog and mountain. She often told me later that she always had to especially watch me because of my ability to get into trouble. In the river in Cormagee, she told me, I had submerged three times, when a neighbour pulled me out. And another day she found me pinned to a stone wall between the horns of a very angry cow. So this evening she was in real terror as time went on and I couldn't be located. For some unaccountable reason I had travelled out to the Marlbank road, and then climbed on to the top of Reid's Rock, which is a tremendously dangerous place even for an adult. That is where she found me, and it is a mystery how she ever thought of looking there. I have often tried to imagine since, what she must have went through as she approached that rock which has a sheer drop of at least 150 feet, that would have been between her and me. She was too mortified to punish me, she left it to Daddy. 'De ya think we're all eejits here?' he said, 'What did ya go up on that rock for, ya rotten haverail outa hell ya? Jasus Chrisssht of almighty I've never seen such an odious omidan in all my born days! Get up to bed, and stay there till yar sober.'

One of the most feared diseases, and probably the most feared at this time was Tuberculosis, known as 'T B' or 'Consumption'. This was a disease that respected neither young or old. There would be continual talk of someone near hand being taken to the sanatorium. Going to the sanatorium was like a death sentence, because hardly anyone ever came back from it alive. The disease could be transmitted between people, or picked up from milk or unhygenic conditions. When someone in a family got TB, the family would be to a large extent ostracised by their neighbours who would be afraid of being smitten. The patient in his or her own house would also be confined to a room, having only minimal contact with their family. My father would come home and say such and such a person had 'Tuberculosis Spondylitis' but I think that he said this for effect rather than it being an accurate description of the patient's disease. There were different forms of TB which it is difficult to believe laymen could distinguish between. Programmes of TB eradication in cattle, and the pasteurisation of milk led to the disease in humans being nearly completely wiped out. Thankfully I never heard of anyone in the 'Mountain' succumbing to the disease. But TB is still a greatly feared disease in Ireland, and no one that I know on either side of the border will drink milk from their own cows. It must be pasteurised first.

Even though we had to do atrocious work, especially me and Petie, when we were young, and got many's the good hiding, we had wonderful fun all the same. The house was so large and uncluttered that Rose, Petie and myself used to have great fun racing through it in the dark, playing Blind-Man's-Buff and other games. Petie tripped and hit his head off the bed once, getting an awful cut on the forehead. And after we got the paraffin lamp, Mammy and Daddy would entertain us by reflecting shadowy shapes of rabbits, ducks and goats onto the newly painted wall. Saying the Rosary was another enjoyable event which often started off the evening's entertainment. Now the Rosary is not meant to be enjoyable, and Mammy kept lengthening it to make sure it wouldn't be enjoyable. But Daddy, who could be the epitome of seriousness himself, was always ready to destroy seriousness in others. By the time the Rosary would be finished, us children, would studiously be trying to maintain our balance on the dangerous cliff of seriousness and devotion, and not falling into the void of hell's fire and despair. We would always fail, because Daddy would have us all, even Mammy, in convulsions of laughing, which is sometimes the greater coming out of concentrated seriousness.

Depending how the evening evolved, we sometimes might have recitations, because Daddy was really fond of them. He might have been away in Mayo and heard a new one, or someone like Owen McNulty from Gortmaconnell in Marlbank, could come visiting and then the whole night would be spent reciting and comparing. Often these recitations seemed as if they appertained to parts of our own lives.

Brian O'Linn

Brian O'Linn was a gentleman born,
He lived at a time when no clothes they were worn,
As fashions were out of course Brian walked in -
'I'll soon head the fashions' said Brian O'Linn.

Brian O'Linn had no britches to wear,
He got an old sheepskin and made him a pair,
With the fleshy side out and the woolly side in,
'They'll be pleasant and cool' said Brian O'Linn.

Brian O'Linn to his house had no door,
He'd a sky for the roof and a bog for the floor,
He'd a way to jump out and a way to swim in,
'Tis a fine habitation' said Brian O'Linn.

Because Rose, Petie and me never had shoes, only wellingtons, and because our clothes were just ragged patches, rhymes like this always stuck a chord with us. But a good recitation wouldn't be finished when we adjourned for bed. Not at all . . . Not likely . . . Mammy and Daddy would be in one bed, the rest of us in our own beds, and the fun would continue finishing the rhymes we had been at earlier, or making other ones up ourselves. Daddy always made a point of 'doing' his recitations in a blood curdling dramatic fashion, and after hearing one of his versions, you wouldn't forget in a hurry. So he would continue under the bedclothes, tormenting Mammy . . .

Brian O'Linn, his wife and wife's mother
They all lay down in the bed together,
The sheets they were old and the blankets were thin,
'Lie close to the wall' said Brian O'Linn.

Brian O'Linn, his wife and wife's mother,
Were all going home o'er the bridge together,
The bridge it broke down and they all tumbled in,
'We'll go home by the water' said Brian O'Linn.

When Hugh Melanophy came to see us he often sang, 'The Dying
Ranger'. Even though I didn't really understand the words, the tone,
rhythm and melody, as well as the illiteration of the words, never
failed to paint a picture of a great red sun, and the ground covered
with the blood of the brave young dying ranger far away in the
wooded west.

The sun was sinking in the west
And it fell with lingering rays,
Through the branches of a forest
Where a wounded ranger lay!
'Neath the shade of a palmetto
And the sunset silvery sky,
Far away from his home in Texas
They laid him down to die.

When they stopped his life's blood flowing
They found 'twas all in vain;
The tears rolled down each man's cheek
Like drops of gentle rain.
Out spoke the noble ranger,
'Boys weep no more for me,
I'm crossing the deep waters
To a country that is free.

Hospital

I was supposed to start school after the summer holidays 1948, but I became very sick. I was delirious for a time. The doctor came but couldn't find out what was wrong with me. I remember well when the nearest neighbour Mrs Mick Dolan came to see if she'd know what was wrong with me. This time I wasn't in the horrors' but was singing away for all I was worth, as I tend to do when unwell. She said to Mammy 'In the honour of God and The Blessed Virgin Mary, the cub is raving mad. He needs to be taken to hospital' . . . Daddy ran across the bog in the black night to John Gilmurray's, for he had the only car in the 'Mountain', and then Daddy ran back and carried me over hedges and dykes out to Hughes Gate on the Marlbank road, where John was waiting. Daddy will talk about the trip to the hospital to this day. We went from Hughes Gate to the hospital in Enniskillen in the unbelievable time of fifteen terrifying minutes. I was operated on straightaway, and found to have a ruptured appendix. The doctors maintained that in another few minutes they could not have saved me. John was a genius at many things, not least pulling Tug-O-War, and then coaching the Marlbank team. But above all he was a brilliant driver, and a gentleman, and after three weeks in hospital, him and Mammy came and took me home at a more leisurely pace . . . I would have to wait another year before starting school.

While I was in hospital Cavan reached the All Ireland Final once again by beating Louth at Croke Park on 22nd August 1948, and Mammy and John were recalling the match on the way out from Enniskillen. But John was also bemoaning the fact that Marlbank-Greentown were beaten by the RUC at the Tug-O-War in Belfast. For some reason I listened in awe as he explained the technicalities of the defeat, for even then I had a great interest in Tug-O-War. But when I returned home I felt very weak and vulnerable, and for a long time there was a weariness about me which was exaggerated by Petie having usurped me as Daddy's chief helper.

One night before the All Ireland took place, we had an invasion of visitors. 'Connor' came showing off his new hobnail boots, and as usual he was trying to rise Mammy. Charlie Cha was there with his latest girlfriend, to hear Mammy playing, and Hugh Melanophy was also there. Mammy played and Charlie and his friend and Hugh danced around the floor, and they all had great fun until this rip started. Hugh must have got fed-up with 'Connor's' mickey-taking, and the next thing they were knocking hell out of each other. But our greater interest was held by the fireworks arraying from their boots. They sent rays of sparks from the floor as they slithered uncontrollably about. Cups and plates, and even the table was smashed before their tempers subsided. It was lucky that Daddy was away, for his ferocious temper would have made it a complete disaster, nevertheless, it was no place for children that night I can tell you.

On the 26th of September 1948, the All Ireland Final took place between Cavan and Mayo. There were a few changes from the 47 Cavan team, but all Mammy's favourites were in action, with John Joe O'Reilly captain once again. Mammy had her batteries well charged up and the wireless was working well, as Michael O'hEithir began . . . 'The teams are ready! The referee throws in the ball! And the game is on!' Michael O'hEithir was one of the greatest gaelic football and hurling commentators that the game in Ireland has ever known. His passion for the game was so intense, his speech was so clear and precise, and all this was enhanced by his wonderful and unique descriptive powers. He was such a master of his art that one could clearly visualise exactly what was happening on the field. His commentary was littered with strange words like 'schemozzle', 'bamboozle', 'paralellogram', which you would rarely hear in a commentary today. This was a tremendous see-saw match with Mammy hanging on Michael's every word. Sometimes Rose or Petie, or even sickly me, who all had other interests besides football, like setting fire to the chimney, would get on her nerves and spoil her concentration, and she would let a shout at us. 'Shut up!' 'Will youse *shut up*!' Anyway it was soon all over, and Cavan won 4-5 to 4-4, but maybe there was a threatening omen there because Mammy's favourite, the great John Joe had to come off and be replaced by a substitute.

On the 7th of October 1948, Bridie and Frank were born. Granny was in residence to oversee the event, and during the day of the 8th an air of apprehension prevailed. Late at night Daddy was ordered to go for the midwife, who lived in the lowlands ten miles away. In the middle of the night the drama reached a crescendo, leaving us young ones even more scared than we were already. Granny was everywhere with pots of boiling water and eventually the business was completed and the excitement had subsided before the midwife came. So Frank and Bridie were the first McGourty's to be born in the 'mountain'.

By Christmas 1948, I was recovered enough to walk with Mammy out across the hills of Landliss, and past 'Ould Farrell's house, all the way to Killnagh Chapel for midnight mass. Daddy met us at the chapel and afterwards we alternated between using his bicycle and walking, to get back home early in the morning. This was the first time I remember Santa coming, and he had left the tiniest presents, but they were there. Shortly after Christmas, a parcel arrived from Aunt Jeannie from Long Island and it was filled with the most beautiful sweets and treasures. Rose got shoes and dresses, Petie got something along with a jews harp. I emerged with a yo-yo and a mouth organ.

Trouble With Sheep

Work on the road and drain had progressed intermittently during the last part of 1948, mainly because Daddy had so many other distractions. Mammy having twins, me getting sick, Daddy away most of the time after sheep, meant there was little time for other work. But from the start of '49 there was an all out attack on both road and drain. Mammy's brother Paddy came to work on the road, he thought it was time he had a bit of a holiday, but he gave up in less than two weeks. He believed that what we were doing was madness, and said 'You'd need a miracle to get a road across that swamp' . . .

But in the spring of '49 we were confronted by even more work, as it now became imperative to fence our land. This had become necessary because Daddy had so many sheep now that they could not be persuaded to stay on their own pasture, but roamed all over the mountain causing rows with neighbours. This fencing meant Daddy cutting posts in the lowlands, and then getting someone to transport them on a horse and cart to Mick Dolans. From there Daddy, Petie and I had to carry them all around our land, the farthest part up in the mountain being more than a mile away. Not only had the farm to have a fence around it, but also across it to restrict the movements of the sheep.

It was in the early summer of 1948 that Daddy had a tremendous walk with sheep. He bought fifty ewe lambs in Collaney, in Sligo, and because he had no more money left he had no option but to start walking with them. I wasn't able to appreciate the ordeal he must have gone through, but I couldn't help hearing the visitors discussing it and concluding he was mad. He had to walk through Sligo, Roscommon, Leitrim, Cavan and Fermanagh, tending to his bunch of sheep, and then he was only able to have a couple of hours sleep before having to gather sheep on our own mountain and walk them to the fair of Dowra on the Leitrim-Cavan border.

CHAPTER 2

OFFICERS OF THE STATE

Because of Daddy's wandering sheep, a farmer sued him for trespass, and one day investigating detectives came out to the mountain to ascertain the extent of our sheep's ramblings. Amazingly, on that day as the detectives examined them, all our sheep were where they should be, and stranger still, intermingled with them were sheep belonging to the complaining farmer. This was very embarrassing for the detectives, as their main objective was to collect evidence against my father. Nevertheless, Daddy, was ordered to round up the sheep in a bunch, and in their presence on the side of a hill he was surrounded and questioned by the three detectives. 'Are these your sheep?' Dad, 'Hmmm, I suppose they are. That one there's not mine!' Det. 'It's easy to tell who that one belongs to, she's marked . . . How do you know yours? I don't see any marks on them!' Dad, 'Oh I know mine by looking at them.' Det. 'Have you got names for them; do they come to you when you call them by their name?' Dad, 'Sometimes I have,' Det. 'Look at this one here, this one with the long horns, what's her name; 'Susan, Biddy, Mary - well?' . . . Dad. 'Oh no . . . no, no, no, that's a ram!' Det. 'Well, well, what about this one then, this one here beside the stone?' Dad. 'That's Paddy Pat John Tammy Pat Mickey Vicky's two year old wether lamb out of Hugh Mickey Frank James's spreckled headed Donegal horney that he bought from Sonny Petie Pat Jack that came from the fair of Bangor.' This interrogation went on for about four hours and in the evening Daddy was ordered to round up the sheep once again and take them to the sheep dipping pens at Tromogagh.

So Rose, Petie, even Mammy came, Daddy and I and the dog Lassie, all set off with the sheep to Tromogagh, not knowing if we would ever get them back again. It was a strange country, as we went along the Marlbank Road, but the sheep were mad, running across hedges and ditches, and kept us so busy that I had little time to study the terrain. We all went home, to await the arrival of the detectives next morning. Daddy went off to the pens next morning, and Petie and I followed on later and forlornly stood at the pens while the detectives questioned Daddy up on Gilmurray's Hill. Eventually a woman came to the pens and brought us to her house which was near the pens. It was a low, small, thatched house, very dark inside, and filled with other adults and small children. This was Terence McGovern's house (Terry's) and the woman who had brought us in and given us a good feed was his wife who was always affectionately known in the 'Mountain' as 'Mrs Terry'. Of course at this time both Petie and I had extreme difficulty in understanding what strangers were saying to us, and they had even greater difficulty in understanding us. But all the same 'Mrs Terry' told us that the detectives had tormented Daddy all day, some of them grilling him while the others ate their meals. Petie and I went back to the pens where Daddy and the detectives came down off the hill, and the conversation between them was going something like this. 'Det. 'And how long are you living here in Marlbank?' Dad. 'A good while.' Det. 'How long is a good while?' Dad. 'Ah, it's a horrid length!' Det. 'Yes, I know it's a horrid length, but could you say how long precisely?' Dad. 'Arragh a'm there a fierce length!' Det. 'Mister McGourty, you know nothing, maybe you know how many sheep you have then . . .could you tell me what number of sheep you own?' Dad. 'Ah I have a good lock.' Det. 'But how much is a good lock?' Dad. 'It's a fare few.' Det. 'Yes, but could you put a number on them?' Dad. 'Arragh I have a horrid dose'. Det. 'Mister McGourty, you have a horrid dose of sheep, we know that, but if someone had to count all the sheep that you own, what number would they get?' Dad. 'A fret of sheep.' Det. 'I know that, but how many?' Dad. 'A sight of sheep!' The reason the sheep were in the pens, and the reason they were questioning Daddy was because they were determined to seize the sheep. And Daddy knew that his only avenue of escape against these officials was to play ignorant. 'Mrs Terry' often told us later how they had all watched out of the window helpless as the detectives grilled my father for seven hours at the dipping pens and on Gilmurray's Hill. But for all their efforts they were unable to bamboozle him, and had no option but to allow Daddy, Petie and I to go on home in the evening with our sheep.

When news of the incident got around 'The Mountain' it seemed to induce the natives into a far more sympathetic attitude towards us. After all we were 'blow-ins', but now people seemed to be always sending us something like a side of bacon or a bottle of milk, a few potatoes or maybe a chair. And they also began inviting us to come and 'ceili'. Some nights when Daddy would be away, we would all set off in the pitch darkness with Mammy to go to Mick Dolan's, or Sheerin's, or Mick Cha's, where Charlie's father lived, for a few hours. Sheerin's had a shop then and there would be a great crowd there. There were always people from the 'Barrs' there, trying to exchange their few eggs for a bit of bread, or flour, or a little meal for their calves. This 'ceilidhing' was an awful ordeal for me, because of my excruciating shyness, but my fear was always tempered by the knowledge that we would get something nice to eat. Mammy would often bring her fiddle and play a few tunes to the assembly. Paddy Fitzpatrick from the Marlbank Braes would also play, and if Owen McNulty was there he would tell stories or give a few recitations. One of his favourite recitations was 'The Ghost in Boho'.

> One Hallowe'en night as the moon shone low,
> And dimly lit the graves in Boho,
> A peasant fated for exile,
> Leave-taking, crossed the temple stile,
> But in the graveyard, about midways,
> A ghostly spectre met his gaze.
> Just by the grave of Seamus Dhu,
> It stood erect as a ghost should do.
> Now startled by this ghostly sight,
> McFadden shivered with the fright,
> And turning round to flee the place,
> To his dismay the ghost gave chase!
> Now hard he runs to gain the stile,
> But the ghost gains on him all the while,
> Ah, such a hurried and reckless race.
> Never was seen in any place.
> But, alas for Jim, he got a fall,

And went heading over the graveyard wall,
The ghost pursuing in his track,
Went headlong over McFadden's back.
Now seeing Jim was nearly dead,
The ghost stood back and calmly said,
'Sure I only meant it just for fun,
To show you how a ghost can run.'
'Run' said Jim, all out of breath,
'And you're a sprinter, by my faith!
I was the swiftest man about,
And you would run me out and out!'
'But come, we'll stop these monkey tricks,
And we'll chat a bit about politics.'
And, this said, the ghost quite leisurely
Leaned his back against a tree.
'Tell me how the fighting goes,
And are the landlords still your foes?
They were the victors long ago,
And tyrannised the folk in Boho.
And is the law as bad of late,
As it was in '98?
What do you think of Lawyer Dan,
Is he an honest hearted man?'
'Ah that he is indeed' said Jim,
'I wish we had a score like him.
Tis' on this account my mind is troubled,
My rent, today ten pounds, is doubled!
Ah this was far too much to pay,
For a bit of bog and a rocky brae,
So tomorrow morning I must go,
No wonder that my spirit is low,
To seek my fortune on Columbia's shore
And lave ould Ireland I do adore.'
'You will not go,' the ghost replied,
'Rest, there's a turning in the tide.
For this very night, away I'll walk,
And with your landlord I'll have a talk,

And if he proves unkind to you,
I'll show him what a ghost can do!
So if you'd like a bit of a spree,
Perhaps you'll just come along with me.
It was a saying in my living day,
'A chat makes short a longsome way'.'
To see this fun, Jim's heart was bent,
So their hats they set, and away they went.
O'er highroad, byeroad, meadow and stile,
They travelled on for many a mile.
O'er hill and marsh, and woodland too,
Till at last a big mansion rose into view.
'Stay here' said the ghost, 'I'll enter alone,'
As they stood upon the landing stone.
He gave the rapper such a knock,
That McFadden shivered with the shock.
A window opened overhead,
And down, a voice like thunder, said,
'How dare you come in the middle of the night,
And set my household all in fright!'
'Shove out the bolt, for the night is thin,
And I'll speak of the matter to you within.'
The window fell into its place
And deathly silence came over the space;
Then footsteps sounded in the hall;
The ghost had walked straight through the wall,
And up the stairs he did quickly glide,
And the bedroom door flew open wide,
And as the ghost poked round his head,
A pistol shot came from the bed.
At that the ghost gave a scornful laugh;
'You might as well be throwing chaff;
Your shot has no effect on me -
I'm bullet-proof as you can see.'
And as the ghost walked through the door
The pistol fell upon the floor;
The hair stood straight on the landlord's head

As he paled, then fainted on the bed.
The ghost then over the landlord bent,
Saying 'How dare you raise McFadden's rent?'
'Ah' said the landlord, 'go way from me;
I'll lave it now as it used to be.'
'But' said the ghost, 'It was too dear;
He'll give the half, five pounds a year.'
The landlord frowned, but still in dread,
He muttered feebly from the bed,
'I will instruct my agent so.'
'No' said the ghost, 'That scheme won't do;
The plea must now be signed by you,'
To prove his point, he quickly then,
Produced a paper, ink and pen.
'Five pounds a year, for McFadden's land,'
Was written and signed with a trembling hand.
The ghost then seized the document
And down the staircase quickly went.
Now there was sorrow in McFadden's heart,
For he feared the ghost from him soon would part.
Then came a sound both loud and clear
Which rang through the world both far and near.
'Hark' said the ghost, 'do you hear that crow/
Goodbye McFadden for I *must go*?'

Mass at Gowlan

But our integration wasn't just confined to the Marlbank community,
because by now, Rose, Petie and I were able to accompany Mammy
or Daddy on alternate Sundays to mass across the border in the
'Barr' chapel at Gowlan.

God's Holy Wee House in the Barrs
By Phil McCaffrey.

Beside Gowlan cross you'll see as you pass a chapel of lovely
design.
Tis here our prayers do free us from cares and bring holy peace to
the mind.
A peaceful wee spot on Tom Briney's lot, far from the torment of
wars.
The troubled in mind true peace they will find in God's holy house
in the Barrs.

From hill and from dale they will come without fail, when God's
holy Sabbath comes round.
The young and the old they join in one fold, their faith is right loyal
and sound.
In modest attire with fervent desire, they come not in gay motor
cars.
But travel the bills on right willing heels to God's holy mass in the
Barrs.

The mass rock we see in old Mullagbee still tells us the pitiful tale,
Of bad days gone by, when tyrants did try to crush the true faith of
the gael.
But now we are free to bend our knee to the sun of the Bethlehem
star.
No darkness or light shall dim the true light of God's holy faith in
the Barrs.

With kind loving care young maidens fair come here at the close of
the day.
It is their delight to keep looking bright their chapel on Puttygarris
Brae.
They polish and clean with brush and with broom, till it shines like
beautiful stars.
That twinkle above the Temple they love, God's holy wee house in
the Barrs.

The natives round here are truly sincere, their faith in God's Heaven
is real.
When nearing life's end they wish for to send their maker this honest
appeal
That God in his love, when he calls them above to his home mid the
heavenly stars,
Permit them to see, as their soul He sets free, God's holy wee house
in the Barrs.

There were two different routes in the 'Barr' chapel. With Daddy we
went straight across the bog, then across the border into Eire, some
more bog and fields until we came to Melanophy's. Our way from
Melanophy's went across springy, moss fields, and dark meandering
avenues through endearing, small, softleaved sally bushes,
eventually bringing us to a road at Fee's. Mammy brought us down
by Mick Dolan's and across the fields to Duckfield, where there was
a cobblestoned road to the chapel. These two different ways were on
each side of a valley, mainly separated by Gorvagh Lough. The
straggling lines of people on each side of the valley were visible to
each other in the distance, and each side would be the subject of a
humorous but scandalous denunciation by the other as their progress
was monitored.

When we arrived at Melanophy's with Daddy, Alice would
be long gone, and Hugh and Francie would be in the sorry state of
confused dressing. Hugh would be on the street shaving, with his
gallices hanging around his knees, and every so often he would have
to sharpen his cut-throat on a strip of leather hanging on the door of
their implement shed. He would be barely recognisable because of
the mixture hiding his face, and the scapular that he wore around his
neck would periodically splash into the basin of water. Hugh was
always ready first, because Francie had to wait for the razor.
Sometimes there would be an explosive and oathfilled argument
between them as Francie got impatient waiting for the 'fucking
contraption of a razor' . . . I would often hope they weren't
'receiving'. At last Hugh would splash brilliantine on, and there
would be a shine off him as we all set off. Francie Bruiser (Maguire)
would join us, then Tom Jimmy (Maguire), Paddy Bruiser, Mick

Bruiser, Hugh Jimmy, Frank Jimmy, Johnny John Dan, Paddy Fee, Paddy A Corries, Jimmy A Corries, Terence A Corries, John A Fills's and the wife and children, so that by the time we got to the chapel, the few that started had grown into a large crowd. As we wended our way towards the chapel, many subjects were unearthed for discussion, and the conversation wasn't always about religion or devotion. The group would be having great fun recounting the bawdiest and most vile jokes, or satirising a recent serious event. My father was the worst of them all, always trying to bring about a revival when a particularly 'good' subject seemed to have been worn out.

Our excursion with Mammy, on the other side of the valley, seemed to progress with a far better class of people. Here it was tall men with straight backs, and ladies. No smut or dirty jokes in this shining, sanitised and exclusive company.

When these two groups converged at the chapel, it just didn't seem right. One expected a window to break, or a chimney top to fall off, because of the unequal clash of the colourful costume robed women, and the ragged, baggy, wellington attired men. The clash was magnified by the arrival of two other diametrically advancing contingents, from Glan and Stranamort. These warriors would be parading the adornments of a far better class of society. They would be outrageously bedecked in the most outlandish hats, with their bodies covered in gleaming brooches, pins and jewellery, binding all before them.

The mass would be in Latin, and good while it lasted. Actually I often thought that there were two masses going on. For a long time I thought Daddy was saying mass in the back. But it was different to that up the front, because the congregation seemed to be answering him, or at least a good many of them. It took a while for me to realise that they were all arguing about the economy and the price of sheep. One day the priest took his life in his hands, but he stopped the 'mass' that was going on in the back. I watched him as he purposefully marched down the aisle and grabbed my father by the ear, and led him outside like a bad child and told him to stay there. From that day on, mass there was changed completely.

But mass was a reverent and serious business, and the men knelt on boards on the right, and the women on the left, and Rose, Petie and myself had to go up near the front and do our best to look the picture of holiness and devotion.

On our way to mass, as we monitored each individual, I soon found that it was possible to tell when their psychological clock was off balance, and this would often manifest itself in some drama in the chapel, at a critical moment. One day I noticed Paddy O Dowda coming up the 'Ould Glan Road' and it was just that bit late to set the alarm bells going. When he did arrive at the chapel, he knelt down beside me, and everybody prayed, and heard the Gospel, and what have you. Mass went very well indeed until the collection box came round, and of course Paddy, with his timing that bit off, missed the box with his penny and off it went rolling along the floor under the seats. Instead of allowing the incident to quietly pass, Paddy bent down into all sorts of excruciating angles trying to locate the penny. Because of his exertions under the seats, his activities interfered with the concentration of the rest of us, and soon the whole chapel was in uproar as more and more people commenced to search for the penny. After some time, with the penny still not found, things calmed down and mass carried on into communion. Right in the middle of communion, when the previous fuss had been forgotten, Paddy suddenly stood up and shouted, 'Aha . . . I have her,' and he held up the culprit between thumb and forefinger for all to see, as if anyone cared if he never again had seen the bloody penny. The chapel went into pandemonium, and I always made sure not to sit near him again; I had quite enough of the limelight for the present, thank you.

On our way home from the chapel with Daddy we were always invited into Melanophy's, where we would get big mugs of strong tea, and a plateful of fadge bread and homemade butter. Melanophy's was a thatched, flag-floored house, which sat right alongside a clear gurgling stream. Just outside the house they had the machinery installed in the ground for making butter, and its by-product buttermilk, and this machinery was powered by their great Clydesdale horse, walking around it in circles. Melanophy's was sparsely furnished inside, and we sat on 'wee creepie stools' in front of the open fire. Even so, their house always gave me a feeling of comfort and contentment. They were always well supplied with their own homemade bread, butter, milk and potatoes. Both Hugh and Francie smoked and got 'The Anglo Celt' every week, and then Hugh had his accordion. I would have thought then, what more could anyone want. Our way home with Mammy was more sedate, and accompanied by far less sociability, as we went straight home with much more determination.

To feed our cow and calf Daddy took meadows from Pat Fee at the corner of Gorvagh Lough in Gowlan, which would provide them with hay. Pat Fee was an old man, living in a thatched house that was ready to fall. It was too dangerous for us to have our tea there, so Daddy and I would go over to Ned's (Cassidy's) and they would make it for us. When Pat Fee died Daddy took McCaffrey's meadow which was opposite and just across the road from the Barr Chapel. In the corner of the field near the chapel there was a little tin shop run by Bobby Armstrong.

Mammy would fill bottles of tea in the morning, and we would all set off for the Barrs to win the hay. We would get loaves of bread, and butter or cheese, in Bobby's shop to take with our cold tea. We would have a tin can filled with water and then coloured with milk, for drinking, and we were always afraid and wary about this can of drink in case we had offended a weasel and he would come and spit in it and poison us all. The McCaffrey's had no father, but even so, they were very jolly, and their mother was a fine looking woman who looked as young as her daughters. Sometimes we would have our tea in their house, and often they would help us with the hay.

Mickey The Widow bought their farm, so Daddy got a new meadow just across the road and right alongside the Barr Chapel. Only Daddy and I ever came to work in this field, and then we used to have our tea made by Pat Maguire's wife Anna. Their children were of a similar age to the one's in our house, and from then on our families have been very closely linked together.

School

In September 1949, Petie and I started school at the Marble Arches Primary School. Mammy accompanied us on that first day. She got us signed, sealed and delivered, and away she went. We were absolutely terrified as the rows of little faces arrainged and indited us for our future trial amongst them. The Marble Arches School was a stone built, one-roomed small building, on the side of a hill along the Marlbank Road, in Tromagagh. The playground was bounded at the back by weather-beaten sally trees, and at the front it ran steeply to the Marlbank Road. Inside the school, each row of pupils sat at a single desk. There was about thirty five pupils of varying ages and they sat in front of a large blackboard and fireplace, which was partly blocked out by the generous figure of the school-teacher, Mrs Gilmurray. Mrs Gilmurray had originally come from Sligo, as Miss Christina Moore, and then married one of her pupils, John Gilmurray. Because there were so many pupils, she used to delegate teaching duties to other pupils, and I was fortunate in being put under the care of the gentle Mary Nolan from Clynnagh, who was nearly finished. Mrs Gilmurray ran the school in a very humanitarian way, and used to scold her pupils rather than cane them, when they failed to attain her standards. On really cold days she would send a pupil off to her house to tell her husband John to bring us warm milk, and bread and jam.

As Petie and I progressed and integrated into the school, it soon became increasingly clear, both to the teacher and ourselves, that we had been instilled with a remarkable degree of stupidity, or in other words, we were complete dunces. Strangely, because of our different personalities, this defect had differing consequences on us as we 'advanced' through the school system. Petie was self-assured and more open in his ways than me, but he had a single-minded and determined streak in him. This meant that every time he was chastised at school, this chastisement was added (in his mind) to the collective quantify of injustices inflicted on him, and therefore, this great obstacle reared up in front of him every so often, to prevent the mutual co-operation and co-ordination of teacher and pupil necessary to gain knowledge. The outcome then of Petie's years at school, was that he learned very little. On the other hand, it has not prevented him from being a very successful farmer, who built a lovely dwellinghouse all on his own, as well as constructing a massive conurbation of sheds to ensure his animals live in comfort.

I was so extremely shy and quiet that Mrs Gilmurray saw me as a 'good boy'. I usually did as I was told, and kept well hid on the times when a rebellious class was inclined to give the teacher 'ould guff. The truth was though, that I soon knew on which side my bread was buttered, and that my shy and withdrawn countenance hid a far more freakish nature than Petie's. The fact was that I had a vile temper, a wicked broadmindedness, and an almost unswerveable determination, and it was only about this time that I was becoming aware of these peculiarities.

A lot of our time in school was spent on religious education, and this was complicated by the fact that three of the children belonged to a protestant family, and had to go outside while this was on. At the time it seemed to me an awful punishment, and later, a scandalous inditement of religion, that because they were protestants they had to go outside in the hail, rain, snow or wind and stay there, just because we had a few prayers to say. On the other hand, because they were happy and cheerful characters, they used to gaze in the windows and have great fun laughing at us, their carefree spirit a contrast to our apparent seizure and immobilisation with our veneration for religion.

Then we had singing, which our teacher loved. I can see her still as she conducted us with her rather severe and dangerous looking cane. Later, when unfortunately I had to attend another school, I often found myself having the rather nasty thought, that this same cane which Mrs Gilmurray put to such good use, attuning our ears to sweet music, could become like a device out of hell in the hands of other educators. But this wasn't our teachers way, and we all got on with our singing. This was one of her favourite songs.

John Brown's Body

John Brown's body lies a-mouldring in the grave
John Brown's body lies a-mouldring in the grave
John Brown's body lies a-mouldring in the grave
And his soul goes marching on.

Glory, glory, hallelujah,
Glory, glory, hallelujah,
Glory, glory, hallelujah,
And his soul goes marching on.

He's gone to be a soldier in the army of the lord,
He's gone to be a soldier in the army of the lord,
He's gone to be a soldier in the army of the lord,
And his soul goes marching on.

John Brown's knapsack is strapped upon his back,
John Brown's knapsack is strapped upon his back,
John Brown's knapsack is strapped upon his back,
But his soul goes marching on.

Another of her favourites was Danny Boy, (Or The Derry Air), and we must have sung these songs thousands of times, as Mrs Gilmurray conducted us with her cane, but I could never understand what they were about.

One day she arranged us and said, 'I'm going to tell you all why that gap is in Cuilcagh, because I don't want ye going down into the lowlands, for people to be making 'gaumbs' of ye because ye don't know why there is a gap in your own mountain!' 'In the olden days,' she continued, 'Cu' Chulainn and his men lived on Cuilcagh, and Cu' Chulainn had a magic cow that would always fill whatever vessel the men took to milk her. One day a cheeky warrior thought to himself that he would trick the cow and began to milk her into a vessel with a perforated bottom. After some time the cow began to wonder why the vessel wasn't full, and then saw her milk running along the ground. When the cow saw this she became very angry and kicked the vessel out from under her, and then she made a giant leap, taking a piece of Cuilcagh with her hooves as she went. Labourers stood transfixed on the fields of the mountain as Cuilcagh weaved and shuddered, and the light of the sun dazzled them, as they tried to see the magic cow and the enormous boulder passing overhead. The boulder landed at the foot of the Hanging Rock, and still lies there. The cow was never seen again.

We also worked with plasticine, learned to do sums, and recited poems like the following.

Lord Ullin's Daughter (T Campbell)

A chieftain to the highland bound,
Cried, 'Boatman do not tarry
And I'll give thee a silver pound
To row us o'er the ferry.'

'Now who be ye, would cross Loch Gyle,
This dark and stormy water?'
'Oh I'm the chief of Ulva's Isle,
And this Lord Ullin's daughter.

And fast before her father's men
Three days we've fled together,
For should he find us in the glen,
My blood would stain the heather.

His horsemen hard behind us ride
Should they our steps discover,
Then who will cheer my bonny bride,
When they have slain her lover.'

Out spoke the hardy highland knight,
I'll go my chief, I'm ready;
It is not for your silver bright,
But for your winsome lady:

And by my word, the bonny bird,
In danger shall not tarry;
And though the waves are raging white,
I'll row you o'er the ferry.

By this the storm grew loud apace,
The water wraith was shrieking;
And in the scowl of Heaven each face,
Grew dark as they were speaking.

But still as wilder blew the wind,
And as the night grew drearer,
Adown the glen rode armed men,
Their trampling sounded nearer.

'Oh haste thee, haste' the lady cries,
'Though tempests round us gather,
I'll meet the raging of the skies,
But not an angry father.'

The boat has left the stormy land,
A stormy sea before her,
When, oh too strong for human hand
The tempest gathered o'er her.

And still they rowed amidst the roar
Of waters fast prevailing,
Lord Ullin reached the fateful shore,
His wrath was changed to wailing.

For sore dismayed, through storm and shade,
His child he did discover
One lovely arm she stretched for aid,
And one was round her lover.

'Come back, come back,' he cried in grief
'Across this stormy water,
And I'll forgive your Highland Chief,
My daughter, oh my daughter!'

In vain. The loud waves lashed the shore,
Return, or aid preventing.
The waters wild sweep o'er his child,
And he was left lamenting.

Just because we were going to school, didn't mean our work on the drain ended. If anything it got worse, for now it had become imperative to finish it quickly, because all the other things that had to be done. By the end of September 1949, the bog was filled with people and asses bringing home the turf. For instance, Bertie Sheridan would draw away his turf on from fourteen to seventeen asses, and many other families would have similar numbers. The hooves of the asses inflicted terrible damage on the passes in the bog, and this forced Daddy to issue a proclamation. He announced that anyone coming to the bog with transport, ie horses and carts and asses, should not come empty-handed, as it were. They should ensure that every time they came, they were armed with suitable material, such as stones, boulders, tree roots, etc. to help to fill in the swamp. Of course many of them grumbled, and why wouldn't they, but they usually done what was asked of them, and of course eventually they themselves would benefit by having a road right into the bog. But when all these workers went home in the evening, Petie, Daddy and myself still worked on, on the drain, into the pitch black night. From about this time onwards, I always wanted to stay up late, so that I could hear the Soldier's Song, which was played at the end of transmission on Radio Eireann.

On the 25th of September 1949 Cavan was beaten by four points in the All Ireland Final by Meath. I think that Mammy had already realised that Cavan's greatness was gone, and she was subdued rather than devastated at the result as she saw that Cavan had been well beaten. Just a few days after the match, Paddy Pat Oiney from Glan was coming to visit us, and in the dark he fell into the drain. The drain was half full of water and Paddy had to struggle for three hours before he at last got out of the drain. He came hammering on our door in the middle of the night, and such a sight I had never seen. He was just like a moving hulk of black bog, and when he dried himself and recovered, he vowed never again to cross 'that bloody bog'. And he never again did. But next day I was feeling completely uncharitable for him as I inspected what had been the perfectly perpendicular sides of our drain, that we had worked so hard on, which he had now destroyed with his clawing to escape. Daddy too, who was never one to let charity interfere with his amusement, entertained us for hours as he satirised about poor Paddy. 'What sort of an omidan is he? . . . Eh? . . . Even you wouldn't walk into that John, as blind as y'are - The sooner he gets a pair of glasses the better!' Petie said, 'He'd need a stick as well.' Dad, 'He might as well get a dog to lead him while he's at it . . . Or better still get an ass to carry him: he couldn't go wrong then.' . . . Then Petie put his big mouth in it. He said 'But what if the wee ass tripped into the hole, Daddy?' Dad. 'Will ya get up on that bank ya rotten cluuson ya, and throw them turf a bit farther out?'

In 1949, the discovery of white sand on Maggie Duffy's land at Aughnahoo made it look as if 'Klondyke' like riches were about to hit the 'Mountain'. The report below, in 'The Ulster Herald' on the 29th October 1949 describes the discovery, as well as relating something of the history of the 'Mountain'.

****

RICHES COME TO THE FOOT OF CUILCAGH

Rare Sand for Glass-Making, Discovered by Expert at Aughnahoo, Wheathill. A Fortune may be lying in a ravine in wild mountain country at the foot of the Cuilcagh Mountain in County Fermanagh.

To a gentle, slim middle-aged lady, and her nephew, occupying a 34 acre farm at Aughnahoo, Wheathill, Florencecourt, it may mean the difference between working a small mountain farm and considerable prosperity as owners of the best-quality white sand for glass-making in these islands.

The white sand pit, almost without limit as to quantity, has been used by the Duffy's, owners of the farm, and their neighbours, for generations for building purposes, and for such domestic uses as scouring pots and pans. It is only six weeks since a young Antrim expert, exploring almost at random through the wilds of Cuilcagh for a sand that is now becoming a rarity in these islands, 'discovered' the layer at Aughnahoo, and only a fortnight since the samples he took were pronounced of the finest quality for the purposes required. Owners of the Cuilcagh source of promised wealth are Miss Margaret Duffy, Aughnahoo, and her nephew Cornelius Boylan, a native of Holywell, Belcoo, who has been living with his aunt, who is unmarried, for eleven years.

The story of the Duffy good fortune reads like a fairy tale, writes our special correspondent, who visited the remote country in which the valuable sand-mine is located, and interviewed Miss Duffy. The past year said Miss Duffy, was the year in their lives that made news, both good and bad. It opened badly with the death of her brother, Charles, in the late summer of last year. He was working out in the fields, apparently in the best of health that he usually enjoyed. A burning sun was shining throughout the day. Mr Duffy complained of severe headaches when he came into the small, three-room thatched cottage which is their home. Within a short time he was dead. There were tears in Miss Duffy's eyes as she told me the story, because her only brother, Francis, died also unexpectedly, eleven years ago, aged only forty-eight. She showed me his photograph, framed, which she treasures - and it is that of a refined, good-looking young man, who might be in appearance, Miss Duffy's twin.

As with typical Irish country hospitality, she put the kettle on the turf fire on the hearth to boil water for our tea, she told us the Duffy story. The little house on the mountain had been the Duffy home as far back as the family history goes - to Miss Duffy's great-grandfather. Her grandfather was Charles Duffy, and her father, Peter, who married Margaret McKernan of Holywell, and had two sons and two daughters. The two sons, Charles and Francis, were well-known cattle dealers in the North-West. Neither married, and both lived with Miss Duffy at Aghnahoo all their lives. Miss Duffy, quiet, cultured, well-informed, has managed the home alone since the death of her mother, and the marriage of her only sister, Mary Ann, who is now Mrs Boylan of Holywell, Con's mother. Con came to live in Aghnahoo, on the death of Francis eleven years ago, when he was a boy of thirteen. He is now twenty-four.

****

UNLUCKY YEAR

Not long after her brother died, Miss Duffy was taken seriously ill, she told us, continuing her story of the past year. Priest and doctor came, and she was not expected to live through the night. She lay seriously ill for months. When she was up and around again, though still weak, Con was out on a neighbouring hill at his work when he collapsed, seriously ill. He had a burst appendix and it was several hours before he could be got to hospital in Enniskillen. He lay in hospital and at home for several months. He was taken ill in April, and indeed has not yet fully recovered his strength. Then their springing cow, one of six they owned, died. They looked upon it as the unluckiest year of their lives - until the first days of September, when Mr William Boyes, of Co Antrim, landed in Aghnahoo to continue explorations he had begun in the district some weeks before. Some fortunate chance brought him to the Duffy farm, and the end of his search, because on the hill above the cosy little house, with its fields of aftergrass sloping from the shelter belt of trees that protect house and fowlhouse and byre, he was shown the great chasm, with rocks rising sheer to a height of eighty feet above the gurgling little Aughandran (Aghanran) river, where the sand is located.

****

RIVER BED EIGHTY FEET DOWN

I walked and slithered down a steep slope, dotted with thin sally bushes, down twenty or thirty feet. Beneath our feet, covered by a thin layer of soil, was the sand. And then we came upon a dazzlingly white sheet on the face of the hill, where Con Boylan and his cousin, Terence McGovern of Glangevlin, had uncovered the sand to take out fifteen tons for sampling. The white face is twelve or fourteen feet deep, as many wide. There seems to be no limit to the depth but

47

rough estimates place it at least eighty feet. It may be a hundred yards long and as many wide. But all these are minimum figures. it is certain that there are many thousands of tons of the precious sand in the mine.

Up we went to the top of the rocks, and we could look up to the top of towering Cuilcagh, behind which lies Cavan. Down in the valley lay the twin towns of Blacklion and Belcoo, and the broad sheet of Lough MacNean at the foot of the Hanging Rock, the back of which we could see, across miles of undulating mountain fields, with rocks jutting up here and there between. Down the eighty-feet high banks you could look to the Aughandran river, and about halfway down, like a big round white sheet lying against the slope was the part of the sand-store that had been bared.

The river is the boundary, on that side of Miss Duffy's farm. The sand-bank is, therefore, just inside her territory. In that funnel-like depth may be a fortune such as is conjured up by stories of a gold rush.

****

USED FOR BUILDING

At the home I saw a new byre in course of construction, the mortar used being a mixture of lime and white sand. It seems a sturdy structure, and Miss Duffy showed me with pride a figure of the Virgin and Child, part apparently of a holy water font, which had been found in the middle of the walls of the old byre, and which is affixed to the wall above the door of the new structure. Around the house were Miss Duffy's hundred hens, thirty ducks and thirteen turkeys. She got a first prize at Enniskillen Show for brown hen eggs several years ago, and about the same time a first prize for her homemade butter. They manage a prosperous and happy life up in the mountains, even if there is neither lane nor road of any kind to the house. They must cross fields and a little footbridge to reach the nearest road several hundred yards away. A donkey and creels are their only means of transport for heavy goods.

But it was worse when Miss Duffy was a young girl, before the five or six miles of road was made to the mountain from the main road, below the Hanging Rock. Her brothers worked at the making of it when they were lads in their teens, getting 11s (shillings) a week, and glad to get it. 'Now they want 11s a day and their keep,' said Miss Duffy. The road was made about 1906.

****

BUTTER 6d A LB IN BLACKLION

Before that they had to trudge the six miles through the fields to reach their home. And she remembers when her mother, in the old days, and she herself, as a girl, in the not-so-old days, trudged into Blacklion every week to sell butter at 6d a lb (pound) and a couple of dozen eggs to get ready money for the household purchases. Times are changed for the better since then. Two years ago, Con Boylan had to fight his way through five miles of deep snow to get a bundle of hay for the cows to save them from starvation, when the big snow isolated the district for a fortnight. The road was cleared but a snowslide filled it up again. They have to walk three miles across the fields to mass in Wheathill Church every Sunday. The making of little over two miles of road - a continuation of the new mountain road - to Wheathill would convenience them and would shorten the eight mile roundabout that lorries and cars and carts have to make to reach fifteen mountain families in the district. Down below Florencecourt way - are Fermanagh's best roads. They feel it strange that a few miles up the mountain they cannot even get a road at all to their homes and must make a three mile journey across the fields on Sundays to mass.

Once in a while they have mass in the Duffy home, when the Very Rev. John McGrail, P P their pastor, celebrates on 'the stations'. Mass is celebrated in the room and neighbours throng in from miles around. A whole pot of eggs is boiled for the after-mass breakfast in which all the neighbours participate.

But their travel difficulties may be solved by the discovery of the sand, for the young engineer who found it thinks that it may bring work and prosperity to the district. It will be necessary to make roads into the mine, if it is developed. And the possibility of riches from the mine is rather more than a dream.

From 'The Ulster Herald' 29 October 1949

****

Sadly, or maybe it was for the best, the high expectations held for Duffy's sandpit were never realised, and the whole event fizzled out without any practical results whatever. On the other hand, our lives at Bailey's Folly took a significant turn for the better when our father arrived home one day with a device called 'Ale Plant'. It consisted of a large glass container with a plant sitting inside it. When water and sugar was added to this plant it began to bubble and ferment and after a day or two the contents turned into a very enjoyable cider type drink.

One night in the spring of 1950 two strange men arrived at the door, and Daddy brought them in. They were dressed in grey belted overcoats, with black hats, and looked for all the world like Chicago gangsters. As usual Petie, Rose and I hid under the table, just like the dogs, as we warily watched and listened to the men. They were trying to sell Daddy a farm up in the County Leitrim, and also trying to do a deal over a coalmine that was on it. After much arguing and wrangling, Daddy bought the farm of nearly one thousand acres at Barlear, in the Lacagh Hills, but he refused to sell the coalmine. The farm was always known to us as 'Jimmity's'.

Smuggling

Smuggling was going on a lot at this time, and people used to come from Glan to our house with boxes of eggs that they had carried across the mountain. We would put the eggs into our loft until we were ready to take them out to William Armstrong's shop-lorry that travelled on the Marlbank road on a Saturday evening. This smuggling meant that there was a constant threat of being raided by the police, and it was rarely, if ever, that the police received a respectful reception at our house. Sometimes Daddy would have the loan of a 22 rifle to shoot foxes, because they killed the sheep. And one day an unfortunate policeman arrived. 'Where's this gun you have? Have you a licence for it?' Dad. 'What rotten gun? . . . What are you talking about?' . . . Policeman. 'We have information that you are going mad about the place with a gun, so where is it? . . . I want it now!' Luckily enough Dad had returned the gun before the policeman came, and he said 'no frigging gun here!' Oh he was in a rage, and he put his rough unshaven face up close to the policeman's. 'Now what are you going to do about that?' The policeman said, 'I'll search the whole bloody place if I have to.' And he did, but he found no gun.

A few days later, Dad was after bringing home a flock of sheep he had bought in Eire, and of course this was 'something you should not do'. The next day a Gardai arrived from the Irish Republic in an awful panic. 'Yi's are goan to be raided! Quick, where's the boss? Where the hell is he?' Mammy told him that Daddy was away in Mayo. The Gardai said, 'Jasus Christ woman does he ever lave bloody Mayo?' Mammy asked the Gardai what was wrong. He said, 'Have you'se sheep here from the State?' Mammy told him that there was, and he said, 'Well they must have heard about them, you'll need to get rid of them quick!' When Daddy came home late that night and Mammy gave him the message from the Gardai, he erupted into a fury, and denounced them all with a tirade of oaths. He maintained that every uniformwearer should be shot on sight. Guards, Policemen, Custommen, they were all the bloody same. 'Not Willie Brown Daddy: not the postman who brings all our letters and parcels.' 'The friggen' postman and all.'

Early next morning the police were trying to break down our door, and Daddy jumped out of bed and ran and opened it. Oh! They were all business. Straight up into the rooms where we had been sleeping, and they searched under us while we were still in bed. They could hardly have expected the sheep to be in bed with us. Daddy said, 'There's no sheep in here!' The Sergeant replied, 'We're not looking for sheep. Ah no . . . not sheep . . . eggs: and we know exactly where they are!' So then two constables and a sergeant rushed up the narrow, angled stairs, and thundered onto the rotten floor above, and straightaway, six big black boots appeared on the ends of six bare, cut and bloodied legs. The one policeman left with us below could not contain himself and burst out laughing, though he made sure he regained his composure before the enraged sergeant appeared back down the stairs. We never had more eggs hidden than on that week, and because there were so many was the very reason that we had put them into our cavernous cavelike well. The policemen slunk off, like dogs with their tails between their legs, and never again came back to raid our home.

But Smuggling was a serious business, and John James McHugh from Barran, describes his part in it in his book, 'A Tale of Generations'.

****

. . .'When the war went on a little while, everything here (in Eire) was rationed, and several things could not be got at all, you had to leave your ration book in a particular shop and then you could get nothing in any other shop. Every person was allowed a quarter stone of war grade flour or two loaves per week. You were also supposed to get a quarter pound of sugar and a half ounce of tea, but there were several weeks you could get none of these items.

There was a big black-market trade at the time where most things could be sold at double or treble the price. We smuggled all, as there was plenty of everything to be got in the Six Counties. Strangely enough, Customs men on our side of the border wouldn't let anything in. If you were caught you would lose your stuff and you would also be fined. We were never caught, as we went across the mountains which were six miles of the roughest walk anybody could travel. The Customs men went up there several nights, but we always managed to escape them. It was very hard work but there used to be a crowd of us together and we thought it was great fun. You wouldn't think it could be much fun carrying four or five stone weight on your back in the dark of the night over six miles, but it was some good crack that kept us going.

Owen Sheerin was the man we used to deal with. He was a very polished old man and always had a great welcome for us. We used to assemble in the kitchen and go down in our turn to the shop. Every time I went down he always kept telling me how good looking

I was. By this time I was nearly beginning to get proud of myself. However, one night when I came up out of the shop a neighbour of mine went down and to my dismay didn't he also begin to tell him that he was good looking. It was then that I saw that he was a very bad judge of good looks or else it was a way of pleasing his customers. I never gave much heed to anything he said after that. Whatever about his bad judgement in that line, he was very useful to us in other ways. He kept us in plenty of white flour and feeding stuff. We also got sugar and jam and sometimes we could get paraffin oil which wasn't to be got at all on our side. We also got plenty of loaf bread. Even though all this involved a lot of hardship, it was better than hunger and want.

People were denied a lot of luxuries during this time. Cigarettes and tobacco were very strictly rationed. In fact there was some shops where it was only seldom you could get any. Dried tea leaves and docken leaves were a common smoke for many. A strange thing was that nobody around here went off smoking during that period. When there was plenty of cigarettes on the market there was far more people going off them. Petrol was another very scarce commodity. Nobody would get a licence for a private car unless they were a priest or doctor or someone in a very important position. The horse and cart trap and the bicycle were the only means of conveyance. It was the first time ever that people were brought on a level and they remained that way ever since. When the war was over and when cars were allowed back on the road, every Tom, Dick and Harry found themselves in a position that they could afford to have one, thus leaving it that in appearance, that there was no difference between the poor man and the rich man. There is no difference in any way only that one has a bank account and the other one has none.

Well the rationing continued all through the war time and smuggling became more widespread. People started travelling twenty miles with horses and bringing two or three bags of stuff on their backs. This continued until it was brought to an end by what is now known as 'The battle of Gowlan'. One night when they arrived at Gowlan crossroads with their loaded horses, they were ambushed by a crowd of Customs men and Guards. Then the battle started. The smugglers threw off their loads, mounted their horses and tried to charge through. As the foot patrol was no match for the cavalry, they failed to arrest any of them. Sergeant Rock from Blacklion grabbed one horse by the bridle. The raider struck him across the head with his staff and knocked him down and rode across him. They all busted through them but when they come to Cornaha Cross they encountered more Guards who had the road blocked with their cars. They then took to the hills with their horses and escaped home safely. Soldiers from Manorhamilton arrived on the scene after the battle was over. Some neighbours living near hand gathered bucketfulls of the flour which was scattered along the road.

This didn't put an end to our smuggling. We kept at it all the time. There wasn't much danger on the pass we used to travel. It was all a wild mountain where the Customs men were not likely to be found on a dark night. The only place we used to be afraid was when crossing the road. We were always very careful then. When we got across, we knew we were fairly safe. However there was another problem. We were always told that smuggling was a sin and we were well aware of that at the time. It seems that we left religion aside during the war years and that we intended catching up with it again when the war was over. I do know one thing, that anyone who didn't commit the sin of smuggling at that time, should be canonised. I can understand why God is against smuggling, but I was always very surprised at how determined our government was to prevent people from bringing in essential goods that we couldn't get any other place, even for money. They claim that their idea was to make the country self productive by growing everything at home. They should know that the wheat we would sow today would not be made into bread tomorrow.'

From 'A Tale of Generations by J J McHugh

****

Halloween

Our lessons weren't the only thing we took an interest in while we were at school. Some of the other children in my class were, Bridget Maguire, Mary Ellen Maguire, Ronnie Moffat, Tom McNulty, John James McNulty, Paddy (Hugh) Maguire, Pee McManus, Tommy Dolan, and Frankie Dolan. Some in Petie's class were, May Sheerin, (Dec) Maureen (Connor) Maguire, Jamsie (Connor) Maguire, John James Sheerin, Peter Fitzpatrick, Eugene McCaffrey, Rose (Johnny) Maguire, Richard Moffat, (Dec) Thomas Moffat, May Boles, Anna McCaffrey, Bridget McManus, Noel McGovern. As Halloween approached, Tom McNulty wanted to know whether we had a good supply of carbide for the event. I didn't know what he was talking about, for I had never heard of the stuff before. So he told me how to put it into a can on a Halloween night and it would make big bang. He even gave me a bit to try at home Petie and I tried everything at home to make it work, but got no response, and soon became fed up with it. We told Tom that we couldn't get it to work, and he said, 'I'll show you,' and he did. At playtime he got a can somewhere and set it on the path to the toilet. He put in the lump of carbide and told me to spit on it. Straightaway it started to sizzle and smoke, with a terrible smell off it. Tom shouted, 'bang the lid on it!' I jumped on the lid, and then ran. *Bbaaannngggg.* . . . It shook the school. Mrs Gilmurray ran out in a panic, and it was the only time I ever heard her use a naughty word 'Jasus Christ of Almighty, what in the holy hell is going on?' I don't think she ever found out what happened, because there was no evidence. The canister had disappeared, never to be seen again.

But certainly this carbide was wonderful stuff, and by chance, Daddy, not aware of our new found knowledge of physics, landed home with a big lump of this carbide one day. Well; We were sending 'Dried Milk' cans in all directions. The sky was full of exploding cans, and the ground was littered with destroyed ones. The best cans were, Andrews Liver Salts and Tate and Lyle Golden Syrup cans, and they stood much abuse before we eventually caused their destruction. Petie and I became so proficient at this work, that we soon came to the conclusion that it was sort of silly just doing it at Halloween, and very often we conducted some of our best experiments on the day that Christ was born, Christmas Day.

CHAPTER 3

SCHOOL

Once Petie, Rose and I went to school, we were immediately exposed to the regulators of society. It was as if we were rabbits with everyone in authority ready to shoot us as soon as we dared to put our heads out of our burrow. First, our headlong gallop into hell, as it were, was halted by religion. We were threatened with 'hell and damnation' by Mrs Gilmurray if we didn't learn our catechism before the priest came on his visit. When Father John McGrail came, he decreed that there was to be no more going to the 'Barr' chapel. We must attend our own chapel in Wheathill. Father McGrail used to come regularly to the school, driving there sedately in his sleek and shining car. It was hard then to believe that he had any comprehension of our existence. Petie and myself arrived at the school in the most outlandish looking rigouts. Mammy done the best she could making our clothes, but she had only scraps of worn cloth, and my short trousers were often sewn together with six or more different coloured pieces. Then we had only wellingtons, to wear to school, or anywhere else. And I never remember having a sandwich, only a lump of dry bread, that would have become completely repulsive by our lunch break. Daddy didn't think much of the priest's orders, but Mammy was a saintly woman, and eventually began to take us to mass at Wheathill.

Then there was what Daddy called, 'The predator that stalks the land', The Schools Attendance Officer. The School Attendance Officer in my time was a Mr Drugan. He would appear around the door of the school, his trouser legs anchored by steel cycle clips, his shiny shoes making a disagreeable and un-harmonious sound on the well worn wooden floor. As a result of his walk up through the Marble Arch Glen, he would always be red-faced and puffing. This put him on the defensive, manifesting itself in pompousness and irritability. He always made sure to appear early in the morning, about 10 o'clock, to catch out the latecomers, or alternatively catch out Mrs Gilmurray, as she delayed filling the 'roll book' until the last stragglers had arrived. He was a stern, sneering and uncommunicative individual, who totally looked down on us and the teacher. Schools Inspectors and Attendance Officers may have been a necessity, but the contrast between our obligation to go to school and kow-bow to this most unfriendly official, and the greatness of our necessity to be at home working on the farm, could not be more profound. But it was true, I missed a lot of time off school, and Mammy was summoned to the court a few times, but Daddy's need on the farm for help was so acute. My attitude then to the Inspectors, was that when I did make the effort to attend, did they not know that my chores at home would multiply.

Environment

But going to school did have its good points. For instance, it gave me the chance to study the social activity of the community we lived in. In the good weather, Petie and I went across the bog, then skirted the rock down to Francie Connor's house. Francie would be feeding calves or weaning them with a bucket of milk. Mary Ellen, his wife, wearing wellingtons and a headscarf, would be flitting between getting the children ready for school, and milking the cows. They all always seemed happy and in good humour, and always had a welcome for us in the morning, and invariably offered us tea and a homemade bun. I always consistently refused these pleasures, because of my awkward shyness. But Petie, and all the family who in time came after us, were more sociable. Eventually, Francie 'Connor's' became a sort of half-way house in the morning as we waited for their school goers.

The 'Connor's' were probably just as poor as us, and indeed the economic situation was such at that time, with rationing, recovering from the war etc. that it was almost impossible for farmers in the 'mountain' to escape from penury. Yet it did seem that the 'Connor's' were attached to a somewhat higher rung of the social ladder than us. They had better clothes, their hair was neatly cut, they had shoes and handkerchiefs. And they had porringers, and sandwiches that they could eat at school. There was therefore, a more polished look about them, than the rag-tag bedraggled army that came from our house. Francie 'Connor' for all his mischievous ways, was an amusing and heart-warming character. And when the young fellows of the 'mountain' began to grow up, some of them would test themselves by being cheeky with him, and he never liked it. I on the other hand, not having a cheeky nature, inveighled myself into his good graces at an early age. I profited from this friendship in many ways, but especially by learning about Tug-O-War, Football and Boxing. I often felt that Francie wasn't cut out to be a farmer at all. His mind seemed to be somewhere else. I think he yearned to be a great runner, or a cyclist or a boxing champion. That made it all the more praiseworthy, that he stuck with farming, and eventually made a great success of it, under the most difficult circumstances. And I always admired him, and we always remained the greatest of friends.

The lane to Francie 'Connor's' house carried on towards the mountain to Elly Macs (McManus) house. Macs was a low thatched house at the foot of a hill, and occupied by four elderly sisters, Mary Ellen, Rose, Kate and Bridget. As we went to school, we could see them spaced out working in different quarters of the farm, foddering cattle, milking cows or chivvying away trespassing sheep, such as ours. Rose McManus was the only native of the 'mountain' 'ever to teach in the Marble Arches school.

Our second route to the school, took us along the track of what used to be a padroad, that headed out for Hughes Gate. When we got to 'the big stone' we turned right and joined the Marlbank road at James Nolan's gate. James's house was hidden behind rocks and bushes, about two hundred metres away from the road. It too was a low thatched house, with a small flower-fringed garden wall in the front, and then a large cobblestoned yard, surrounded by outbuildings. Along with James lived his wife Lizzie, who had a bad limp, and son John and daughters Mary and Sarah. The Nolans had a nice small farm, with a very deep well in the bog. As we usually went this way in bad weather, we would often see John and James carrying great loads of hay on their back, struggling to make ground to their cattle against the bitter wind, rain or hail. The Nolan's were comfortably off, and advertised their position in the social hierarchy by having a trap to take them to mass. Then as we carried on, Phil McManus's was on our right, and then Biddy McGrath's was on the left, alongside the lane into Johnny McGurns, and separated from the school by a rugged, hazel wooded, rocky promontory. Biddy was a widow, and lived with her son Paddy in this thatched house that seemed ready to fall, and it had great gaping holes in the roof. It was an eerie, shadowy place, surrounded by pine and overhanging larch trees. They had a small uneconomic farm, and we used to get the water for the school tea, from 'McGrath's well'.

In really bad weather, such as when there was snow, either of these routes was too dangerous, and so we went by a third route. This way was about three times as long as the first, and followed the direction of our new road, passing closely by Mick Dolan's. Daddy would often accompany us, to work on the road, and we would somewhat forlornly leave him until we returned in the evening. Mick Dolan's was also thatched, and sat a bit away from our track. Mick was dead, so Mrs Dolan lived with her sons, Packie, Michael, Frankie and Tommie, and daughters Rose and Kate. Dolan's had a good sized farm, half heather half grazing or meadow land, and Michael and Packie done the farming. As we passed, the cows would be lined up like an army troop, at attention, as they all hung their heads over a low wall, and sedately waited to be called to milking. Frankie and Tommie would join us as we carried on to school. Two hundred metres away, up the rocky slope lived Hugh Maguire (Cha) and his wife, and only son Paddy. Hughes farm was also one of two halves, one half meadow or grazing, and the other, a humpy, heathery wilderness. Paddy would join us, and never was there seen going to school anywhere in the whole universe, a more serious, studious, or subdued group of schoolchildren. Anyway, the next house we came close to was Dolan's of Clynnagh (The Clerks) And in the morning their house was always conspicuous by never showing the slightest sign of life. No lisp of smoke curled towards the sky on the white-frosted morning. No sign of a lump of hay moving across the white snow, towards the hungry and looing cattle. Nothing. But I did know that people lived there. Mrs Maggie Dolan lived with her sons, Jim and Paddy, and daughters Rose Alice, Kathleen and Manie.

From there we carried along the Marlbank road to school. The whole place would be crawling with rabbits, and every so often, at a safe distance, they would prop themselves up on their hind legs and groom their faces with their front paws, almost daring us to disturb them. Sometimes there would be ground mists, that we were able to rise above, and look along them as their silvery wisps filled the valleys. And Cuilcagh was always there. As we took the road to school, it seemed to grow larger and more magnificent, as our aspect of it changed. It seemed that its personality changed with the weather, or as some in the 'mountain' used to say, 'When Cuilcagh changes, the weather changes.' If Cuilcagh was black and glinty, cold was coming. If it had shiny mirror like patches, you could expect showery rain with a bitter wind. A blue azure radiation, and you could expect fine weather, while a mist on the top, according to its density, could be interpreted either as good weather, or dull showery weather. It was no wonder that there used to be many violent arguments over what Cuilcagh predicted, when farmers would be wondering whether it was safe to cut their grass to make hay, and if they made the wrong decision, it would spell near disaster.

Wheathill Chapel

In keeping with Father McGrail's wishes, Petie, Mammy and I eventually set off for mass in Wheathill one fine summer morning in 1950, all kitted out in our wellingtons, for we had no shoes. Happily, we headed out across the bog towards Francie 'Connor's' and then we took the lane past McGrath's house that brought us through Crossmurrin and then to Johnny McGurn's. Johnny and the wife made us tea, and then accompanied by them and Ellie Mac, we all headed off for the chapel. Our way from McGurn's took us into the wood of the Marble Arch valley. For newcomers like us this was a terrifying and awe inspiring place, as we were suddenly enveloped in a world of thunderous noise, rushing frothy water, massive cavernous chambers and dangerous holes underfoot. This is where the Marble Arch gets its name from, where the limestone has been worn and formed by countless years of rushing water, into a natural arch, over which our pass led. Our journey continued through the wood, precipitously above the rushing river, and every so often, where the side wall and pass had slipped into the river, we had to crawl dangerously across the disturbed ground. Gradually we descended to the level of the river bank, to a continuous, but harmonious commentary from the birds and insects, as they went about their business, or warned their relations about our coming. As the area that we walked in along the river widened out, park like, my senses were sent reeling by the magical, carpet-like phenomenon of millions of beautiful flowers. It was like a shimmering rippling sea, as the slight breeze caressed the flowers into breathing, weaving undulations. Lovely Primroses, Daffodils, Dahlias and Bluebells all combined to make this one of the most enchanting places that I have ever been to.

We came out on the main road at Claddagh Bridge, and carried on past 'The Red School', then the Post Office, and the Church, before at last reaching the chapel. If you can imagine, as we went along this road, more and more people joined it, on their way to mass. And progressively, Mammy, Petie and myself became more and more unsure and self-conscious, because of our ever-growing certainty of the conspiciousness of our footwear, in contrast to the gleamingly robed and footed strangers that emerged from the lanes and houses of Wheathill.

This was not a chapel to be compared with the 'Barr' chapel. For instance, Gowlan chapel stood on a bare hill, bleakly exposed to all the elements. I often heard people say that 'A shnipe wouldn't live at it.' But Wheathill chapel was discreetly secluded on low ground, behind reverentially leaning palm trees. The crowd of people lined along the road at the chapel, waiting for mass, seemed to be occupied with a more sedate and deferential countenance, and the three of us paraded through them like models at a fashion show, exposed and terrified until we got to the safety of the chapel door. But when mass was over we forgot our deficiencies, as well as our wellingtons, as we became encompassed in a state of happy euphoria, that mainly radiated from Charlie McTeggart and his family, as they furnished all and sundry with countless cups of tea and cakes and friendly chatter. Every time we went to mass in Wheathill it was the same, we would always be treated to tea and friendship.

One Sunday I went to mass alone, and two rather disconcerting things happened to me on the way back home. As I was homeward bound, and passing 'The Red School', there were youngsters there attending Sunday School. When they spotted me, the interloper, from a different religious establishment, they began to attack me at the hedge in front of the school. One lot on one side of the hedge would kick me through the hedge to the other assailants waiting on the other side. They would then kick me back again. This went on for some time, until someone came and stopped it. I was hurt in both mind and body, and sore all over. As I carried on, I consoled myself, and when I came to the 'Marble Arch' I rested and reflected, thinking on what had been done to me. In a temper I got hold of a boulder and hurled it through the opening of my feet. Suddenly and frighteningly, I heard a shout from amidst the scattered boulders away below in the depths of the river. I quickly focused my eyes on the foaming boulder strewn river, to see that my missile had shattered on a boulder inches away from a man and woman, who were trying to make their way to the massive caverns beneath my feet. The man was making threatening exclamations and gestures, so I thought it better to make a hasty departure. Later I realised the enormous danger the man and woman had been put in by my unthinking action.

I ate a bellyful of crab apples during the school summer holidays of 1950, and had to be rushed to hospital once again, this time by ambulance. As we passed Reid's Rock the scene of my earlier adventure, I was wondering if I would ever see it again. People stood along the road to see the ambulance, which was a rare sight in the 'mountain'. After three weeks in the hospital I returned home once more.

Then Daddy and I set off one evening to Jimmy Burleigh's of Beighy to look for stray sheep. To get there we went across the bog, past the school, and the dipping tank, and then into Legnabrocky, which was an impossible rocky, wooded area, unless you could find the pass that had been hewn through the rocks. Then we passed Johnny Maguires, a wee thatched house, where Bridget and Mary Ellen, and the rest of them lived. Monstrous high rocks reared up in front of us, as we came nearer McNulty's, and then we were clambering up the humpy hills that led us to the top of Benaughlin Mountain. From there we were able to see Burleigh's in the distance below. We came to it and in we went, and it wasn't long until his housekeeper had us struggling to put away a wonderful feed. Then we looked at the suspicious sheep, and luckily (thought I) it wasn't one of ours. On our way back, it was pitch dark as Daddy knocked on James McNulty's door. What a place! Nulty's was a low thatched house, and Jimmy and his wife lived with their two sons, Tom and John James. Jimmy's brother Owen also lived with them. They all enveloped us immediately in such a friendliness and warmth that I had never experienced before. Mrs Nulty cooked us a lovely feed, which we heartily enjoyed. But my interest was totally taken over by the glorious conglomeration of items residing about the house. There was harmonicas, accordions, banjos, drums, flutes, tin-whistles, nose flutes, jews harps and a violin. They had every sort of maps and designs and a ball shaped map of the world. They had cameras, magnifying glasses, binoculars, even a ship's compass. They had wonderful 'National Geographic' magazines, Readers Digests, and hundreds of comics. I never wanted to leave. And then an amazing thing happened. Somehow, I suppose through praise and ingenuity, they inveighed Daddy to try the tin-whistle. I was totally bewildered to see that he could play it perfectly, something which I had never known before. Reluctantly we left in the early hours, but I came home most of the way on air, after such an amazing night.

The Fair

Now that me and Daddy seemed to have struck up an agreeable and satisfying partnership, when it came to travel, we went and embarked on an another excursion. Taking the lambs to the 'Fair of the Black' on the 22nd September 1950. Daddy called me at four in the morning, and he had thick bacon rashers and eggs ready, which we ate before the great open fire. As we tried to gather up the sheep in the dark, my weak and undernourished constitution left me feeling very fragile at this unearthly hour. We eventually reached 'the Black' at about half six, and it was crammed with animals, buyers and sellers and merchants. The thing to do was to find a place to hold the sheep in a good market position, and consequently we arranged ourselves on the road opposite Armstrong's Handball Alley. Some of the other sellers used hay rope to tie the sheep's necks together, but we didn't have any of that, so we done our best to contain them with our outstretched arms.

When a buyer came along, he would circle and stalk about the sheep, and eventually engage Daddy in conversation. He would talk about everything except sheep, but at last he would say, 'How much do you want for them lock Farrell?'

Dad. 'Fifty bob apiece.'

Dealer. 'Jasus Christ Farrell, you're raving. You won't get anything like that for them. They're just ordinary mountain lambs. At that rate of going, I couldn't make you an offer.'

What used to happen then was that an independent onlooker would enter into the fray, and this provided a very useful device in finalising a sale.

The 'Newcomer' would say, 'What are you giving Farrell for these sheep?'

Dlr. 'I'm giving him nothing. He's asking an outrageous price for them. You couldn't deal with him!'

'Ncmr. 'Farrell what do you want for your lambs?'

Dad. 'I'm asking fifty bob apiece for them.'

Ncmr. 'That's a bit steep Farrell.' Ncmr to Dlr. 'What will you offer Farrell for his sheep?'

Dlr. 'I'll give him twenty eight and six for them, and not a farthing more!'

Ncmr. to the dealer 'Put out your hand,' and he gets ready to slap it. 'Say you'll give Farrell thirty five bob for the lambs.' He whacks the dealer's hand. The dealer thinks about that for a while, then he says, 'Well, alright so. Thirty five bob.'

Ncmr. 'Farrell, he's giving you thirty five bob for them. It's a fair price. Will you take it?'

Dad. 'Whissht will you. I won't take it. I'll take forty five bob. Take it or leave it.'

Ncmr. 'Jasus Christ, you'se are two fierce ignorant men. Give me your hands!' And he gets ready to whack them. 'Divide the difference!' Neither of them agree, and lope off in different directions through the throng. Time passes, and eventually the 'newcomer' reigns them in again.

Ncmr. 'You'se are a horrid pair to have anything to do with! Split the difference or upon my troth, I'll never be seen at another sheep fair! Give me your hands. Now split the difference, and Farrell will give you a good luck penny. You know there's no one dacenter than Farrell. Now spit on your hands and clinch it!' If at this point the combatants show any inclination of agreeing to the proposition the newcomer makes their minds up by saying, 'Good luck to you'se now, you'se have made a great deal.'

But selling the sheep and cattle was just one part of what went on at the fair. The main street of the 'Black' would be thronged with a mass of people, animals, merchants, hucksters, trucksters and gypsies, all seemingly fused together in a heaving inseparable multitude. For the first tine in my life I ate an ice-cream, and then Dad said it was time I had a dinner or something, and he deposited me into the rush and confusion of Farrelly's busy Restaurant, where, quietly and subdued I waited for attention. The nearness of strange faces, being adjusted into all sorts of comical grimaces, as their owners ladled soup, stew or semolina into them was disconcerting. It was a relief when I too was presented with my dinner. But what I was supposed to do with the cutlery that accompanied it was a problem. However, by sneaky and secretive glances at the other diners in the room, I gradually found out what to do with the sharp and shiny implements. But Mrs Farrelly was a lovely friendly and helpful woman, and she took great pride in telling me that her husband was working on the Suez Canal, widening it, and that it was already more than a mile wide.

Fed and full-bellied, I came out into the throng once more. Dad was nowhere to be seen, but someone said that he was in the Bushman's, a pub, and I went to find him there. He was right merry, and asked one of his friends to show me the Blacklion Creamery. The Space Shuttle ready to take off at Cape Canaveral could not have been more fascinating to me. The place was predominated by an intricate network of scrupulously clean, shiny, steel pipes. At various valves along the pipework, hissing and spurting steam erupted, and at other places milk sizzled. The various floors were reached by clinically clean steel stairways, and on the top floor in a corner, there was an office to do the books. The creamery was fuelled by an enormous coal boiler, which I was allowed to attend for a time. A tremendous heat radiated out from it, as I shovelled coal into the voracious and cavernous furnace. The creamery was run by a Mr McCauley and John Dolan (The Prince) who in later years used to cut my hair, and was one of those people who make you feel better for having met them.

When I returned to the fair, the crowd seemed to have taken on an air of apprehensive brooding, because many of them were unsteady and rambling, and becoming gradually incapacitated through intoxication. When I at last found my father, beyond the end of the anxious and heaving crowd in the 'Bushman's', it was obvious he was 'well on it' and he gave orders to someone to direct me home. When he got up out of bed the next day, he was a mass of cuts, black eyes and abrasions, all the evidence of a violent fight. None of us however, had the nerve to ask him for details about it.

One day Mammy prepared to go to Enniskillen, and I was delighted when she decided to take me with her. We dressed up in our finest gear and set off walking to Belcoo where we would meet the train that would take us to Enniskillen. Except for the clouds of steam and hissing of the train at Belcoo, I remember little of the journey. Enniskillen was very thronged, with everyone rushing about. I managed to get lost for a while, and when I was reunited with my mother I was somewhat disconcerted by the many admiring glances at my mother, coming from the men as we walked along the street. It struck me as very strange the number of one-legged and one-armed men that roamed about the street. I didn't know then that they were victims of the Second World War. Mammy's sister Annie was working in the Royal Hotel at that time, and we met her briefly out on the street, all dressed up in her white apron, and hat. Mammy bought a box of lovely silver knives, forks and spoons in a silverware shop, and then she bought a kettle, as well as sweets for me and the rest at home and soon we returned to Belcoo on the train.

After leaving the train we began our homeward journey down through the main street of Belcoo, and then turned right for Blacklion, where a *Stop* sign across the road soon showed us where the Northern Ireland Customs office was located. It was only in later years, when I had to pass through these same Frontier Posts, that I gained some inkling of the apprehension with which Mammy must have approached the Customs Posts on this day. As Mammy and I were travelling towards the south, and Eire, we would not have been perceived by the authorities to be as great a threat to the economy as if we were travelling with goods in the opposite direction. On the other hand, seeing as we came, apparently, from the south in the first place, the occupants of the Northern Ireland Frontier Post would want to know what we were doing in their country, and so we were called in. Along with the usual questions such as 'Where have you been?' I'll always remember them saying to Mammy, 'Why have you this cub with you?' I began to wonder, maybe little bucks like me weren't supposed to be out wandering about like this. The custommen let us carry on, and we continued across the bridge between Northern Ireland and Eire and soon saw another *Stop* sigh across the road. This was the Eire Customs Post, and there was no way we were going to get past it without an examination. We were intercepted and shown into the customs office. 'Empty out the bag!' The kettle, sweets and cutlery made their appearance. 'Mother a jasus! Where are you going with these things? Is our own stuff not good enough for you?' Mammy explained to the custommen that we were only travelling through Eire in order to get back into Northern Ireland at Mullaghbane. Eventually we were let go, with the custommen warning Mammy that they would be watching to make sure that she turned left in the 'Black', and that if she didn't they would follow and apprehend her. When we turned left in Blacklion Mammy told me to look after the kettle and stuff, while she sneaked back around the corner to get fags, which were cheaper in Eire. We then carried on out the Unapproved road towards Florencecourt, and crossed the border into Northern Ireland once more.

Once we passed Arthur Elliott's house at the border we felt much better, away from the prying eyes of the authorities, and Mammy lit up one of her newly purchased cigarettes and sent plumes of smoke skywards. We travelled over the top of Arthur Elliott's hill, and at the bottom we would turn off the road into the lane on the right, which was a nearway up to Marlbank. When we turned right into the lane we were shocked to find a police sergeant and his bike nonchalantly leaning up against the hedge. This was no ordinary policeman, but someone who was well known and feared far and wide. 'Well good afternoon,' says he 'and where might you be going?' Mammy told him we were going home. 'And where might that be?' Mammy told him. 'Names?' 'Bridget and John McGourty.' 'Now isn't that amazing . . . What have you got in the bag?' Mammy said 'A few woodbines, a kettle, a few implements and sweets.' 'Empty out the bag!' Mammy emptied out the bag on the ground. 'Holy Moses' said the policeman, 'Have you no shame, woman? Where have you smuggled this in from?' Mammy explained that she had not smuggled them at all but had just come from Enniskillen with them. 'Woman, I have just watched the two of you coming down that road. That road comes from Eire, the south. Enniskillen is that way,' says the policeman, pointing north. 'Now let me see what you have here,' he said, poking at the items with his well polished boot. 'They do good stuff in the south, I'll give them that . . . hold the bag open,' he said, putting the kettle into it. Then he threw the remainder of the cigarettes into the bag. He then took two spoons, two forks and two knives, and threw the packet with the rest of the implements into the bag, and handed Mammy the six pieces of cutlery. Then he said 'You have nothing to complain about now have you? I'm confiscating this property on behalf of His Majesty's Government, you can be on your way now.' We continued on our way, but for years and years Mammy talked about 'that hoor of a policeman' and hoped that the day would soon come when 'the crooked hoor would rot in hell'.

Christmas 1950 was a particularly memorable time for me because Aunt Jeanie sent us another parcel from Long Island. The harmonica she sent before, was long since gone, and still I couldn't play. But now she sent a far better one which I appropriated. I was thrilled with its lovely tone, the rich timbre of the base, and its intricate and magical construction. But the present of the harmonica was almost inconsequential, when viewed against my other acquisitions from the box. There were 'Wild West' comics and 'Annuals', something which I'll never forget . . . I couldn't read yet, of course, but the action was so exciting in these comics, so real, that

I just had to learn to read, to know exactly what was going on. I kept these comics for years, to relive again and again yet another adventure. You can forget about your television. These comics were so real you could believe you were there with the Sheriff, as he trailed the outlaw through the mesquite and sagebrush on his little burro, before being bushwhacked underneath the outcrop of Badlands Bend.

One of the most popular men that roamed about the 'Mountain' when I was growing up was Willie Brown, our postman. Willie was a Protestant man from Florencecourt and he was a very amiable and amusing character. He collected the post at Florencecourt Post Office and had to walk all the way through the 'Mountain' delivering post to each house and collecting the letters to be posted. It was a tremendous walk six days a week, and Willie would come to our house when he would often be drenched to the skin with wet. He would have a cup of tea, and everybody would have such a pity for him as he set off already soaking, into a heavy storm of snow or rain. He always managed to be cheerful however and everybody in the 'Mountain' loved him. He was a big, stout, redfaced man, and he had two massive carbuncles on each of his ears. When he met anyone out on his travels, whether they were eight or eighty, his usual cheeky greeting after he said hello was 'How's your mother?' This often got him into trouble when young children told their father that Willie wanted to know if their mother was alright. Sometimes, in the Marble Arches School, Willie would knock on the door and Mrs Gilmurray would send out a pupil to collect the letters. Willie would engage the child in amusing conversation until Mrs Gilmurray shouted at the child not to be loitering on the doorstep. As Willie started to go he would say loudly to the child, so that Mrs Gilmurray could hear 'and how is your mother keeping now?' and this would send the whole school into uproar. Willie was postman in the 'Mountain' for many years, and when he retired it was calculated that he had walked at least a quarter of a million miles as a postman.

Daddy was spending more and more time away, and those of us at home had to look after the sheep, as well as getting on with our work on the drain. We always awaited fearfully Dad's return, because he would cross-examine us severely before inspecting our work in the morning. If we had produced any defect whatsoever, we would be almost obliterated by his venomous wrath and ridicule. The twins, Frank and Bridie were growing too, and crawling about in Spring 1951. Frank however was a 'donny cratur', and had Mammy nearly distracted because he was sick most of the time.

Jimmity's

Daddy, who always seemed to have had a preponderance for walking, decided to take me on an outlandish walk in the spring of 1951, when I wasn't even ten years old. This was to walk to our new farm at Jimmity's. Mammy and him discussed it briefly, but she was totally against the idea. I however, of little knowledge, was all for it, so away we went. We crossed the bog, and into Cavan, the same way as we went to mass. Out past the 'Barr' chapel, and then we took across the rough, stubbly hills of Stranamort, meeting many of Dad's acquaintances on the journey. Somewhere along the way, a small pebble got into my wellington, but I couldn't face telling my father, because I'd be holding him up. I suffered silently, but increasingly, which made me fall behind, and eventually Dad relented and stopped to find out what's wrong with me. At last we came to my Grandmother's house in Roo, where I had never been before, and she had a great welcome for me. My feet were very bad, and all skinned, and cut where the pebble had been. Granny bandaged me up, and gave me socks, for I wasn't wearing any, and despite her protests for me to give up, we carried on. Granny lived on a lovely green, lowland farm, but from there on our journey became a remorseless upward struggle. After an hour or so we came to men cutting turf on Ben mountain. We stopped briefly while Daddy chatted to them, and then we had to carry on again. Eventually, the result of my pursuit of the heels of Daddy's relentlessly disappearing wellingtons, manifested itself in loud wails from my throat and chest. My ill nourished body just could not take in enough air for the effort needed, and from time to time, retching spasms and being winded made me unable to continue. Painfully, and stubbornly we carried on, our only company being the odd sheep and the eerie wind. We made for a corner of Ben, where the sides of the mountain were going away from us. One side of the mountain was continuing towards Dowra, and the other side towards Manorhamilton. An enormous expanse of country became visible to us, though I wasn't really in the mood to admire it that day. Still the mountain went treacherously upwards, as we struggled to reach the top. Finally we got to the top, and rested awhile, and Daddy pointed out our own mountain at home, now so far away. As we crossed over the top of the mountain, a valley appeared away below us, but Dad told me that we were not in sight of our new mountain yet. As I stumbled and tripped my way over this barren and godforsaken land for miles, darkness came, and still we weren't near 'Jimmity's'. The pitch black night came upon us, and still Dad drove relentlessly on. I sloshed along behind him, wellingtons full of water, and my body a mass of pain. But I couldn't stay there, so I had to go on. At long last Daddy opened a door in the pitch darkness, and I heard him muttering, 'There must be a candle here someplace.' And then I heard him say, 'Where did I leave them hoors of matches?' The dim candlelight showed me a damp, unplastered stone-built old house, with an uneven flagged floor, and low cobwebbed ceiling. The fireplace was at one gable end, and Daddy got the fire going, but we had nothing to eat. Daddy went off in the darkness saying, 'I'll be back soon.' After an hour or so I ventured to look out, but there was nothing but overpowering darkness, and it was beginning to rain. Daddy barged in with a saucepan of cold porridge, and a can of milk. It didn't look very appetising, wobbling about like a jelly, but I was ravenous.

Dad told me to stay there, and off he went once more, and I wondered where he could go in this all consuming blackness. I pondered . . . and was seized briefly with a sensation of terror, but soon settled down, and hoped the house wasn't built on the edge of a cliff. I attended to the fire, and found a sort of a bed in the dimness, made up out of a bundle of coats and rags. Tiredness compelled me to try the bed, and soon I fell into a stupor, out of which I was rudely awakened by a terrific explosion. Nothing more happened for the moment, and I concluded I was dreaming. Then all hell broke loose, with flashing bright lights and a ferocious thunderclap, which completely unnerved me, though I was quite used to thunderstorms. The lightning would dart about the ground, and the static crackling, and the pungent smell of the cordite were overpowering as the lightning fused and lit up the whole earth. Immediately the thunder would start in one area of the sky, and then travel through the heavens in increasing loudness, until with a massive whistling velocity, the shock would hit the earth. It was a dreadful storm, and for me was physically and psychologically draining. The lightning allowed me to see the torrents of rain coming down, and when at last it subsided I went back to bed and slept fitfully.

In the morning I was starving but there was nothing to eat, or no way to start the fire. The house was at the top of a valley that went as far as the eye could see, and it was beside a violently rushing torrent of a river. On the other side of the house there was another, less powerful river, and they converged farther down in the valley. Jimmity's was a desolate and barren place, with not one other house to be seen, but it was a wonderful and exciting place too with these spectacular and dangerous rivers. My hunger became acute as the day wore on, but still Daddy never appeared. As I wandered around the land near the house, I found a coalminer's bogey, and I wondered where the coalpit was, that I wanted so much to see. Still the day wore on, and I was becoming frantic for food, when suddenly I heard a shout in the distance. This was a redheaded youth that Dad had met someplace, and he had sent him to cook me something to eat. Bacon and sausages and tea and bread, never tasted so good as on that day. This youth was called JJ and that was the only name I ever knew him by, but he became one of my greatest childhood friends. Daddy returned later that evening, and soon we were homeward bound across the mountain once again. When we got to Granny's I stayed there until I had recovered. Dad went on alone.

Integration

As Petie and I progressed at school, and our relations with the other pupils were consolidated we began to visit their houses off and on. Our first unchaperoned visit was to Johnny Maguire's of

Legnabrocky. Along with Johnny and the wife, there was Bridget, Mary Ellen, Rose, John, Joe, Michael and Julia. Johnny worked as a herd on Legnabrocky, which wouldn't have been a very well paid job. Nevertheless, Johnny and his wife were two very happy, amiable and generous people, who would give you the last thing they had. Their children too. They were all so close and happy that I often wonder are there any families like that now. I had a crush on Mary Ellen, so it was nice to be able to visit there for the first time. We played games all night long, including cards, and Mrs Maguire cooked cakes and Boxty for us. We had a great night, but alas it had to end, and we sadly headed for home. Nothing came of my crush however.

Another house we liked to go to was Ernie Moffat's of Tromagagh. To get there, we went across the bog, and then hoped we would be able to get across the Shru Croppa River. Moffat's was a great house to go to, because no matter how exciting, adventurous or rumbustous our fun was, there was never any sanctions put on our pandemonium. Mrs Moffatt was as bad as any of us, and would join in our fun with gusto. She would cook us an enormous meal, and then we would start all over again. Ernie was a tall skinny man and wore a hat, and his wife was a medium sized auburn haired woman. To see them out, they looked sober and sedate, but when they were at home with their children, they energetically joined in their fun. I often thought that it must have been the best and happiest place in the world to have been brought up.

We would also occasionally go to Mick Dolan's where Tommie and Frankie lived. They were fairly sober chaps, and this meant that our fun and games were enacted in a more restrained and serious manner. This usually turned out to be playing cards, or learning to play Draughts. Sometimes they would come to our house, and Daddy, the demolisher of seriousness would soon have them enjoying themselves in abandon.

One of our most looked forward to events, was a visit by Mary Ellen Maguire, (Mrs 'Connor') and the children, Jamsie and Maureen. It gave some sort of significance in our house, when people like Mrs 'Connor' came to visit us. Mrs 'Connor' and the children, like Francie, were our great friends, and as she spoke with her slow, soft voice, it was soothing and comforting for us all. She would always bring some delicacies for us, and then Mammy and the rest of us would walk home with her, because she was afraid of the dark.

It is strange how fate maps out the course of our lives. In the spring of 1951, I got a yearning to learn to cycle, and consequently, whenever Dad would bring home his ould Raleigh, I would be trying to learn how to cycle on it. Petie however took the wind out of my sails by secretly learning before me. Of course our legs were far too short to go over the bar, so we had to reach one leg awkwardly under the bar to the pedal. My problem was that I was uncoordinated, and unable to synchronise the shift of pressure from one pedal to the other in order to force them around. But Petie's learning made me ominously determined, and from the day I first learned to cycle, our lives progressed with a far greater independence of one another. When the summer school holidays of 1951 came, Daddy had arranged for Petie to go to Phil McGovern's of Drumkeerin, and I was left at home with Rose, the twins, and Farrell.

One day however, when Daddy sent me to 'The Black' for a message, I saw my chance to see a bit of the world. I had heard that John Nolan was just after getting a brand new Rudge bicycle and I went out and asked him for the loan of it, telling him that Dad needed medicine from 'The Black' urgently. John, and his father James were worried, and well they might, for I could easily be killed going down the Marlbank Braes, yet, to them, it would have been almost unthinkable to refuse. Anyway they discussed the ins and outs of my request, and eventually gave me the lovely, shiny bike. When your legs are too short to stretch over the bar of the bike, you make progress in a strained and ungainly manner. All your weight is on your right foot, and you have to propel your left through the frame, under the bar, hoping to force around the pedal. So all your body, except the left leg, hangs out precariously from the side of the bike. Anyway, off I went. Down the hills, a couple of indiscretions, but no problem. It was a lovely day, and I was nearly at 'The Black' yet hardly any time had passed. I could see the mountains far off in the distance, across the lough, and I began to wonder . . . I thought to myself, looking at the road away from 'The Black'. I wonder where would that road lead me. Off I went into the unknown. Across Brockagh Bridge, and the Arney River, and then I came to the cottages at Florencecourt Railway Station. Feeling rather thirsty, I went to the door of a house to ask for a drink. The woman who answered the door, evilly scrutinised me and said, 'Get ta hell outa here ya tramp ya! We want none of yeer lot round here! Begone! or I'll put the bloody dogs on ya!' I carried on then, through Letterbreen, Mullaghdun, and then past Carson's Quarry at Crenaghoe. Finally, I reached Belcoo, and then 'The Black'. There was a fierce uproar when I got home, but from that day on, every chance I got, I was off on John's bicycle. When Petie got home from his holidays in Drumkeerin, he made me right envious, relating how the people there were the nicest, the friendliest, their children were out of this world with manners and sociability, and you would never want to eat anyone else's apples, after tasting their's.

As our work on the drain, the road and the sheep continued, there were also other things happening at home. We had got a lovely little pig, and I loved carrying him his feed, and having a little chat with him. He grew at a tremendous rate, and every time we let him out, there was pandemonium. The dog would be facing him at his shed, daring him to come and when we opened his door, but he would barge, squealing through us, dog hens and all. His little legs went at a furious pace, as he raced across the fields, and torpedoed into the bog with his snout. He would spend time hurling lumps of turf up into the air, and then he would abandon himself to the bog, rolling about to his heart's content. When he had enough of the bog, he would saunter leisurely back to his shed. As he spied us looking at him on his way back, he would blink his little red eyes conspiratorially, as much as to say, 'well you'se have to go to the bog to relieve yourselves, why shouldn't I?' But now 'Doomsday' had arrived for piggy. Dad had made arrangements with Paddy Corrigan at Wheathill to come and kill him. Rose, who had just started, Petie and I, took the day off school for the event, but later we wished we hadn't. For the killing of a pig, first you have to collect all your available pots, and get them ready with boiling water. We done all that. Then the pig cannot be killed while immobilised, he must be taking part in some activity, like running. Mammy and the rest of us young ones watched fearfully as Dad and Paddy advanced on our dear pig. They led him out of his shed. He ran. They caught up with him, and Dad was trying to hold him while Paddy plunged in the knife. Paddy stuck the knife into the pig, and then amidst the most terrifying screams, I have ever heard, they let go of the pig, or in other words, the pig got away from them. Well! The pig ran out and up the hill, with the blood gushing out of him, and him giving the most heart-rending and blood-curdling screams. He disappeared from view, and we found him down in the bog, dead. When he was taken home he was put up on a table, and shaved or scraped with knives. Then he was cut up into square pieces, which were bedded in salt, in a tea-chest. The bits and pieces, called griskins, were collected into bags, or sheets of paper, like fish and chips, and we cooked some of this for weeks. Paddy Corrigan got a bag of griskins, and we gave some to all the neighbours. It was the same when some other mountainer killed a pig. They would give us a bag of griskins. One part of the pig was very useful and lasted longer than all the rest. This was the queer-smelling pig's bladder, which we used to blow up and use as a football.

JJ from Jimmity's came to stay with us, and work on the road, while he was waiting on a better job in the lowlands. Then we got a 'Tilley' lamp before Christmas. Our sheep were crossing over into Hugh Melanophy's green fields, and he used to come to our house in a temper, and 'lacerate' us and Charlie Cha. Daddy would usually be away. We had so many sheep now that they were escaping out from our land in all directions. They used to go down to Sonny Dolan's, Mick Dolan's, and Phil McManus's meadows. And many a morning Elly Mac woke us as she stood on the mearme fence berating us at the top of her voice about our 'unmannerly hoors of sheep'. 'Why can't you'se get cattle like normal people?'

Cuilcagh

I asked Daddy about going to Cuilcagh on my own, and one day I set off. I headed up past the 'ould house' and on to 'the rocks'. Then I walked on to the top of Screg Na Connell, where I deviated left towards Lugadiff, before eventually coming to the Shru Croppa river. The ground was heathery, rough, and slippery with many swamps. I followed the river and came to 'Connor's Walls'. The walls of the old house were still standing, along with what had been the little outhouses. Around the house one could still make out the shadowy contours of cultivations of a former age. The crane was still in position over the redundant fireplace, and I wondered about the people who must once have sat around it, as the women baked the bread and the men smoked their pipes and told stories. There were still the little cubbyholes scooped out of the wall, where the women and the little ones would have kept their treasures. Saddened I carried on. Beside the house there was a cascading waterfall, and the bed of the river had changed from that of strewn boulders to one of flags and shale. The going became more steeply upwards, through interwoven rushes that grew way above me. As I got higher and higher, and a vast countryside opened out before me, there wasn't a sign of life other than the odd sheep, and the eerie stillness was only occasionally broken by the plaintive bleating of a lamb calling its mother. As I went higher still, the steepest ground on the approaches to the summit was made up of ribbed hard sprat and slippery shale. My heart was beating at an enormous rate, and my lungs pained for air, as I alternated between resting and continuing to the top. As I reached the pinnacle of every new proturbence, which I expected to be the top of the mountain, I found that yet again, Cuilcagh had receded into the distance. At last I was on the top and my most immediate reaction was great surprise at the force of the wind. There is always a stiff and penetrating wind on Cuilcagh, even when it is a stifling hot day in the foothills below.

The vast and immense magnitude of the view was breathtaking, and I was able to see the shimmering Atlantic ocean at Lissadell, in County Sligo. One fifth of all Ireland is said to be seeable from the top of Cuilcagh, and I would believe that. Our own house nestled so tiny, far off in the valley below, and I was able to see every other house in the 'mountain'. The top of Cuilcagh is made up of an enormous upheaval of massive rocks and boulders. It looks as if a giant knife sliced down through its top, leaving these magnificent leaning rocks, which were once obviously attached to the main mountain. The upheaval has created mighty caverns the size of houses, which, when one enters them, fills the inquisitor with feelings of melancholy and depression.

I made for the eastern end of the mountain, towards Swanlinbar, and was able to gaze down on black reflections of the clouds, in the murky, lonely and largely uninhabited Lough Attona. But the eastern end was very far away, and a mixture of extreme hunger, loneliness and tiredness, conspired to drive me homeward. Though my trip was uneventful, I can vouch for the fact that Cuilcagh is no place for the unwary, and since that visit I, as well as my father, have had many scares on it. The greatest danger is fog, or mist, as we used to call it, which can suddenly envelop one. When that happens, unless you are completely sure of where you are going, the best thing is to stay put. Then there is snowstorms. If you are caught in a snowstorm on Cuilcagh it is difficult to know what to do. If you take shelter in a cavern, you are likely to be snowed in, and if you decide to brave the snow, you are just as likely to have a serious fall as to freeze to death in the cold. The last danger is more likely to happen on the descent from Cuilcagh. In descending from the top, you are faced with a myriad of possible routes. Some of these ways are made more attractive by being beaten down by the travels of the sheep, and so one follows one of these tracks. Often, before you realise it, and when it may be too late, this trail has led you onto what we call an 'Alt'. These 'Alts' are massive banks of shale, which are completely treacherous when you find yourself on them. Otherwise, Cuilcagh is a wonderful place. Remote, wild, exciting, it makes the visitor feel small and vulnerable, yet when you descend from it, you feel completely exhilarated and enervated.

The following is Alan Warner's account of his walk to Cuilcagh.

****

First, Alan Warner relates the amount of trouble he had in 'The Black' (Blacklion) in trying to find anyone who would be able to direct him towards the best route to Cuilcagh. Then he carries on . . .
'At the abandoned school (Marble Arches) I cut off into the fields

and headed up the Sruh Croppa river valley. It was fairly easy going over small fields and small ditches, but later I came to heathery hills and bog. I lunched on a hillside, finding what shelter I could from the wind. Below me in the valley was a sheep lying very still. A grey crow cawed and flew close over the sheep, but it made no move. A little later two men and a dog, presumably looking for lambing sheep, came up to it. The sheep then got up and revealed a new born lamb, still wobbly on its legs.

As I went on, the Cuilcagh ridge came into sight, dramatically covered in snow. The clouds were increasing behind me, and they looked ominously dark, but I thought that I could surely have no trouble following the ridge, once I had climbed on to it. My plan was to ascend the western end and walk along to Cuilcagh Mountain at the eastern end, then to descend and walk across the bog to pick up the Gorthnalughany road. I reached the top of Tiltinbane soon after 3pm and began to walk along the ridge. Almost at once it started to snow, but I decided to push on, thinking I could follow the ridge even in poor visibility. Soon I was floundering in deep snow up to my knees, with drifts here and there much deeper. Now I thanked God I had a stick. I was able to probe the drifts ahead of me, before I plunged into them. Sometimes I failed to touch bottom with the stick, and worked round another way. The snow ceased for a short time, then started again and turned into a blizzard. The cold increased and the visibility was reduced to a few yards. My gloves were wet, my hands numb, and I became quite uncertain of my direction. There seemed to be deep, rocky crevasses all around me. I managed to get out my compass and I found that I was going more west than east. For a time I was worried, even a little frightened. I realised that I must abandon my plan of following the ridge, and get off the mountain in the direction of the road. But there was nothing except the compass to give me any indication of direction, and all around me were forbidding clefts, cliffs and crevasses. I couldn't seem to find a promising slope to work my way down. Finally I got to one and had a glimpse of snowy ground beneath me. I was unsure how deep a drop there might be below, but I worked my way cautiously down, feeling great relief of getting off the ridge. The snow ceased again, but visibility remained very poor.

Finally I got a dim impression of Benaughlin in the distance, and I made a beeline for it, as far as I could across heavy bog. The going was very wet in places. There were some deep gullys with swollen streams rushing down. I was in a fairly sodden state, but still relieved at being safely off the mountain. I never even saw the peak of Cuilcagh, which I was originally aiming for. After nearly two hours of bog-trotting I became aware of turf stacks in front of me - a welcome sign of civilisation. Soon I found a green turf-track and this led me to the tarred road. Walkers usually try to escape from tarred roads, but I was heartily relieved to see this one.

Extract from Alan Warner's book 'Walking the Ulster Way'.

****

Christmas 1951 passed and our attention was constantly on the wireless as we listened to the daily accounts of the awful ordeal of Captain Henrik Carlson, of The Flying Enterprise, which was stricken by a terrible storm off the south coast of England. After the rest of the sailors were taken off to safety, Carlson and a young sailor refused to abandon the ship for twelve terrible days, until in fact it sank. Mammy had us constantly praying and saying rosaries for these two brave men.

Our winter nights during those years were often spent 'lamping' rabbits. We had no torch of our own, but Jim Dolan, (The Clerk), John Nolan, or Eugene McMorrow (who lived in Sheerins) would come with their torch. These torches usually contained six one and a half volt batteries, making about nine volts, and the brilliant light was adjusted to a precise focus point. Sometimes two torches were connected together to give an even stronger light. I would be in a high state of excitement and apprehension with the thought of the chase, as a crowd of us, accompanied by our sheepdog, set off into the tunnel of light. It was no problem to find rabbits, because the place was crawling with them, and when we located one, the bright light completely mesmerised him. The sheepdog would then run and catch him, and gently hold him until we caught up. One of us then held the rabbit up by the hind legs, and gave him a vicious karate chop to the back of the head, from which he usually died instantly. Some people were apprehensive about this sort of execution, but I was a dab hand at it. I also used to make rabbit snares, from the special fine wire, and I would then position it on a rabbit run, where it would soon ambush an unfortunate victim. This was the way I earned my first money, and it was nothing for us to be taking five or six dozen rabbits out on our backs to the Marlbank road, where Gillen or Gracey (meat buyers) would give us about two shillings a dozen.

As work on the road progressed, Carson's lorry used to come with stone, which Petie and I would spread after school. At that time Carson had two Commer lorries, and the engine of the Commer had a very distinctive sound. At that time there used to be an Esso advertisement for fuel, *'Put a tiger in your tank'*, and these Commer lorries for all the world reminded one of what we imagined to be the crazy throbbing growl of that tiger. But these lorries couldn't come near our house yet, only to Dolan's land. The very first vehicle to come all the way to our house was Jack Crozier's tractor. This was an old Fordson, a spluttering, noisy monster that scared the life out of us young ones as well as Mammy, and we kept well away from it. Jack and his son Byram, stood up at the long steering wheel, that reached up to their shoulders, as this cumbersome, but powerful machine easily drew along a trailer of turf. I suppose one could say, that from that day on, we had drawn that bit nearer to civilisation, noisy as it was.

The Ram, Granny's

A rather humorous event occurred about this time, or at least Daddy thought it very funny, and afterwards he got many a good evening's entertainment by expanding, exaggerating, and re-telling it, accompanied by suitable guffaws. A strange ram appeared in our land, and Daddy sent out enquiries so as someone would tell whoever owned it. It transpired that the ram belonged to someone in 'Glan', across the top of Cuilcagh, and one day he arrived for his sheep. This man, Judge, brought with him a large bottle of poteen, and as him and Dad hadn't seen each other for a while, they had many things to talk about. As the day wore on, they interspersed their conversation with liberal doses of the Poteen. At last, the man reined in his ram with a short rope and amiably they both set off. When the man got to the approaches of Cuilcagh, he recklessly decided to cross over the top of a steep 'Alt'. For some reason, the ram, who had been a pretty agreeable companion so far, suddenly flew into a rage, or became disagreeable, with the result that both the travellers cannoned down the 'Alt'. They came to rest at one of its intermediate pinnacles. The man holding the rope was helpless on one side, with a two hundred foot drop below him, and balancing him, and keeping him from falling was the ram attached to the rope on the other side, with a similar drop below him. For hours the man held on to the rope, until the sheep grew quiet, and then he slowly inched his way back onto the apex of the 'Alt'. He could only watch as he let go the rope and the ram thundered down the side of the 'Alt', and then he continued on for home. Sometime later the ram was found dead at the bottom.

Another incident that took place at that time, goes some way to illustrate how backward we were. One day Francie 'Connor' came with news that there were two merchants circulating in the lowlands, selling wares like clothes and cooking utensils. He took great delight in telling Mammy that they came from the East, where the 'Three Wise Men' came from. He said that people from the East travelled around on magic carpets, and that when they took a dislike to someone, they were likely to put them in a bottle, like a genie. He told us that these merchants had enormous big heads, about the size of the pot we boiled our spuds in. Granny was there at this time, and as she and Mammy discussed this 'news, they got themselves into an awful state of nervousness, and thought it would be better to evacuate the place for a while until the danger had passed. But when Dad came home he told them not to be such 'woeful omidans', and for a time their fear subsided. After a few days however, Dad began to put on the pressure again, with reports of sightings, and fearful depredations, as the merchants got nearer. Finally he said that he had heard that they were coming to our house on such and such a day.

I'll tell you, it wasn't just Mammy and Granny that were frightened, I was fearful, we all were, as the dangerous day drew nearer.

On the day that the merchants were expected, we abandoned the house. Mammy and Granny took the young ones up into the mountain, from where they were able to observe whoever came about the place. Petie went to McCorry's in the Barrs, and I went to Melanophy's. No merchants came, and so the next day we done the same thing again. Still no strangers appeared, and it was only then that Mammy began to have doubts about the truth of the stories about these strange men. She told the world in general, and Daddy and Francie 'Connor' in particular, 'Jasus Christ but you'se must think we're all complete eejits! Merchants from the East! Wise Men from the East! Fakirs from the East! Friggers from the West! Merchants from the East me arsh!'

On the third day (now where did I hear that before) bright and early, arranged around the stony floor of the house, with the dilapidated brown cradle containing the baby in the middle of us, we found ourselves being surveyed and scrutinised by these strange and quaintly garbed men. They had indeed great turbans on their heads, and as they moved about there was many accompanying tinkling sounds from their trinkets and accoutrements. But we soon found out that there were was nothing to be afraid of, as they were both very friendly and amusing characters, and not the ogres that we were led to believe they were.

One day Daddy said to me, 'There's a bicycle at granny's for you.' I was delighted. No, I was more than that. My excitement nearly led me to distraction, until I eventually got a chance to go and collect it. One day I set off walking, and soon came to Granny's. The bike was there in the hayshed, and no man or woman ever before seen such a horrible and ugly bike. It was a woman's bike, constructed of thick, rounded, rather than straight, tubular bars, and painted a sickening yellowish green. This man that my father knew, who had a shop in Glenfarne, had snapped up a bargain by buying these bikes which the Germans had abandoned in the war. Very soon the main road was a place to be avoided for anyone with a weak stomach, or who had lately eaten a dish of suspicious origin, because it would be full of riders busily commuting on their stomach-turning machines.

But I got my own back on the bicycle man. When I began travelling on my newly acquired 'treasure' I soon found it had a problem in the freewheel mechanism, and I took it back for the cycle man to put it right. This man was renowned far and wide, because he was the possessor of a fearful temper, and as I had already heard of him, I proceeded to his place in Glenfarne with some trepidation. Naturally, he recognised the bike, and said, 'And who are you now?' I told him. 'Sure, I know your father for years. Isn't it a lovely bike he got for you? Is it going all right?' It wasn't going all right at all, and I told him that. 'Wait there' he said, 'I have other things to do.' Jasus! I thought to myself, he's a lovely man, what do they be talking about, saying he's bad-tempered. At last the man dismantled the bike, and took twenty four ball-bearings from a large box that sat on the bench. As the man fiercely concentrated on the freewheel, he noticed that I had got closer to a can of grease that was on the floor. He said 'Will you keep away from that tin of grease for fuck sake!' I jumped with shock, and sent the can of ball-bearings crashing to the floor. *Aaawwww!* For Jasus sake. There were ballbearings everywhere, thousands of them, and I freewheeled myself out on top of them as I ran to the door. The cycle man nearly exploded. He was incoherent with rage, and his incoherence fearfully evolved itself into the fairly coherent conclusion that, 'I always knew it! I always said it! Everytime you see a fucking cub, hit him, for if he is not after doing some depredation, he is on his way to do it! Now take yourself and your fucking bike outa here, and never let me see you again!' I'll tell you one thing, after getting such a lacerating I felt very small. If I was a dog, I would be slinking away with my head down, and my tail between my legs. But still . . . There was a gleeful tingling surging through me, and I was soon overcome with a feeling of gladness and happiness, and thought to myself what a marvellous day it had been.

But bike or no bike, Granny's was a lovely place, and whenever I came there I always tried to prolong my stay. In comparison to the frenzy that always prevailed at home, life at Granny's house passed by in a completely different, and far more unhurried manner. Uncle Francie worked for the County Council, on the upkeep of the roads, and he used to provide stones from his own land. I remember often as him and Packie Dolan, a neighbour, and I, broke stones. We would all sit down companionably on the already broken stones, and armed with round-headed hammers, we would proceed to smash to smithereens the rocks we had placed in front of us. I really liked this work, and was usually reluctant to leave it to go to dinner or tea. In the evening, Francie and I would go along the well worn pass to the well for spring water. This pass went through lovely fields, and blackhorn and furze covered grazing land, and the well was under the embankment of the railway. This was also the way we went to Frazer's shop, and in the evening crowds of farmers would be making their way along this pass to the shop. Some of the people were. John and James Murray, John, James, Packie, Charlie, Bridie, Michael and Mrs Dolan. Johnny and Charlie Monaghan, Peter, Annie and Mary Jane McLoughlin, Dick, Willie, Jack and James Johnson, Paddy and James Cox, The Donnels (Granny's) and many more. The path that carried on from the well then crossed the Sligo Leitrim and Northern Counties Railway, an angled steps took one over the fence. Then the pass continued down a green rocky slope, alongside a splashing river. A bridge then crossed over the river at Dolphie Gaw's house, and the track still continued on the other side of the river, passing through a dark wood. Then came a sodden field of about a hundred metres, which was lined with flat-flag stepping-stones, and at the end of this field was the Blacklion-Manorhamilton road, and Frazer's shop. There used to be crowds at the shop, stocking up with their groceries, and Sweet-Afton and Woodbine cigarettes. Even when I didn't go to the shop, Francie always brought me home a packet of Black-Jack sweets, you got six of these for a penny. Looking back now, the way to the shop seemed to be a very magical, romantic, spell-binding course, along which to perambulate or make one's way, and sure enough, on one particular day I myself had an 'emotional experience'.

When we, (Mammy, Petie, Rose, me etc.) came on holidays to Granny's, Mammy, Granny, and the visitors that used to be there, would play cards or tell ghost stories. The 'conviction' with which they related their 'experiences' made them for me completely believable. And as Granny's house was a rather eerie and foreboding place, and the land was full of fairy trees, burial sites, and other lonely places, my perception of life there was predominated by a certain sense of unreality. Often, as I walked about on my own, I expected something to spring up out of the ground in front of me. So this day, as I was coming alone from Frazer's shop, I was immersed in a world of my own, and enjoying my Black-Jack sweets. Suddenly, as I was about to exit the wood, I heard a shout. Down below me, standing in the eye of the bridge was the most beautiful young girl holding up one of my favourite Kimberly-Gang biscuits, and beckoning me to join her. I didn't know her. I wasn't even sure if she was real, and of course in my innocence, I hadn't a clue what she wanted. I ran like fuck. The girl was real enough, and I later found out who she was.

At home we continued to cut down ash trees, and the crows became increasingly noisy and spiteful, as we progressively diminished their nesting area. Then we used to have football matches, when neighbours like Francie 'Connor', John Nolan, Jim Dolan or Charlie Maguire (Cha) would join us. And on the slippery ground, Daddy would take great delight in bundling four or five of the 'defenders' plus the ball, past Mammy the goalkeeper. Then Francie 'Connor' began teaching football, and we used to play at his house, with Jamsie, Jerry, Pat and Hughie. Then there was John James Sheerin and Jerry, and John Joe Maguire. Paschal, Jimmy and Phillip McGovern (Terry) used to play, and sometimes Thomas Moffatt.

Daddy had to mostly walk to Barlear in those days, until Charlie Cha (Maguire) had a bright idea and got a motorbike. Dad always had a keen sense of self-preservation, and always detested motorbikes. Still it was a fast and energy-saving way to get to Jimmity's, so he joined Charlie as a pillion passenger. As Charlie became more proficient, his speed rose accordingly, and as the two of them went along, above the noise of the bike, Daddy could be heard constantly shouting 'Will you go easy, for God's sake/' One night, for some unknown reason, Charlie failed to take a corner at Newbridge Hall, and went through the hedge into a field, and ended up in a dyke. Both were injured, but not badly, and Charlie went on to scare the wits out of all in 'the mountain' with his dangerous speed. Daddy however, never went on his motorbike again.

In February 1952 Daddy and Mrs Gilmurray fell out, and Rose, Petie and I had to change schools and go to Moneygashel School in 'The Barrs'. This school was completely different from the Marble Arches in that it was run with a frightening authority. It was permanently pervaded by an evil tension that periodically exploded into brutal punishment. There was less emphasis on religion than in the Marble Arches, but then we had to learn Irish, of which I and my brother and sister knew nothing. Our days at this school were overwhelmingly conducted in a state of nervous apprehension and petrified expectancy, where the most innocent indiscretion was punished with instant and terrible retribution. One day, a beautiful girl, Bridie Maguire (Hugh Aleks) was punished mercilessly by repeated caning and continuous banging of her head on the desk in front of her, which was covered in blood. During lunchtime in the playground, her punishment continued, with her being kicked around the playground by a psychopathic schoolmaster, whose brutality nearly killed her. Our father and mother got to hear of this brutality, and we were sent back to our precious Mrs Gilmurray, troubled but wiser children. Other children from across the border were also removed from Moneygashel School, such as Peter, Rose and Bridget McManus, and came to the Marble Arches. For some however there was no escape, and I often thought how did they survive as they put in their time there.

Jimmity's Again

On the 17th March 1952, Pat was born in 'the mountain' with no one except Granny as a midwife. It was about this time that Daddy asked me to go to Jimmity's to look at the sheep, because he was going off to Mayo to buy more. In one sense I was delighted because it meant freedom to see a bit of the world, but I was also quite nervous at the prospect. Dad gave me directions, then I took his bike and set off. Down I went to Blacklion, and then I headed for Glenfarne, where the bad-tempered man with the garage lived. When I got past Glenfarne, who should I meet on the road but an evil looking, big buck goat, with enormous horns, and he made straight for me, and knocked me off the bike. As he stood back momentarily admiring his work, he then readied himself for a new attack. Luckily, a farmer came out of the field at just that moment, and shooed the goat away. I was cut and bruised, and continued my journey in a more fretful disposition. Later, for some reason, I became sick and feverish, and as I turned left at 'The Big Bog Cross' for the mountain, I was in bad shape. Amazingly, a man whom I knew, because he used to come to our house, shouted at me from his doorway. This was Bertie Siberry, and him and his wife made me a good meal and I left there feeling much better. I wasn't even sure if I was going in the right direction, but the Siberry's assured me that I was. I carried on the zig-zag steep road up the side of the mountain, and eventually came to the top, where I sat down beside Doo Lough to contemplate my weariness.

I was still in bad fettle, as I carried on down into the mountain valley where Jimmity's was. I looked at some of the sheep wearily, for it would take me about three days to see them all, because the amount of land we now owned there was well over thirteen hundred acres. When darkness came, I made my way to a house that had been hidden behind a hill. This was where Johnny, James and Paddy McGovern lived, and as they had a massive pot of porridge ready, we all armed ourselves with appropriate sized spoons, and heaved the porridge out into bowls, where it was made even more enticing by being mixed up with liberal quantities of milk. They tried to persuade me to stay there for the night, but no, I was too important, and proudly independently and fearfully I made my way back in the dark to Jimmity's. There was no food. No fire. I fumbled about until I found the bed that I had used on my earlier visit, and slept peacefully. When I awoke early next morning, I was full of life. Out I got, and began busily looking around me, admiring the place. Jasus! I thought to myself, but I could run today. By God, I'll soon have these sheep sorted out. Stand back and let me at them. So off I went, up into the wilds, recconitreing and counting the sheep. First I concentrated on the upper part of the land, and headed out by Lough Avanney. But by the time I got to the top of the mountain, overlooking Creevela, I was becoming ferocious hungry.

What I was going to do for eating I didn't know, but some inner force propelled me towards McGovern's once again, and they said to me 'Arragh sure where were you! We're looking all morning for you. Sit in there like a good cub and eat your fill.' And I did. It took me all the rest of the day to collate the sheep on Jimmity's, and then the next day I carried on with the work on Peter Ann's land, which was almost completely surrounded by rivers. When I had finished in Peter Ann's land, I headed back for home in the 'Mountain'.

As Petie and I continued to grow up, we became incredibly fleet-footed, and when we had business of our own to do, like going after rabbits, or quarrying stones, we took great delight in escaping from Rose. We thought we had men's work to do, and didn't want her around, and when we began to run she couldn't keep up with us and had to go back home. I loved running, freely and abandonedly through the heather, the created breeze cooling my flush face. I felt as if I could go like the wind. But I was a relatively slow runner in comparison to Petie, and one day our different abilities were tested. Some people were at our house doing something with smuggled cattle, and one of the bullocks got away and headed off for the 'Ould House' and the mountain for all he was worth. Petie and I took out after him, trying to bring him back, but he just kept going. Eventually Petie gave up the chase, thinking it was madness to continue, but I steadfastly went on to pursue the bullock, past the 'Ould House' on to 'The Rocks' then to the top of Screg Na Connell, where he turned back to run along the border. As the chase went on, I became more and more determined that I would get the better of the bullock, and at last he grew tired and exhausted, and was forced to lie on the ground. When he had rested he was a changed bullock, and demurely accepted my wishes and agreeably walked back to the house. All at the house were as amazed as I was myself, and for the first time ever, I noticed an almost imperceptible glimmer of pride in my nearly impossible to impress father. But our increasing fleet-footedness became especially noticeable to us when fathers and their young fellows from the lowlands at Enniskillen came out to the mountain to shoot pheasants or foxes. While these people seemed hardly able to walk to where they wanted to go on the mountain, Petie and I ran rings round them, as swiftly and nimble-footed we traversed the rough humps, hills and other proturbences as fast as the fleetest-footed hares or deers.

Before the turf were drawn home from the bog in 1952, there was an all out attack on the road. Tommy Sheerin used his cart to carry large boulders from his quarry to the swamp. The Mick Cha's, Phil, Michael and Charlie, carried trunks of trees to the swamp. Dinny Nolan and his sons, Phillip, Tommy and Jerry came with bushes to even out the rough bottom of tree stumps and boulders. Even Hugh Melanophy came with his great Clydesdale horse to slipe boulders and trees to the roadway. Then lorry after lorry load of stone came from Carson's quarry, and sometimes there would be twenty or more mountainers levelling it. Eventually the swamp was crossed, and the road continued to the top of 'the hill', where it stopped for the time being. This road had the effect that now the amount of people who cut turf in the bog multiplied, because they were able to bring them away easier, and it also meant that we were able to sell some of the enormous amount of turf that had come from the drain. Jack Wallace of Moneen was one that began to take these turf away, on his new Ferguson tractor and trailer. He would be accompanied by is nephews Clarence and Gordon. They would have pots of Lemon Curd jam with them, and we would be delighted when they usually left some after them. Sometimes they left the tractor out the road and went home by car, and once again by some devious means, Petie had learned to drive it and I still hadn't a clue.

The 'Pink Witch'

So by the middle of 1952 our bog suddenly became far more accessible, and this manifested itself by increasing numbers cutting turf. However, there was still no road to the house, and despite the numbers that worked in the bog, we had, with a sense of isolation, to doggedly carry on with our seemingly never-ending work on the drain. But if Petie and I had only known, it was as if Daddy had received Divine information as he planned the completion of the drain. But all this turf-selling we were at, finally erupted in one of our first gestures to the trappings of luxury. Mammy had seen some catalogue, and she thought to herself 'I could do with some of that' and she went and ordered a new 'Pink Witch'. She had us all guessing for weeks as she grinned and joked about her 'Pink Witch'. She used to say 'And don't think that any of you'se are going to be going about with her.' At last, when we could wait no more, a message came that the 'Pink Witch' was at Mick Dolan's. Petie, Rose and I, Bridie, Frank and Farrell all went with Mammy, who carried Pat, and arrived like an army at Dolan's to escort the 'Pink Witch' home. Mammy's 'Pink Witch' was a brand new ladies bike, of many luxurious colours. It was lovely no doubt, with modern straight handlebars, and cable supported caliper brakes, instead of the old steel rod mechanical lever brakes. To some degree the little bike, dressed up in its rich and garish colours, seemed lost, inappropriate, incompatible with the dull and greyish dampness of the mountain. But Mammy had no such qualms about her precious acquisition as we all headed back towards home. Every so often the boldest of us would try to cajole and enamour her to let us have a go on 'the bloody bike' and she would resist vehemently. 'Get away from my bike ya crooked-footed omidan ya,' or 'If ya don't get your dirty feet away from it I'll brain ya.' But Mammy had a problem in that her original single-minded determination usually disintegrated at an early stage where we were concerned, and very soon, Rose, Petie and I commanded almost complete authority over the bright and colourful 'Pink Witch'. But no matter what hurry Daddy was in, he always resisted the temptation to take the 'Pink Witch' because he knew that it was one certain way of making himself look completely ridiculous.

In November 1952 came the tragic news that John Joe O'Reilly had died at the early age of 34 in 'The Curragh' Hospital, Kildare. We were all shocked, sad, but Mammy was devastated. Her hero, that stood for everything that was manly, brave and good, her and Cavan's inspiration, that had battled through to triumph on so many occasions gone. I think that Mammy died a little the day she heard the news. She had prayed so much, and so fervently for good things to happen in the world, and then this tragedy took place. She never was the same after John Joe's death, and became disillusioned with the world. She began instead to do the football pools, as if she had rejected belief in the spiritual for the more material things in life.

At Christmas 1952 the Mummers came to our house. They had been there before, but I was too shy and hid in the room, so I didn't see them This time however, I bravely stood my ground and thought, 'what the hell, let them throw at me what they will,' or something similar. The presence of Mummers nearby is registered by hearing a sort of light tinny drumming, and intermittent phases of distant plaintive melodeon playing. As the Mummers come closer to one's door they are accompanied by an increasingly clamorous and erratic noise. As soon as the Mummers get the attentions of the occupants of a house, they arrange themselves into a military-like stance or disposition, and the Captain of the Mummers addressed the head of the house.

'Any admission for Captain Mummer.' The residents, who by now will be agreeably disposed to witnessing the satirical entertainments of the Mummers, bids them enter.

The Captain of the Mummers enters.

'Here comes I Captain Mummer, and all me men;
The door is open; we shall enter in.
Room, room, gallant boys, give us room to rhyme,
And act out our activities, for this is Christmas time.
Christmas comes but once a year,
And when it comes, it brings good cheer!
We'll act the young, we'll act the age;
We'll act what was never acted on any stage;
We'll dance within, we'll dance without,
We'll dance your house all round about!
And if you don't believe in what I say,
Enter in Oliver Cromwell, clear the way!

Enter Oliver Cromwell,
Here comes I, Oliver Cromwell, as you all may suppose,
Many nations I have conquered with my long copper nose.
I've made the French for to shiver, and the Danes for to shake,
And I've beat the jolly Dutchmen, a hard crew to break!
If you don't believe in what I say,

Enter in Beelzebub, clear the way!
Enter Beelzebug.
Here comes I, Beelzebub,
And on my shoulder I carry me club,
And in me hand a drippin' pan!
Amn't I the jolly old man?
If you don't believe in what I say,
Enter Prince George, clear the way!

Enter Prince George.
Here comes I Prince George, from England I have sprung;
Man noble deeds of honour, to value I have done;
I've saved bold Caesar from his stake,
What more could mortal man undertake?
For England's rights, for Ireland's cause,
What is the man before me'll stand
But I'll cut him down with my right hand.

Enter Grand Turk, (Bad humour)
Here comes I Grand Turk, from Turkeyland I came,
Seeking for the champion, Prince George is his name.
I'll beat him up and hack him, as small as any fly
And throw him to the devil to make a Christmas pie!
If you don't believe in what I say,
Enter in St Patrick, clear the way.

Enter St Patrick.
Here comes I St Patrick, all dressed in armour bright,
Amn't I the gallant champion upon this very night?

Prince George.
What are you but St Peter's stable boy, who fed his horse on hay
For seven days, and then he ran away!

St Patrick.
That's a lie Prince George!

Prince George.
Take out your purse and pay sir!

St Patrick.
Take out your sword to try, sir!
I'll run my dagger through your heart
And make you run away sir!
            And Patrick stabs him.

Captain.
Doctor! Doctor! Any man for a doctor.

Enter Doctor.
Here comes I, a doctor pure and good,
And with my sword I'll staunch this young man's blood.

Captain.
And where have you travelled doctor?

Doctor.
I've travelled England, Ireland, Scotland,
Upstairs, downstairs, from the bed to the po,
Seeking for that which you all do know.

Captain.
And what can you cure doctor?

Doctor.
I can cure the Big Plague, the Little Plague,
The Plague within, the Plague without;
The pip, the pop, the palsy and the gout.
Moreover I can make an old woman on critches
Burst her britches
Leppin' over stone hedges and whitethorn ditches!

Captain.
And what medicine do you use, doctor?

Doctor.
The heart and liver of a creepie stool,
The brains of an anvil,
The giblets of a dishcloth,
Put that in a Wran's bladder,
Stir it up with a cat's feather,
Take that fourteen fortnight's before day
And if that doesn't cure you, I'll ask no pay.
Moreover I have a little bottle in the hip pocket
Of my waistcoat called Hocus-pocus (S) ally campane,
Rise up dead man and fight again!
   Prince George rises.

Captain.
Cocks crow in China, echoed in France,
Come to old Ireland to see Irishmen dance!
Ho! Music!

Enter the musician.
Here comes I who didn't come yet,
Big head and little wit.
Although my head is big and my body small,
I'll play you a tune that will please you'se all.
(They all dance).

Enter the Wran.
The Wran, the Wran, the king of all bords
Was caught in a forest last New Year's night!
The Wran she is small, but her part it is great!
And I hope Mr McGourty, you'll give us the price of a trate!
If your trate is small,
It won't go round the Wranboy's all.
But if your trate is big and of the best,
Then I hope in heaven your soul will rest!

Enter in Miss Funny, clear the way!

Enter Miss Funny
Here comes I Miss Funny,
With a long leather purse to carry the money!
Money I want, and money I crave,
And if I don't get money I'll bring you all to the grave!
If you don't believe in what I say,
Enter in Jack Straw, clear the way.

Enter Jack Straw.
Here comes I Jack Straw,
If I don't get money, we will have law!
Meal, flax, hemp or tow,
Pay the Mummers or out you go!

Captain.
Come on, pay up, all silver and no brass,
And you can stick your pennies up in your ---!
We're not the daily beggars that go from door to door,
We're just the neighbours children, and you've seen us all before!
With our pockets full of money and our barrels full of beer,
We wish you all a Merry Christmas and a bright and prosperous
New Year.

When the Mummers had done all their 'Mumming' they would buy
a barrel of stout with the money they had collected, and then
organise a 'Mummers Dance'. This would be held in one of the local
houses, and everyone around would be invited, where they could
dance the night away, drink their fill, and eat plenty of homemade
sandwiches.

Myxomatosis

The winter of 1952/53 was very cold, and in January and February
there was a snow whiteout. Petie and I had spent our Christmas
school holidays carrying bundles of hay from Hugh Melanophy's to

our house, to stock up in order to feed our cow. The cow of ours was a rather unsociable creature, and kept well away from the house. The usual nature of cows, and cattle in general obliges them to seek out human company when they get cold and hungry, in the hope of receiving food or nourishment. Our cow however would be no place to be seen, even on the worst days, and from our experience we always knew that she would be trying to graze at the farthest extremities of our land. Some of us would set off in the snow with a bundle of hay for her, calling at the top of our voice, 'Suuk, suuk, suk, suk, suk. Suuk, suuk, suk suk, suk. Eventually the cow would materialise in the distance, and it would be a picture, as the ambling cow and the person with the load of hay, the two dark hulks in the monotonous whiteout, approached each other and converged in silence.

To have any shame at all during these whiteouts was a severe disadvantage. For instance, on the way to feed the cow both sets of tracks told clearly where they had converged and the cow had eaten her hay. Not only for that day, but for many previous days, the tracks were clearly there. If, when the hay-carrier felt like a rest, or had to relieve himself, there was the evidence sprinkled about in a thin yellowish zig-zag line cut into the snow. Around the house there was no place to hide even for the most private functions, and when one had no option left but perform them, there was the story in the snow just as if you wrote it down and gave it to your co-habitees. Even the foxes, badgers, hares or rabbits, could no longer go undetected, as their criss-cross tracks led straight to their dwelling places. The poor rabbits didn't know then that their world was just about to be destroyed by that terrible and malignant disease, myxomatosis.

In the spring of 1953 the first signs of the disease showed itself in the mountain, by the rabbits seemingly becoming slow and lethargic. They could be caught easily without undue exertion. As the disease progressed, the rabbits hunched up their backs, and drew their paws together underneath, probably with pain. The dogs, who earlier asked for nothing better than chasing them, were now repelled, and shied away from them. As the disease gained on the rabbits, their faces and bodies became covered with the most awful lumps and sores, and they would sit sad-faced looking at us as they continued towards their dying agony. I know that farmers were angry with the rabbits, because they chopped up enormous amounts of grass, but this was an evil and terrifying disease, and if rabbits could communicate among themselves, they would tell their descendants about the horrible plague that man manufactured to obliterate them off the face of the earth. Although I myself used to kill and eat them, like most people, I didn't see them as enemies, but more like cheerful and cheeky companions, whose numbers sometimes got out of hand. For me Myxomatosis was a scar that disfigured the conscience of humanity, and its effect will be felt for generations. For myself, I haven't tasted a rabbit since, nor never will.

On the 1st of February 1953 we heard from Radio Eireann that the Princess Victoria had sank in Belfast Lough the day before, with a loss of 128 lives. 44 people were saved. We were all very sad, and soon Mammy reigned us in and began saying rosaries for those who were lost, as well as for their relations. One of my favourite programmes on the radio was The Balladmakers, which used to be broadcast on a Saturday night at about 8pm. It was made up of music, song, recitations and storytelling by a Seanniche, who used to tell the most outrageously unbelievable stories that usually began with the introduction. 'In my father's time.' One of the recitations that used to be often on was, Hanrahan. 'Oh we'll all be roo'ned' said Hanrahan, 'before the year is out.' Another of my favourite programmes was 'The School Around the Corner.' This was a hilarious comedy about a schoolmaster and his cheeky pupils, who were trying to put one over on him. Paddy Crosbie done all the voices, and his ingenious accenuations for the individual speakers gave an added dimension and cheekiness to the already very distinctive Dublin accents. Then Mammy had a great interest in music and would listen to the top songs on Radio Luxemburg. 'The Station of the Stars'.

CHAPTER 4

THE MOUNTAIN ROAD

Life in the 'Mountain' in my early days was to a great extent dominated by an inanimate object, 'The Mountain Road'. Even before my generation came along, tremendous amounts of energy were put into efforts to compel the authorities to provide a 'mountain road'. A road through the mountain was discussed at length from 1880 onwards, but always rejected by the authorities. Andrew Elliott from Corry, Mullaghbawn, a highly intelligent man, a sort of a poor man's lawyer, fought the mountain men's case. In November 1891, at Letterbreen Courthouse, the 'road' was once more rejected and Andy composed these verses entitled, 'The Glenawley Mountain Road'.

The Glenawley Mountain Road

At Letterbreen on Monday last another row occurred
About the famed Glenawley Road, it was, upon my word
The court was densely crowded, and it wasn't hard to do,
For the shabby little shanty, accommodates but few.
The magistrates all took their seats just at eleven o'clock
And round about them was a crowd from near the Hanging
Rock.
All signed their declaration like thorough businessmen,
And the cesspayers were ordered up by genial Bobby Glen.
A road by Mullylusta, it soon was carried through,
It leads from Derrygonnely, convenient to Belcoo.
This road is badly needed to connect those little towns,
And Mr Archdale promised to subscribe fifty pounds.
Then No 2 presentment, the Glenawley mountain road
That was supposed to run so close to poor Pat Tight's
abode.
But poor Pat Tight is dead and gone, ochone, it was the
pity!

100

He was the boy could raise the row, his sayings were so
                                                    witty.
Pat would have made a councillor, Tim Healy he'd outstrip,
And let me see the gosson to tackle him with a whip.
He was the boy could make a speech of knowledge he'd a
                                                    store,
He'd lectured on the mountain road for seven years or
                                                    more.
A veterinary surgeon, he was the best, by far
From Glangevlin to Blacklion, and then to Swanlinbar.
He was a judge of poteen, no better could be found,
From Timbucktoo to Tubber, and Thomas Vicky's all
                                                    round.
He was a thorough carpenter, the best I'll freely bet,
1000 pounds to a pinch of salt, if you lose you need not fret
But an eulogy on poor Pat Tight I'll write another time,
and now here goes, by jingo, to put the road in rhyme.
The road was advocated right well by Hughie Dolan,
The services of the notices was proved by Joseph Nolan.
There was no opposition till Mr Nixon of Belcoo
Enquired very quietly if this was the old horseshoe.
The question it caused merriment, as you can plainly see,
To call a road a loop line as crooked as can be.
This nasty insinuation, to use the expressive word
Of Mr Johnny Sheridan, who could not well be heard.
He would not now reply to, although he did indeed,
When behind backs he was tackled by Mr Thomas Reid.
A fair amount of Billingsgate these gentlemen let fly,
But who came off victorious I could not then descry.
Then Rev Father O'Reilly addressing thus the chair,
A more isolated country was not here or anywhere.
The old people are shut in and cannot go to mass,
Except they walked on stepping stones they had no other
                                                    pass.
Did Mr Nixon want the people from the mountain down to
                                                    fly?
For Mr Andrew Elliott, his reverence could cry.

Then Mr Christopher Wilson saw things were getting hot,
And what the people wanted was a road to the Shannon Pot.
Up at Mr Strawhorn's and over Killesher brae,
But for the upper road, he thought, the people would not
pay.
The rents up there were very high, and before the road
would start,
He humbly suggested Lord Enniskillen should pay part.
Then Mr Smythe looked angry, if angry he could be,
He said the land was up for sale, excepting Gortaree,
And a few other places from that to the lakeshore,
So the tenants would not bother him as they often did
before.
The road was then rejected, why I could not say,
But it is not lost forever, they'll be at it again in May.

In May 1892 another inconclusive meeting took place in Letterbreen
Courthouse, and once again Mr Andrew Elliott arranged an account
of the proceedings into verses.

Glenawley Mountain Road (2)

Oh! the day was charming, the rain not harming
The mountain men as they came along,
To the Read Sessions to make confessions
Of the hardships they had endured so long,
And Mr Johnston, sure he was wantin'
A road to accommodate every man
To Legnabrocky, over hills so rocky,
Up to the mearing of Aghanran,
To serve white Murty, who ties so purty
So many acres of Curragh grass.
With what precision he makes division,
And put four bundles on every ass.
Then there's Patrick Nolan - he's always scolding -
He took exception to all that was said,

I well remember last December
I made a mistake when I said he was dead.
But he's still living and says he's giving,
A large amount of County Cess.
For nine long years, gains't doubt and fears,
He's fought, but failed, I must confess.
And it's really a pity, for Pat's so witty,
Without him the session would be quite flat -
They may contradict him, but they can't evict him,
For he knocks them into an old cocked hat.
But the day is comin' when Pat will be runnin'
Along the road through Trimogagh,
By the Marble Arch he'll daily march,
From Cuilcagh mountain to the lough.
And Audie Elliot, (the truth I tell it) -
Will have an avenue through his land.
And Pat McGurn will go through crossmurrin
Probably driving four-in-hand.
And grocery stores will be built on the moors,
And fairs will be held in Clyinagh Park,
And Charles Maguire won't slough through mire
When going home just after dark.
It's my intention now to mention
Who served the notices all around,
Young John Nolan served Hughie Dolan
By throwing his notice on the ground.
In Killesher he left one on the dresser,
Mr Strawhorn this denied,
And Mr Bracken and the barracks of Macken,
But Mr Mayne wasn't satisfied.
At Letterbreen this was the scene,
The court was crowded round and round,
And Mr Wray gave extra pay
To his driver who returned to town . . .

And so the story of the efforts to get a mountain road went on. It
wasn't until 1907 that the road reached the top of the Marlbank

Braes. In 1928 it was made to Sheerins cabbage garden at Clionagh. Another piece was added bringing it to James Nolan's gate, then in 1933 it was made just past Marble Arches School. Then another quarter of a mile was added, bringing the road to the Aghanrawn River at Legnabrocky.

Continuous pleas to Fermanagh County Council for the Marlbank Road to be extended led to a tender application being issued in December 1952 for, 'The construction of road through Tromagagh and Legnbrocky. 320 perches. (1 mile)'. This would take the road from the bottom of Kerr's hill to Gortmaconnell Rock. There were few applicants for the contract, but the job was given to the McGovern brothers, Tommy, Eddie and Phillip, whose farm ran alongside ours on the other side of the Border in Eire. Their family nickname was the Michael Neddy's (this was not a derogatory term, but used to distinguish that family from countless other McGovern families).

The road had to be made through what was then the almost impassable rocky pinnacle terrain of Legnabrocky. Then through an area of soft bog and boiling sandy clay at Legg, beside Johnny Maguire's house. At Gortmaconnell there was a high hill (Nulty's Hill) that had to be cut through, with embankments that continually slipped. The route of the road passed within 20 feet of a 100 foot deep canyon where the Aghanrawn River ran.

Tommy Kerr had moved from his house in Tromogagh recently, and the McGovern's took up residence there, where they done all their cooking and slept. They suffered atrociously, working continuously into the night. Often they would find the work they did the day before, destroyed overnight, by moving ground or a slipped embankment. Often when they succeeded in doing good work, the Clerk of Works would find some defect in it, and it would have to be done all over again. Sometimes the McGovern's got browned off with the road and went away for a break. Phil Maguire, Charlie Maguire, Jim Dolan, Paddy Dolan, Eugene McMorrow and Phillip McManus all from Marlbank worked on the road. Phil McCaffrey, John Cassidy and John McBrien, all from the Barrs, also worked on the road. I would often meet these men coming from their work at nine or ten o'clock at night, all wet and covered with muck, their drawn, tired faces still able to produce a forlorn smile of greeting as they pushed the pedals of their bicycles homewards. The McGovern's finished the road in 1955 and widespread praise for the tremendous job they done. This part of the road has always been known as 'Michael Neddy's Road'. Sadly, Tommy McGovern and Eddie both died at a young age. Below is Phillip McGovern's account of the making of 'Michael Neddy's Road'.

****

'My recollection, as one of the brothers, who carried out this contract for Fermanagh County Council in 1953 and 1954, and are as follows. Phillip McGovern.

****

Fermanagh County Council put out for tender this contract in December 1952. The opportunity to work and to make money had great appeal to all three of us, Tommy (RIP) Eddie (RIP), and myself, despite the fact that we did not underestimate the enormity of this task. We gave a lot of study to plans and specifications both on site and in our own home. The cuttings and fillings, contours and gradients were quite a challenge, especially as this was our first encounter into such work. However, we proceeded with lodging our tender with Fermanagh County Council and, to the best of my knowledge, our tender was £5400. This tender was unsuccessful and the contract was awarded to a lower tenderer.

At some later stage Fermanagh County Council put this contract out for tender for a second time as the original contractor who was awarded the contract withdrew his interest. Although our interest was still very keen, though somewhat blunted having failed with our first tender, we gave a lot more serious thought and study in checking out our estimate of contract. Also a very big factor we considered was how we were going to be accepted by the local community and how we would find local labour and manpower. To this end, we had no reservations whatsoever, and time proved us correct on both counts. After consulting with a few different experienced contractors and rechecking our estimates, we submitted our tender, this time at £5300. It seems, after some debate and consultation in the Council Office, our tender was accepted by a narrow majority and we were notified accordingly.

It was now early spring 1953, and time to get preparation and work underway. Our first task was to get accommodation and we considered something like a mobile home. However, we dismissed this in favour of reconstructing an old derelict house belonging to a man by the name of Tommy Carr, who so kindly consented to let us have the use of this. Although we lost some valuable time repairing this house to make it habitable, it was essential to have something like it adjacent to the site. We lived there for the duration of the contract except at weekends when we returned to the family home at Monragh, the Barrs. Those weekend return visits kept us in touch with our parents and our youngest brother Michael who, although he was only a teenager, had the enormous task of doing the farm work, saving the crops and the responsibility of looking after my mother who was in failing health at the time.

It was now late spring 1953 when we commenced work on this contract. In the meantime, of course, we had become quite familiar with the plans and specifications and the strategy we should employ. We employed three or four men straight away, and the only machinery we had was a tractor and trailer and a horse and cart. Picks, shovels, spades and wheelbarrows were the order of the day, and there was no place in the team for the man who couldn't handle these effectively.

As we were progressing through this very rugged terrain, we took on extra workers, and I hasten to add, like the original workers in our employment, were all handpicked men who were hard-working and trustworthy when left on their own. Certainly the work was nothing for the faint-hearted. Our concentration at this stage was on the clearing of scrub, laying of pipes, rock drilling and blasting. However, as always in our minds, the real challenge had to be Nulty's Hill and how we would dig our way through the enormous monstrosity to reach the other side. The answer, of course, was if a bulldozer could be got to the site.

After many days and weeks of digging and, following on a visit by Tommy and myself, we were able to persuade Hamilton and Preston of Enniskillen to hire out a bulldozer, with a driver supplied by the name of Paddy Gallagher (RIP). It was not possible to bring a bulldozer on to the site from the Marlbank side. Therefore, the only hope was the Wheathill side. There was even great risks to this especially travelling across the steep sloping hill of James and Mick Carson. Anyhow, Paddy Gallagher negotiated this route successfully and the bulldozer was safely on the site. After about a week of long hours digging, Nulty's Hill was beginning to take shape and Messers Hamilton and Preston recalled their man and the bulldozer. The remainder of the digging was by pick and shovel and Nulty's Hill certainly lived up to its challenge.

Work was now progressing on different jobs along the entire road site but not at the speed we had anticipated. The main reason for this was that a few of our workforce had to take time off to attend to their own farms. Throughout the summer and autumn, work mainly comprised of rock drilling, blasting, quarrying, opening of new watercourses, laying of underground pipes, fencing, etc. Also, throughout the period we had progressed nicely on what we considered the second greatest obstacle of the contract; to secure a foundation to build a road across Johnny Maguire's meadow. This was soft bogland - in fact a good part of it was swamp land. By the terms of the contract and specifications, the underlying bog, or the greater part of it, was to be removed and replaced by boulder clay or the equivalent.

Throughout the period Christmas to early spring, before our staff returned to work, we were able to complete the laying of the foundation for road pavement in Johnny Maguire's meadow with sandy gravel we found nearby. This proved of immense benefit to us. By completing this section in Maguire's meadow it enabled men and machinery to pass freely from one end of the site to the other. By March 1954 it was return-to-work for some of our workmen, especially those who were not caught up with the spring crops. The job now seemed to be taking on a new meaning as we could at least see the general layout of the base upon which the road was to be built.

Much digging and filling still remained to be done. There was now a great deal of concentration, on quarrying out the solid rock that came in the path of the new road. This was also a means of providing the first layer of stones for the foundation. It also provided the stone for the road surface, as well as the stone crushed dust. I should state at this stage the anxious feeling we all had at the thoughts of transporting a stone crusher on to the site. The weight of these stone crushers are many tonnes and to draw one over the Marlbank Hill was an unenviable task.

However, our real worry was the safety in taking it across the metal bridge at Tromagagh. The bridge itself consisted of two parallel metal girders with railway sleepers covering them. A notice was erected by Fermanagh County Council that the total weight of the vehicle and the load was not to exceed two tonnes. By our calculations the width of the stone crusher on axle and wheels corresponded exactly with that of the gilders on the bridge. To deviate off this line in crossing could prove fatal. A young man by the name of Byrum Crozier assisted us in towing this crusher with our own tractor over the Marlbank Hills and hence across the metal bridge. Byrum led with his tractor, with me in toe of the stone crusher, and Tommy directing operations.

By way of explanation of the width of the span, the first tractor had not cleared the far end of the bridge by the time the stone crusher had arrived on all four wheels on the other end. It was only then that the Council notice about not exceeding two tonnes registered with us. The vibrations of the bridge is a memory that will live on with me. We had now accomplished this task and the stone crusher was safely on the site.

In spring 1954 work became available for us with Cavan County Council for dumper work and rock drilling. It was decided that I should take on the dumper work and later the rock drilling with the help of one of my brothers at various times. Rock drilling by its very nature is rough and tough work, and although this was just intermittent work, financially it was quite rewarding and helped in no small measure to subsidise our expenditure on the contract in Glenawley.

The deadlines set by Fermanagh County Council for completion of this contract was November 1954. It was full steam ahead from here to try to meet this deadline. The main concentration of work was on 'bottoming out' of the first layer of stones to a depth of 15 inches. Although we did not meet the deadline for completion of the contract our main objective was achieved. Because of bad winter weather, work was suspended from Christmas to early spring 1955 when we commenced stone crushing and surfacing the new road with broken stones and 'screenings' from the crusher.

Having now completed our contract as per plans and specifications it was only a matter of time until Mr Archie McClure (County Surveyor) arrived to inspect and pass the contract. Indeed Mr McClure was most lavish in his praise and commendation of us in accomplishing this task. Our feelings, of course, were of a great sense of relief, satisfaction and fulfilment. This feeling was also tinged with a sense of sadness to say goodbye to so many of our workmen who were so loyal and faithful to us throughout the entire period. Good wishes and God's Blessing was expressed by everyone to everyone.

Phillip McGovern.

****

Phillip has also given the following information, in response to a questionnaire. Although the McGovern's came from over the border in the Barrs, Phillip says they were completely at ease about coming to work amongst the natives in Glenawley. Their only trepidation was about officialdom. In fact the County Engineer Mr Archie McClure 'proved himself a true gentleman and most tolerant'. The workmen used bicycles to travel to work and returned home each night. Rock was shifted by using an air compressor, which was powered by a Fordson Major tractor, to drill holes in the rock, which were then filled with gelignite and set off in blasts.

Phillip also says 'I know my late brothers and myself have fond memories of that period. The fun was mighty at times, especially when we assembled for our midday meal at Johnny Maguire's. Social life, in fact, was very good; dancing, especially at the weekends, was quite excellent. The usual ballrooms or dance-halls were, Blacklion, Doobally, Glangevlin, the crossroads at Derrylin, and Swanlinbar, etc. The main topic on each Monday was which dance you were at the previous night and how the matchmaking with the girls went. The comments and descriptions of some of the transactions were very funny indeed. John B Keane, the well known playright certainly would have a field day if he were listening in. The first Christmas we were at the contract, about one dozen of us went out mummering on our bicycles which was great fun. Some of the lads forgot their rhymes and fell down on the job. We covered Glenawley, The Barrs and Enniskillen. We collected a heap of money despite the fact that we were clad in green, white and gold. From the takings we had some great sprees; dancing, drinking and more drinking in Phillip McManus's in the Barrs; a great assembly of young boys and girls. Phillip and his wife were always great hosts, having other great events I would like to recall.

****

Queen Elizabeth II

As we continued work on the drain in May 1953, the storms and rain of the spring had filled it full of water, and it resembled a canal. The drain was almost finished, and soon it would reach the green field at the house. The talk at this time was all about the coronation of Queen Elizabeth II, and while Daddy had no time for royalty, Mammy thought it was great. William Armstrong, whose lorry came to the Marlbank Road with our groceries, gave us a free canister of tea, with a colourful regal portrait of the Princess and Prince Phillip adorning it. Mammy quickly put it in the most prestigious part of the house, which was beside Pope Pious XII, on a high shelf that Daddy had made with a hatchet. All of us except Dad admired this, predominantly blue, colourful royal picture, and it was even better when we got two days holiday from school to celebrate the coronation. On Monday the 1st, all of us except Dad were going to Granny's in Roo, to listen to the coronation on her new wireless, but until then our whole concentration was centred on the drain. On the last day of May, a Sunday, Daddy kept Petie and I out until the middle of the night, until we finally made the drain into the swampy field. Then all that was left was to finish the lower end, and release the enormous amount of water that was backed up in the drain. The next morning the three of us were at the lower end of the drain working like blazes, and eventually there was only a small portion of turf between the backed up water and freedom. Daddy said, 'Some of you'se go up to the house and tell them to come down here quick till they see this.' Petie went off, and soon returned with Mammy, Rose, Bridie, Frank and Farrell. 'Stand up on that bank out of the way,' said Daddy to all of us, and he attacked the remaining obstacle in the drain. Suddenly the force of water burst its way through, nearly engulfing Daddy as it charged towards Johnny Dolan's land. As the water plunged and rushed, and then flowed sedately, it seemed as if an awful strain had been drained away from me. But I didn't have a lot of time for concentrating on myself, because Daddy was in his element. 'What did I tell you'se, ya friggers ye. Didn't I tell you'se that we'd have the drain long finished before we had any frigging Queen ruling over us? Now like a good woman will ya get up to the house and make us all a good feed.' When we got to the house, the Radio Eireann news had just started, and the newsreader said that 'at last man has reached the top of the world.' He continued, 'We have just heard that Edmund Hillary, accompanied by Sherpa Tensing, has reached the summit of Mount Everest, at 29002 ft. the highest mountain peak in the world. They left a Union Jack, as well as a spiritual offering from Tensing.' So it was indeed strange that Daddy had manoeuvred things that we would finish the drain at this particular time. And tomorrow we were going to Granny's to see the Coronation! Could we take much more excitement?

The next day, all of us except Daddy traipsed down to Granny's to listen to the Coronation of the regal, the just, the bright, the beautiful, the ravishing Queen of England. Granny had just got a new wireless, as if specially for the event. 'Jasus but we're a quare people too, leaving our homes in the mountains of Northern Ireland and going into the Republic of Ireland to recognise, respect, relish and revere the Queen of England on her Coronation.' But truly it was a great day. The commentator, the music, the speeches, all combined to give us a sense of the magnitude of a glorious and awe-inspiring occasion. Then with all the excitement of Hillary conquering Everest, it seemed as if fate had conspired to give the English the impression that they still ruled the world, or at least a large part of it. It was strange however that in all this exercise of self esteem and well-being there wasn't one word on the wireless about our drain.

But there was a throng at Granny's, old and young, to listen to the Coronation. They were all there, and when we had went to the bother of going, we would hardly be able to give the Queen enough attention in one day, so we ended up staying the whole week. We knew that Daddy would be furious, but it was an important event, we were excited, so we thought, 'what the hell.' As I've said before, Granny's was an agreeable and relaxing place, and as Uncle Paddy, Mammy's brother, was there, they spent a lot of time, playing the fiddle and exchanging tunes.

Uncle Paddy was an undisciplined sort of a fellow, a wanderer, who used to go off walking down the road and not return for two or three years. He would have spent his time working here and there around Ireland. He was a fearful gambler and drinker, and never had any money. Often when he would return from one of these expeditions, I would be there. And I would know exactly what he was discussing, when he would be impressing gullible neighbours with the most outrageous and scandalous tales of corruption and debauchery, as his wanderings took him through the depravation and prostitution of the country.

One lovely sunny morning, as the milk-cart departed from Granny's house, and a crowd of us were seeing it off, John Dolan arrived with his brand new shiny Raleigh bicycle. Now that was something to be admired, and we all gathered around it, fascinated, and very impressed, as John lectured us on the mechanical and technical abilities of his newly acquired machine. Paddy, being an expert on the ways of the world, and on bicycles, asked John if he could have a go on it. I wished it had to be me that asked him, but I hadn't the nerve, so all I could do was watch like the others, as Paddy, victoriously, gloriously and sedately, the blue smoke from his fag curling upwards in the clear air, and seemingly without any perceptible use of energy, effortlessly glided farther and farther into the distance, and when he took a right turn into the Roo Road he soon disappeared from view behind the whitehorn and larch bushes. Embarrassingly we waited, and when we all grew tired waiting we dispersed with an air of tension and aggravation to our respective places of abode. It wasn't until six years later that Paddy was spotted, nonchalantly making his way along the Roo Road towards Granny's once again, as he completed his journey minus the bike.

Aunt Annie used to come home to Roo frequently from her job in Musgrave Park Hospital in Belfast, and Granny had two more daughters, Jeanie in Long Island and Manie in Connecticut. She also had another son John, who went to England at seventeen and never was seen again. Until the day she died, Granny never gave up hope that one day he would return, but he never did. In the morning, Joe McCauley would come for to collect the milk for the creamery on a flat-bodied, one horse cart. He would return in the evening with the milk can, and the left over skim milk, and whatever groceries he had been told to collect. These would usually be buttermilk, bread, tea and Killasnett Butter, the whitest butter I have ever seen. Francie used to get the paper every day. It used to be thrown from the passing train at Quinn's Gatehouse and Francie would collect it there. He had a great interest in politics and the ways of the world, and sometimes Ned McCauley, a brusque squat, sergeant majorish sort of a fellow, would visit and they would spend the whole night arguing about Communism, Socialism, Marxism and religion. These 'discussions' often went on for weeks, in various degrees of ill humour until they were finished, then they would set about a new topic. They also used to play draughts, and a draughts match between them could easily go on for two weeks. But the most collective entertainment that we all took part in was playing cards, usually 25'.

When we returned home from our unscheduled 'holiday', Daddy took swift and retaliatory action that greatly interfered with our attendance at school. From then on every Tuesday and Thursday, either Petie or I had to go and look after the sheep on Jimmity's, and Dad would go on intermediate days. This meant, on the days that I went, leaving the house at seven in the morning, and Tommy McManus, who was now involved with Daddy in Jimmity's, would pick me up at the Barr Chapel in his Ford Prefect car, and we would head for Jimmity's. We would buy groceries in Dargoon and then call in to 'Big Pat's' house at Dargoon school, where Mrs 'Big Pat' would cook us our breakfast. As we would be eating, Jim, the son, would sleepily get up, soon followed by Tom Mawn, a helper.

No matter how dry the day was, the rushes on Jimmity's and the ferns on Peter Ann's land were always full of water, like as if you shook a tree after rain, and soon our clothes would be soaking to the skin. This wasn't a great enticement to the fact that we still had to roam over the mountain all day long. A day on Jimmity's and Peter Ann's land was akin to playing rugby all day long, because you never knew where the next battering was coming from. I would trip myself up on the rushes and go careering down an incline, usually getting a few good belts from stones on the way. I would go headlong into holes in the ground, or disappear into camouflaged depressions filled with water. Sometimes I would suddenly slide on the treacherous surface, and go cannoning into the stony river, only to once more remove myself and lick my wounds. It was on one of these misfortunes that I damaged the cartilage of my knee, which as affected me ever since.

When Tommy and I were finished on Jimmity's, we would again go to 'Big Pat's' for a feed. This would be at about ten o'clock, and then we would head for home. Most people would be in bed as I walked from the Barr Chapel, but the Melanophy's were usually up and I would give the door a few knocks, so that they knew it was me, and then I would carry on across the dark and lonesome bog. Often, as I walked across the bog, and my fearful imagination began to work, I was certain that I had seen dead bodies of people, and other terrifying monsters. The next day I would have to go and have a quick look to see if they were still there.

Rural Electrification

It was about this time that there was a sudden and noticeable surge of activity around the Barrs and the surrounding areas. Children and old people would stand transfixed as they watched their working men, postmen, farmers and those with no jobs, dig these gravelike holes all over the area. And what, you might ask, were these holes for? Well, they were for the poles that were going to be used to electrify the area under 'The Rural Electrification Scheme'. Then men with rolls of steel wire, connected the poles together by stringing two strands of the wire along insulators on the top of the poles. Soon, the houses in the Barrs were all illuminated, and humming from the sound of electric wirelesses.

Our education, which had progressed favourably, became more intense, as Mrs Gilmurray realised that she now had about her a group of pupils that would surely bring honour and glory to her school. One morning she lined us up and surveyed us, and doubtfully picked out the smartest, who would represent all that was best in the school, by passing the 11+ exam with flying colours. And so the day of fate arrived, and John James McNulty, Mary Eileen Maguire, Eugene McCaffrey, Maureen Maguire, Thomas Moffatt and myself readied ourselves with polished countenances, rulers, pens and pencils, and piled into John Gilmurray's car. It is hard to believe now, that there ever was another group of children going for their 11+ exam, who were more nervous, quiet and tight-lipped, and when they got to the Technical School in Enniskillen, more disillusioned, than our group on that morning.

When we got to the exam centre in the Technical School, we didn't know where we were, or what to do, and I was just like that bull in the china shop as ignorantly, erratically, and uncouthly, I careered into tables and chairs, and sideswiped ink bottles and papers off tables, as I distressfully tried to find my place. At last the exam was over, and with relief and exhilaration we thought to ourselves, 'let the fun begin.'

Once more we piled into John's car, and he took us to McDonagh's Restaurant in The Hollow, where he ordered dinner for us all. By the time we got to McDonagh's we had become a most unruly bunch, each trying to out do the other for boldness. Mrs McDonagh was terrified for her customers as well as for her crockery, as we boisterously played under the table, drummed at the window with knives and forks, and generally laid siege to the place.

The customers soon left, but John was unflustered and took it all calmly, and we settled down a bit when presented with our dinners. As the rest of us greedily fed ourselves, John James began to sing about the man who didn't like soup.

'There once was a man who didn't like soup,
He squeezed at a boil on his head.
Said he to his missus, 'I'm not having that,
I'll have a big sausage instead.'

Then Mary Ellen chimed in with her bit

'And what about Mrs Mullally,
That tethered her child to a goat.'
Said her father from down in Dunally,
She'd be better below in the boat.'

Eugene then had a go.

'Will you'se give me a hand with this table,
And push the thing into the wall.
For if we've more room we'll be able,
To run round the floor and play ball.'

And that was the end of that.

When we'd finished, John paid for our dinners,
And away from McDonagh's we fled.
To continue our life as beginners,
In the mountain we cherished, instead.

As we made our way home in the car, gradually we began to realise the complete idiots we had made of ourselves, and we commented to each other on the repercussions of our actions when the teacher, Mrs Gilmurray heard about them, as she was sure to do. I could just imagine her berating us around the room in the school. 'You'se have let the whole school down! Shame on you'se! We're trying to keep our heads up and do the best we can here, and you'se have to go and drag the good name of the school through the gutters and back streets of Enniskillen! How are we ever going to appear out again, with the whole world talking about us! And what is Father McGrail going to say? I can't think about it! Just don't make me think about it!' But Mrs Gilmurray never heard about our 'fun' or if she did she kept quiet about it, and there were no repercussions, except that I for one failed the exam.

Terry's New House

Early in 1954 the first new house since we came to the 'Mountain' was to be built. This turned out to be a massive two-storey dwellinghouse, far bigger than any other in the 'Mountain'. It was built by Terry McGovern of Tromagagh, by Tommy Nolan of Marlbank and Billy Elliott from Derrygonnelly. Not only was it a massive big house, it was also the first house that Tommy and Billy built. Every morning, as I and the other scholars went to school, we would meet up with Tommy and Billy going to work, and they would always tease us all unmercifully. Nearly everyone in the 'Mountain' and beyond thought Terry completely mad to embark on such an ambitious project. He had only a small farm of middling land, and him and his wife already had six children to bring up. But Terry McGovern was shrewd, industrious and an exceptional visionary, and Terry's house was built, and a lovely and wonderful house it turned out to be, and from the day it was finished in 1955, the 'Terry's' seemed to have taken on a new strength and outlook, and soon 'Terry's' took over from Sheerin's as the new meeting place for the young and old of the 'Mountain' as well as those from farther afield.

One day in the Spring of 1954, two men, two boys and a terrier, arrived at our house with the intention of shooting pheasants on the mountain. They dined with us, and then Daddy went off with them. Soon I saw Dad, with his long loping strides, hurrying for the house. He said that the dog was lost in a hole, and he wanted an ash ember to light a fire. We all went with him, and the two cubs were sniffling and crying about the dog. Dad got a fire going, with the intention that the smoke would drive the dog out. But to no avail.

We could clearly hear the dog barking in the depths, but we couldn't be sure whether he was barking because he was trapped, or because he was still trying to dislodge the badger he had went after to drive him out of his sett.

All day long and into the night, everything they could think of was tried, including trying to dig a way in, without success. Next day Dad decided that the only hope was to send for James McNulty, as he was an expert in the way of animals. James and his son John James duly arrived, accompanied by their terrier. They decided that by sending this terrier down into the hole, the shock of him, and his aggression, might just be enough to encourage the other dog to dislodge himself, if he was trapped. But this had no success either, and eventually the McNulty's had no option except remove their terrier or he too would be lost. Still the lost terrier continued to bark below in the bowels of the hill, though a bark that grew gradually weaker as time slowly passed. All the people met in our house and decided, reluctantly, that the only realistic option was to abandon the terrier. This decision was taken in the knowledge that the dog could be hundreds of feet down, as the area is all part of an enormous cave system. For about a week we all went to the hole every day and could still hear the poor terrier giving the odd plaintive yelp. Then we couldn't bear to go any more, and left it to Dad to give us news. One day he came back and said that he couldn't hear the terrier any more. That was not the end of the story however, because a few days after the terrier could be heard no more, he appeared on the doorstep, bedraggled and hungry, but alive.

L-R
Bridie,
Frank,
Rose and
Petie
McGourty

L-R
Jimmy,
Phillip,
Paschal,
Noel and
John
Thomas
McGovern
(Terrys)

Hugh
Cunningham
and
John Nolan
1947

119

The beautiful Mary Nolan.
Taken in New York city, 1953

Hugh Melanophy and
Kieran McCaffrey

Bridget (granny)
and Annie Maguire

Mrs Bridget (Biddy) McGrath

Mrs Dolan (Packie's Mother)

James and
Lizzie Nolan
with
unidentified
children.
John Nolan is
on right.
1974

John and Christina Gilmurray

Owen Sheerin. Shopkeeper

Mrs Bridget McGourty.
Note partly dug track of
road in background

Johnny Melanophy
(John Dan)

Mr Tommy Sheerin. 1979

Mary Nixon and
Mrs Robert Sheridan
at Gortaree

Tessie Nolan, Mrs Robert Sheridan, Raby Sheridan and friends of Gortaree. 1954

The turf-cutting entertainer. Bertie Sheridan

Mr 'Dinny' Nolan at his farmhouse. 1974

Mr George Sheridan

Miss Maureen Maguire
(Connor)

Marion McGourty
holding her pet goat
about 1965

Phillip and
Mary Nolan on
their wedding
day in June
1960

Mrs Theresa
Dolan
(school teacher),
Mrs Agnes
McCaffrey,
Jim Dolan and
unidentified
visitor

James McNulty,
Mrs McNulty,
Thomas
McGovern
and
John James
McNulty

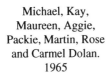

Michael, Kay,
Maureen, Aggie,
Packie, Martin, Rose
and Carmel Dolan.
1965

L-R
Brendan, Terry,
Paschal and
Tommy McGovern

Mrs Keaney
and
Mrs Theresa
Dolan with
their class of
schoolchildren
in the 1960's

The Morlbank
Tug-o-War
team with some of
their cups

L-R
Kevin, John, Bridie,
Marian and Bridget
McGourty

Frozen bog at
Baileys Lodge
with a snow
clad Cuilcagh
in the
background

View of
Baileys Folly
and Cuilcagh
from the
'Big Hill'

Mrs Sheridan,
George Sheridan,
Mary Nolan and
Mrs Terry
McGovern

Carmel, Sean, Lorraine
and Farrell McGourty

Baileys Folly, with Reed's Rock on left and Belmore Mountain in the distance

Road into Baileys Folly

The remains of Hugh, Francie and Alice Melanophys house, with trees growing in fireplace

CHAPTER 5

SHEEP-DIPPING

Sheep dipping

The sheep had to be dipped to prevent them being infected with maggots, which would eat them alive. On the day of the dipping, Peter, Daddy, I and the dog would gather up the sheep, and soon all the place around the house would be white with them. We would then set off to the Sheep Dipping Tank at Terry's with this enormous bunch of sheep. Jasus, but I used to be proud, as we passed the school as pupils made excuses to go out to the toilet to see what was going on, and could see the whole place covered with sheep. I knew they would be impressed, and would tell all the other pupils, and so I was bound to rise in their estimation from this reflected glory.

Of course plenty of other mountain people had sheep. The McNulty's, Moffatt's, Terry McGovern, Francie Maguire, Patrick Anthony, Tommy Elliott, all had sheep, and some of them had far more than us. But to my uncluttered mind they were at a disadvantage, coming from more secluded directions, and so were not able to engage in the public glory, that I thought we must have received as we travelled through the mountain along the Marlbank Road.

It used to be pandemonium at the dipping tank, as sheep got mixed up, and tempers flared. Luckily Terry McGovern was a sort of an overseer, and he had a calculated and organised way of doing things, as well as a calming influence on the more headstrong. There was little ceremony about the way the sheep were dipped. You caught one, and hurled it down into this concrete tank that was brimful of antiseptic smelling liquid. Then, Terry had a wicked looking, long handled, reversed T piece that he used to push the sheep down into the depths of the tank, or alternatively to pull the sheep to the surface again. When the sheep was thoroughly dipped, it was allowed to find the steps that led out of the tank, and the weary, bedraggled and shaking sheep would go off to join its comrades.

When they were all done, we would set off for home with a far more manageable and chastened flock of sheep, that never got their spirits up again until they knew that they were safely back on our land.

The beginning of 1954 saw a snow whiteout in the 'Mountain' and we would trudge down to Rossa in the lowlands in the dark evenings to meet the grocery lorry. Neighbours from across the border, like Hugh Melanophy and Frank Jimmy would join us. They would be wearing hob-nail boots and Sugans. Sugans were straw or hay ropes that were wound around the lower legs to prevent snow wetting the trousers and legs, and to keep feet and legs warm. Often the people in hob-nail boots began to grow very tall as the snow froze and consolidated on the steel and leather soles of their boots, and they would be unable to remove it without some implement. Jim Dolan, Tommy Sheerin, Dennis Curran, James Nolan, and more would join us, and we would all happily make our way down the hills to Armstrong's lorry, hardly feeling the cold at all.

The Outside World

When the snow was over in 1954, once we rose up out of the valley our house lay in, onto the hill at the house or whatever, there was nearly always someone to be seen out on the hills, or attending to their cattle in the fields, or going about the road in Marlbank. Like the Red Indians in the books that Jeannie sent me, translating smoke signals, my brothers and sisters and myself could stand on the hill and deduce where the main activity was taking place in the distance. Maybe it was football at Sheerins, or football or Tug O War at Connor's, Moffatt's or Terry's. Whatever was going on we would be drawn there, usually inveighing Mammy to accompany us, ensuring that we could prolong our stay well into the night.

Tommy Sheerin repaired the Marlbank Road with material from the quarry. We would listen to the iron wheels of the cart in the distance, discerning the varying modulations of the sound as the cart wheels crunched the loose stones and lurched from side to side. When we could see Tommy and the horse and cart far off in the distance, the great black horse and the significantly smaller red cart seemed to move so slowly, as Tommy filled the pot-holes, trimmed the edges and repaired the fence along the road.

As some of us still went to the 'Barr Chapel' with Daddy, we were now usually accompanied by Dennis and Hughie Curran and Con Boylan. They would be able to get fags in the 'Barrs' where they were cheaper. On odd occasions Connor, or Mick Robinson, who worked for the Pat Macks would also come. The priest had some fairly stern sermons for us to think about, in particular the destruction that television was causing in our moral well-being. For the people of the 'mountain' however, their moral good order was safeguarded because they didn't even know what a television was. Another threat to morals was the obsession with Buddy Holly and the craze for his 'new' music. An even bigger threat came with the beginning of the era of 'rock and roll' started by Bill Haley and The Comets. Songs like 'Rock Around the Clock' and 'Shake, Rattle and Roll' led to mass participation where the young were entranced, often acting stupidly and rioting. On Radio Luxemburg the preacher Billy Graham seemed to take on an extraordinary power, in parallel to the rise of 'Rock and Roll' and the anarchic antics of the 'Teddy Boys', as if to combat the serious undermining of the values and morals of mankind.

One of my everlasting loves was boxing, and prompted by Connor, I took an early interest in the career of Rocky Marciano, and we would listen to the fights on the BBC or Radio Eireann. Marciano had knocked out Joe Louis in 1951 and in 1952 became world champion by beating Joe Walcott. He fought Ezzard Charles twice in 1954, beating him. These fights would be eagerly looked forward to, even Mammy was a sort of a fight fanatic, and we would all fervently crowd around the wireless.

Every so often Daddy would present Mammy or some of the rest of us with the other end of the crosscut and another of the great ash trees would be sawn down for firewood. The Blackbirds or Jackdaws would evacuate to another ash tree and violently denounce us, arranged like an army across the front of the trees. The knocking down of a tree never lost its awe for me, and when it had fallen, like wolves, we would attack it and scavenge it until only the great bare trunk was left to be cut up.

Despite all the hard work that Petie and I had to contend with on the road and the drain etc, my hardest day so far came in April 1954, when Tommy Sheerin and Dennis Curran arrived in the bog to cut turf minus their third member, who had failed to turn up. I was drafted in to wheel the barrow from them as Tommy cut and Dennis loaded it. There was no allowance made for my youth, and all day long wheeled the barrow until a halt was called in the late evening. I burst into tears with relief, but my shame at doing so was tempered by my satisfaction that I had survived the unthinkable and not given in.

Before we got our summer school holidays in 1954, John James McNulty's father James had got a new Rudge bicycle, and one day at school John James came up with this outlandish idea that him and I would go to Bundoran on the next Sunday. He had heard someone who had went on the bus talk about the wonderful excitement to be had there, and decided that was the place to be.

I commandeered the 'Pink Witch' from Mammy, met John James on a bright Sunday morning at 'Hughes Gate' with his heavy Rudge, and off we set for the seaside. We had nothing to eat with us, and as we travelled along the lovely shores of Lough Macnean, we soon began to get hungry. We came to Cashel, near Kiltyclogher, where there was a shop open and armed ourselves with a supply of Cidona and a variety of biscuits and bananas, and found a quiet place where we dined voraciously.

Garrison presented us with a dilemma of not knowing which road to take, and we soon found ourselves going along by the shores of Lough Melvin, which was extremely beautiful, set in among green fields and woodland plantations, with scattered wooded islands. Past Lough Melvin, creating an impression of vastness and magnitude, were the Glenade and Benbulbin Mountains. We got lost again, passing out Bundoran and then found ourselves coming closer to it once again along the road from Kinlough.

Soon there was no doubt we were close as we began to meet expansive and colourful advertising hoarding, enlightening us about the merits or virtues of hotels, dance halls, amusements and other wonders of Bundoran. A strange smell accosted both of us. We cycled over the top of hill and there in front of us lay the greeny grey expanse of the great Atlantic Ocean. Between us and the ocean lay the vast built up area of houses, shops, factories and church steeples that was the town of Bundoran.

Everything about Bundoran on that day was magical. The sunshine haze enveloping the town, almost imperceptibly infiltrating with the colour and hue of the ocean, conspired, as it were, to leave no visible distinction between them at a distance. Swarming crowds of people, enshrouded with their finest and most colourful clothes were all seemingly being spiritually propelled towards yet another attraction. The air was permeated by the most wonderful wafting emanations of delicious meals being cooked, accompanied by the strong-scented aromatic smell of coffee.

John James was in his element, taking to all forms of entertainment like a fish to water. I on the other hand, because of my woeful shyness, exhibited an awkward reluctance to enter into the spirit of things. First, John James dragged me onto the shore so that we could go on a trip on the amphibious DUKW. ('duck') We already knew about the 'duck' from our teacher, Mrs Gilmurray, who used to explain how, like a duck, this strange craft could travel on either land or water. In fact one of our chief reasons for coming to Bundoran was to see for ourselves how this strange machine worked. Far out into the ocean we went, with about twenty others. The machine went perfectly if noisily, and it was just as great a surprise to me that this vehicle could actually stay afloat on water, as any other surprise I got that day. The DUKW made a large trough as it turned and then headed for the shore at great speed. Out of the water and onto the sand it went with little perceptible difference in either speed or comfort. It stopped on the sand and we disembarked, much wiser, and thoughtful after such a thrilling ride on a miraculous craft.

John James had to drag me everywhere. We tried all the penny slot machines, ring throwing and one-armed bandits. We also done our stuff on the punch-ball and tried the juke-boxes. 'Lazy Mary' was a 'hit' at the time, and every chance we got, John James or I put it on again. Then we found 'The House of Mirrors'. This was a wonderful place. Thin women that stood near us became two metres wide. Their children grew ugly faces. In another mirror their bulk diminished and they became twiglike. John James and I became prosperous wide-bellied cattle-dealers. Then we became crotchety bent old men with rubbery wearisome features. As we almost burst ourselves from laughing we became matchstick men, with no discernible countenance. We in turn, became ugly, old, bent, evil and amiable looking, and as we laughed ourselves out of the place, we laughed again to find that, as John James said, 'there is damn all difference in us' since we first went in.

As 'Lazy Mary' penetrated every corner of the amusement arcade, we found the 'Bumping Cars'. This was a truly exciting place, which I was enthralled with. But I just could not overcome my shyness and occupy a car, and I was left in contemplation as John James hurtled about the floor, crashing into cars to his heart's content. And so the day went on until evening, when we started for home. When we got home to the 'Mountain' we were very tired, and our thirst for travel and adventure was sated for the time being.

Picking Potatoes

By 1954 I would sometimes accompany Daddy when people from the lowlands wanted us to work the odd day, usually picking spuds. The most usual day for them to come would be a Monday. After resting on Sunday they would be all business on Monday, and arrive out of the blue at our house at about half seven in the morning. We would arrive at a field down about the 'Five Points' and join other strange men and women in picking up potatoes. A machine flung the spuds up in the air and we each had clearly delineated areas that we had to attend to. There was no time wasted with 'elevense's' or any of that crack. There was no social interaction between the individual pickers. My fingers used to be numb with the cold and dirt of the constant catching of the potatoes. These were not occasions for enjoyment, and there was nothing about them that was enjoyable.

At half-past twelve we would be called to dinner with a whistle. My father would confess that he was 'wake with the hunger'. I too used to suffer from a tremendous hunger on these potato picking excursions.

Even from the first time when I done this work, I never failed to be overcome by feelings of unease and disquiet at the performance enacted at the house where we were to have our dinner. One, two, three, four, one after another, all trotted into the house towards their dinners. However, my father and I were shooed off by the farmer in a different direction, thereby disabling us from entering the comfort of the house; or to put it another way, to prevent us from tainting the house with whatever affliction we had about us. My father would get one pound for the day, I would get five shillings, which rose to seven and six.

Increasingly I began to despise these great big, wealthy, pathetic potato growers. The time came when I did not really see them, like I could see through them, as if they were transparent, and did not really exist for me. That did not however stop a great resentment against them troubling me from within, and I eventually made sure that I did not go there any more. Daddy too, though it would have been more of an old tradition for him, soon gave up as well, and could not be enticed to go back no matter how urgent the farmer's needs.

In the spring of 1954 a strange thing happened. Once again Daddy and I were invited down to the lowlands to do work. This work however was for someone we both knew and liked, Bertie Sheridan, the man who used to give 'concerts' in the bog. This was a job laying concrete, and Bertie's usual men had let him down on the last day, so me and Daddy were reined in instead. Anyway we went down to Bertie's, where there was none of this 'crack of starvation or segregation', and the first thing we had to do was eat a big feed. Soon we were at work as the concrete lorries began to arrive thick and fast. As I shovelled the concrete some sort of a demon seemed to have been let loose within me and I began to generate tremendous amounts of power and energy. I was only slightly built, whitefaced and weak looking, yet some amazing energy generating machine was at work within me. I suddenly realised, and so did my father, that a point had been reached where our physical strength was almost equal. This realisation itself did not make me happy. My father was a giant of a man in my eyes. He still is. His quick-wittedness was razor sharp. He was highly intelligent, and he did not shirk from a good 'boxing' match when the need arose. Everyone around 'The Black' and the 'Mountain' recognised him as a special man who had undergone an early life of the utmost physical hardship, and his feats of endurance were well known. As Petie, Frank and I, and the younger ones, like Pat, Farrell and Kevin, grew up, we were always being told by neighbours and others, 'you'll never be like your father.' So really I felt sad and psychologically wounded. A subconscious burden seemed to have been placed upon me, in that I had somehow breached a reserved, imaginary place, and in doing so, I unalterably and unconsciously began to threaten and push Daddy from it. Bertie gave us both one pound.

Marian was born in 1954. A large proportion of the female population born in this year were called Marian, in honour of the Virgin Mary, and because 1954 was called 'The Marian Year'. it wasn't only people that were named after her. There were Marian houses, Marian roads, and a new housing estate in Blacklion was called 'Marian Crescent'. Therefore, when some person, place or thing with the name Marian is encountered, it usually means that they came into being in 1954.

In the 1950's the Forestry Department of The Irish Republic began buying up farms which were no longer economically viable, and setting forests on them. One day in 1954 my father arrived home with a bunch of innocent looking branches which he set on the westward side of the house, very soon these pine 'branches' began to grow rapidly and were soon able to provide a bit of shelter and colour at the house. At the same time Michael Neddy's farm, that mearned ours, was sold to the Forestry Department, and men began to work on it. Phil McCaffrey, who worked on Michael Neddy's Road, then began work on Michael Neddy's land on the 16 July 1955 with fourteen other local men.

First the workers created a fire-belt between our land and Michael Neddy's. Then the farm was cross-hatched with a pattern of drains and furrows, which turned the already rough ground into violently hostile terrain. Then pine saplings were set in uniform patterns two yards apart, giving the 'tree's as they grew, the appearance of a well drilled growing army.

The trees that my father set at the house soon grew tall and provided an increasingly strong windbreak against the wind and squalls that seared across the bare bog. The pine trees in Michael

Neddy's land soon grew tall as well. Intermixed with them, the grass and heather that had now no stock to eat it turned into an impenetrable barrier of brambles and hard grass mixed up in briars. From a distance the forest began to look like a great blank wall, and soon we were prevented, to a large degree, from communicating with our neighbours in the Barrs.

In the early 1950s Mrs Gilmurray asked all her pupils to paint a picture of whatever subject interested them. On the 16th of May 1955, at Kezar Stadium, San Francisco, Rocky Marciano gave Don Cockell of England a terrible beating, and next day the papers were full of gory pictures of the event. I painted my own version of one of these pictures, with the two men covered in blood and Don Cockell's face terribly cut and battered. Mrs Gilmurray thought that my picture was certainly dramatic, but secretly I didn't think she was impressed. However, I put the painting up on the wall of our house, and it hung there for many years.

On the 12th of October 1955 our beloved teacher Mrs Gilmurray retired. As a young girl called Christina Moore she had come from Sligo to the 'mountain' in 1915 to do the job she adored, teaching children. She had married one of her pupils, John Gilmurray, but sadly, they themselves had no children. The greatest part of her life had been spent in the 'mountain' and she had grown old there. In the forty years she had spent teaching in the Marble Arch, not only had she not missed one week off work, she hadn't missed one hour, or even one minute. Not bad for forty years.

At a function in Killesher Hall to thank her for her dedication to her pupils, and to make a presentation to her, Father John McGrail, in a tribute to her said that she had not only looked after the mental progress of her pupils, but also their bodily needs. This was indeed true, for even to this day I can remember when often I was starving Mrs Gilmurray would feed me and the rest of the pupils with large slices of bread and blackcurrant jam, which she had got John, her husband, to prepare. She was totally dedicated to her charges, whom she treated like as if they were her own children, and herself and her husband John will be loved and remembered forever in 'the mountain'.

New Teacher

Our new teacher was to be Theresa McGovern from Drumcannon, Killesher who began to teach in Marble Arches School on 17th of October 1955. A new broom sweeps clean, so what did we make of Theresa, or Miss McGovern. I was about the only one of the pupils with previous knowledge of Miss McGovern, so I was hopeful this foreknowledge would prove an advantage. It happened that one evening I walked out the padroad towards the Marlbank Road, when I spied our good friend Jim Dolan, in his land foddering cattle I presumed, so I legged it across a few stone walls towards Jim, when too late I realised he was accompanied by a lady, and worse still, he was holding her by the hand. I was dumbfounded, paralysed for an instant, as Jim and his ladyfriend tried to put me at my ease. So this was to be our new teacher, and Jim was going to marry her.

On the 17th of October, when Theresa started at the Marble Arches School, prior knowledge proved to be no advantage whatsoever, and every pupil in attendance suffered a severe culture shock on that acutely cool and frosty October morning. Miss McGovern, recently graduated out of Teacher Training College, brought with her all the necessary and attendant attributes of a highly qualified modern teacher. Her teaching methods were based on strict disciple, attention, orderliness and subordination. Straightaway, and from henceforth we were to pursue whatever subject we were concentrating on, with a wonderful interest and enthusiasm, and homework was to be a substantial and essential element of our 'new' education. What she probably didn't know what that at one stroke she had destroyed what had been an important element in our prior academic enlightenment. With Mrs Gilmurray much of our time would be spent in 'secret' discussions, hiding behind other pupils backs, about the price of calves, the merits of a particular 'Wild West' story, or a description about taking a cow to the bull. Miss McGovern put an end to all this 'talking' with the military-like efficiency and orderliness of her teaching. On her first morning she laid down the law, stating what we were to expect from her, and what she expected from us. Everyone had to be on time, with homework properly completed. There was to be no missing of days, no scheming, and absolutely no going to McGrath's well, where once you could while away a peaceful hour or so.

Employment

In May 1956, a few weeks before I was due to leave school, I started work for George Sheridan. George arrived one day at the house, enquiring off Mammy whether I would go to work for him, because his 'boy' Jimmy Nolan was leaving. I was still not school leaving age, and of course I had missed my first year, so Mammy didn't know what to do, and arranged for George to come back the next day when my father might be there. George came back next day, my father was there, and all were agreeable that I would start with George next day. When George was leaving he said to Daddy, 'and what wages would you be expecting for the young fella Farrell?' Daddy said 'arrgh whisht about wages, what wages, won't jaw wages be alright?' And next morning, with my two arms as long as other, I made my way across the hills and fields to work for George Sheridan of Gortaree.

George had a good farm of about 160 acres, which like our own farm mearned the Border. The Frank Sheridan's had just left their farm across the Border and George owned that too. Dinny Nolan, Jimmy's father, a widower, lived just down the lane from Sheridan's, with his other children, Phillip, Jerry, Tessie, Tommy and Bridget.

George's farm was made up of low-lying meadows, ascending limestone rocks and rocky slopes, and at the highest point the land was covered with heather. The predominantly sloping aspect of the farm was facing the East.

My arrival at George's led me to suffer a fairly severe culture shock. George's mother was an invalid, and always sat in an armchair near the heat of the range. I was surprised when George continually addressed her as 'Mother'. I had never heard such a thing. There was a maid who looked after George's mother, as well as running the house and helping with the outside chores of milking and feeding the calves. Our meals were at proper times. The cows would have to be gathered for milking in the morning, except for the winter, when they were inside all the time. One of us would have to find the ass to bring the milk out to the road. The milk would be in ten gallon containers which were attached, one to each side of the ass's straddle. When whoever brought the milk to the road returned again we would have our breakfast at half nine. Mrs Sheridan wouldn't be up at this time. We would have tea at eleven, dinner at one, tea at three, and our proper tea at six. After tea at six we would rest or take it easily until the milking at half seven, which took about an hour. At ten we would have tea or cocoa, or a dish of boiled milk and bread called 'Pinnade'. The maid and I always ate what everyone else had, and were treated as part of the family.

When I first started, Jimmy Nolan still worked there. Dennis Curran from Tromagagh had been there before Jimmy, and left an awesome reputation for the amount of work he done. I thought to myself as I stood near the strong and muscular Jimmy, what do they expect a wisp of a weakling like me to do?

The first day I went there, I was sent to Belcoo for bluestone, because George thought it looked as if the potatoes might become blighted. George gave me ten shillings to pay for the bluestone, told me to hurry up, and off I went. It soon began to pour rain and I was soaking by the time I got to Blacklion when I realised I had lost the ten shilling note. I almost walked back to Sheridan's looking for it, but all to no avail. I was devastated and didn't know what to do. And I daren't go back without the bluestone. In a trance I walked towards the shop in Belcoo, as if the bluestone was going to materialise into my hands when I got to the shop. As I walked along in the torrential rain something clicked, and I suddenly realised that Bobby Nixon was not in the little shop at the Barr chapel anymore, he was working here in Belcoo, in Evans's shop where I was expected to get the bluestone. With great difficulty because of my shyness, I explained to Bobby how I had lost the ten shillings, and had no money of my own, and if he would give me the bluestone, I would pay him as soon as I got money. Bobby gave me the bluestone without any bother, but my troubles weren't over. When I got back to Sheridan's, George read the riot act about 'what the blazes kept me'. I was ashamed of myself as George berated me from his very varied and impressive vocabulary, in front of 'mother' the maid and Jimmy. The idea of slinking off home even entered my head.

My early days with George were accompanied by extreme bouts of loneliness and homesickness, and I missed all my brothers and sisters and my parents desperately. I missed the whole unpredictability of home life; never knowing when Granny would suddenly come visiting, or what new enterprise Daddy would want me to help him with, or the latest row about sheep. But really there were many things indelibly ingrained on my brain that could not be satisfied. Our farm was sheltered from the east, George's faced the east. George faced Cuilcagh. We looked up upon it. The sun set differently. The wind felt different. And when we went to bed at night at home, we slept soundly in the knowledge that we were not only protected spiritually by God, but that the mighty outstretched arm of Cuilcagh protected us physically from any harm that might come our way, and so in my loneliness at George's many were the days when I didn't think it was so bad to be poor. This was a seven day a week job, but sometimes of course, after the milking, I would go home for an hour or so, but the time was so short, and sometimes there would be no light at home, so I couldn't see anyone properly, that I would often have to return to George's somewhat deflated.

I began to fit in, got on all right with George, and had my own room, a new luxury. I still had desperate periods of homesickness, and would gaze longingly across the valley, where I could see our land but not our house, which was hidden behind 'The Big Hill'. Soon I was able to do the normal things like milking cows and feeding cows, calves and the outlying cattle as well as clearing out the byres. Two of the most hated jobs were, pumping water and finding the ass. There was a lovely spring well gushing out of the rock beyond the byre at George's. This water was taken by a pipe to a reservoir on top of the rock near the house, from where it was able to flow by gravity to the various taps around the house and outbuildings. The pipe between the well and the reservoir was connected to a mechanical pump to pump the water into the reservoir. It would take hours to fill the reservoir as one just stood there pushing the handle of the pump forward and back. The ass was everything that asses were reputed to be. Stupid, obstinate, awkward and vicious. Someone, usually me, would have to go and find him in the morning to bring the milk to the road, which was the only work he done. He would always make sure to be at the farthest extremity of the highest part of the land. If he wasn't there, and he heard one coming, he would make for some faraway fence as fast as he could. He especially acted up with me, kicking and trying to catch the creamery cans in the whitehorn fence in order to knock them off, 'because' said George, I 'didn't know how to handle him.'

Some Sundays I had to cook the Sunday dinner. The maid would go to early mass in Wheathill or Killinagh, and George and his sister Rabie, who was a nurse in Enniskillen, would go to Church in Killinagh. Mrs Sheridan would give me directions on how to cook. I always got on well with her, though initially she seemed Victorian, austere, forbidding, all dressed in black. However, it probably made a change for her to show her usefulness in guiding me doing the cooking. She missed nothing. If the potatoes weren't properly washed, or a carrot poorly scraped, or a knife out of place on the laid table, she would lever me out of the way with her rapier-like walking stick, and point out the defect. She also used the stick with swordsman-like skill to confine the cat to its own territory instead of wandering aimlessly about the kitchen. I got used to cooking and actually became quite good at it, and eventually the churchgoers were able to return in the knowledge that a properly cooked dinner would await them.

Life at George's soon settled into fairly mundane routine. Sometimes I felt as if there were unseen oppressing forces preventing me from bounding recklessly out into the world. George would go off in the evening on his bicycle to the pictures in Enniskillen, or to some other destination to enjoy himself. Roisin had a bicycle too, though she rarely went out during the week. Roisin was a very beautiful, quiet and refined girl of eighteen. She always wore a dress that went to her toes making her very delicate and feminine looking. Even so, she worked as hard, or harder, than any of us.

George's house would have many visitors at night, especially in wintertime, as those were the days when ceilidhing reigned supreme. Bertie Sheridan, George's cousin, the man who gave concerts in the bog, would arrive, amidst thunderous noise, slithering across George's street in his hob-nail boots, roaring with laughter at the fun of his own jokes. It's amazing to think back to them times. Now all you can hear about is your health; butter is bad for you, so is sugar, salt and fatty foods. In other words, there is damn all eatables going that are actually good for you. George and his mother and Bertie used to have continuous arguments about what food was good and bad for you too. Roisin, who would always be in fits of hysterical giggling, whenever Bertie was around, would cook us all a great feed of bacon, sausages, fried eggs, fried bread, black pudding, and what not, and set it out for eating. She would say to George, while hovering over the table with a frying pan full of lard oil, 'do you want little bit of the oil George, to dip your bread in?' and George would reply indignantly, 'goodness gracious no! no, no no! It's not good for you, that oil,' and Roisin would retreat with the pan. Bertie would then speak up. 'Come back ta' hell here with that pan! Don't waste the good oil - please. Throw some unto the plate like a good girl.' A few minutes later Bertie would demand the rest of the oil. George would say with a sort of bemused sarcasm, 'laws a day mother, I'll be blowed if he's not going to kill himself. There's nothing worse than too much of that oil you know. Far be it from me to warn you, Bertie, but if you keep going like that you'll blow the bloody belly off yourself.' Mrs Sheridan would growl, mostly to herself, about big idiots, while Bertie carried on unconcernedly, finishing his meal, and leaving the plate the cleanest one on the table. Then he would proceed to lecture us all on the finer attributes and merits of oil, eventually summing up with his minutely studied and well considered conclusion, 'I'd be only half alive if I didn't dose myself daily with a dollop of good thick oil from the frying pan. That's what keeps a body warm you know . . . . If you ladle lakes of oil in to you, you'll never be cold in the winter, you know.' Bertie lived until he was about eighty. Mrs Sheridan also lived to be a great age, and George is very much alive and he is eighty four years.

Another night time visitor was Dinny Nolan, George's next door neighbour, a fairly domineering character, and he came at least twice each week. Dinny and I had never got on well since one day I met him in Blacklion he gave me a rope to hold that was tethered to his wild ass, and the ass took off. The ass galloped for Belcoo with me on the end of the rope. All I could think to do to stop that ass was to try to go anglewise to his direction and hope to wind myself around a telegram pole that was approaching swiftly. I was whipped against the pole with a terrific wallop and forced to let go the rope. Instantaneously, and probably wrongly, I thought that Dinny had done this to pull a fast one on me, the young cub. And so, when he came to Sheridan's, I would be furious because he would interfere with our night's entertainment. For instance, our only entertainment was the radio, and certain programmes like Din Joe, or the Balladmakers on Radio Eireann, or Double Your Money, with Hughie Green on Luxemburg would be eagerly looked forward to. The milking times for the cows would even be changed so we could listen to these programmes. There we would be listening intently to whatever was on, and Dinny would walk in and start complaining about the 'noise' from the radio. The radio would be turned off and the rest of the night would be spent discussing the price of heifers, rates, taxes, the immoral state of the world, what the hell 'Rock and Roll' is, and what subsidies could be wheedled out of the government. Our entertainment vetoed, Roisin and I would usually invisibly retreat to our respective corners. I would go to bed.

Retreat slowly, into the dark, blank night,
Where the creatures of the day seek out their rest.
But dreams of savagery and rolling thunderballs prolong the fright,
Then, silently, the dreams retreat as darkness vanishes into the west.

Because of complete full-time working with George, with no days off, the one day off in the year, Christmas Day, was eagerly looked forward to. In 1956 I helped with all the morning work, like milking the cows and foddering the cattle, then went home after 11 o'clock mass in the Barrs on Christmas morning. Christmas Day was always a very special day in our house, the one day in the year when we all had a wonderful dinner, and always with jelly and custard or cornflour afterwards. We always had a wonderful Christmas Day, playing our games, and seeing our parents.

Christmas Day 1956 was the first ever Christmas when the complete family were together. Petie, Rose, Bridie, Frank, Farrell, Pat, Marian, Kevin, Mammy Daddy and myself. This was one of the best Christmasses ever, made better by my being able to be there. With families there is some deep, indefinable, psychological link that locks into place when the family is all together, complete. When a member is missing, especially at a time of celebration, like Christmas, there is a sense of an almost imperceptible, but indescribable loss that creates a feeling of lonesome desolation. There was no feeling like that on this day and our fun proceeded unabated into the evening. However, our fun had to stop about 10 o'clock because I had to return to George's for work the next day. Mammy and all begged me to stay, 'won't you be time enough tomorrow?' but I had to go. When we looked out into the black night there was a total blizzard. Off I set, and almost everyone in the house came with me down to the gate out of our land, continuously trying to cajole me to turn back and stay with them until morning. Then I was on my own, in the darkness, and continued my journey into the ferocious wind-whipped snow. As I ploughed my way onward, the snow was rapidly getting deeper and deeper, until it soon became an effort to try and drag one foot out of the snow and force it forward in front of the other one. The snow froze as it fell, freezing onto my hair and clothes, and weighing me down heavily. This was one of the worst short-term snow-storms ever known in Fermanagh and knocked down forests of trees, electric and telephone poles and wires because of the tremendous weight of the freezing snow.

When I eventually got as far as Sheridan's, I was dead beat. George had visitors, and my appearance, covered in freezing snow and icicles proved a source of great amusement to them, prompting me to clear off to bed in a great huff. The conflictions of the day were almost too much to bear. To have had such a happy day; then the wrench to leave the comfort of our own home, the struggle through the snow, and then all those posh people, sitting around the warm fire enjoying themselves, and laughing at me, and not so much as offering me a cup of tea or a piece of Christmas cake, angered me. I thought to myself, by jasus you'se are going to get some surprise when ye decide to go home', and so they did. I could hear them all outside shouting and bawling in the middle of the night as they tried to manoeuvre the car in the snow. I chuckled maliciously to myself as I curled up in the warm bed. Next morning the car was almost covered with snow as it lay with its front buried in a drain.

The 'Mountain' in 1957.

So ten years had passed since we came to the 'Mountain', and it is as well to ponder for a moment while we register some of the changes that came about during that time. Well, our 'drain' was long done; and the 'road' was now made to the green patch just in front of the house. Our land was all fenced, and of course the Forestry Department had put up their own fence in Michael Neddy's land. The 'forestry' fence, coupled with the rapidly growing trees on Michael Neddy's land, soon provided an impenetrable barrier, and the outcome of all this 'fencing' was that we lost nearly all contact with Ellie Mac and her sisters, on one side, and with Francie, Alice and Hugh Melanophy on the other. 'Michael Neddy's Road' was in place as far as Nulty's Rock, and it was possible from that time to travel along the Marlbank Road to Nulty's Rock, and then cut through the fields to reach Wheathill Chapel. Sheerin's shop had closed down, and this resulted in huge crowds from the Barrs arriving at convenient places like Hughes Gate to meet Armstrong's grocery lorry on a Saturday night. Terry's had their lovely new two-storey ' house finished, and from the late 1950s some imperceptible social evolutionary force began to draw the occupants of the 'Mountain' consistently towards Terry's in ever increasing numbers for their collective communal interaction and relaxation.

All in all, life in the 'Mountain' was progressing satisfactorily, or was it? Tommy and Frankie Dolan, our nearest neighbours who I had went to school with had gone off to England or Scotland, and I have never seen them since. Mary Nolan, who taught me on my first day of school, and her sister Sarah had gone away to America. Bridget, Mary, Jimmy, Jerry and Tessie (Dinny) Nolan were gone, Michael, John, Hugh and Charlie (Cha)(Maguire had left. Owen Sheerin who owned the shop had died; and Hughie and Irene Sheerin were in America. And John, Patrick and Baby

McMorrow, who lived in Sheerin's, had also gone to America. Also John James Sheerin, who I went to school with, gone as well. Paddy, Mamie and Kathleen Dolan (the Clerk) were gone. Bertie Sheridan's family had gone from Legolagh, and the Frank Sheridan's, from Legolagh had also gone. John Joe and Baby Curran, Tom McNulty, Bridget and Mary Ellen (Johnny) Maguire and Maureen (Connor) Maguire were all gone. The Sheridans from Tromagagh were gone and had been replaced by Ernie Moffat and his family. Ronnie and Thomas Moffat from that family were also gone away. Charlie Maguire, who was an invalid left the 'Mountain' in 1948.

As well as all those people who had gone off to make their fortunes, many more had gone to meet their maker. Mrs Mick Dolan, who had urged my father to get me to hospital when I was ill with appendicitis, had passed away. .Hugh Maguire, Mick Maguire and his wife, Phillip McManus, (Big Phil) Mrs McManus (Big Phil) Biddy McGrath and her son Paddy. Tommy Kerr, Johnny McGaurin and his wife, Maggie Duffy and Ellie McManus had all passed away. Mary Ann McGovern (Terry A Jimmy's) and her brother and sister were also deceased. And our sister Ann, who only spent a short time in the 'Mountain' also passed away in 1947. My grandmother, Mary McGourty had an accident at home in Gortnaleg and died in the Enniskillen Hospital in February 1956.

Of course there were some replacements for these people who departed from the 'Mountain'. Packie Dolan married Aggie Carson, from the Barrs and their children were Maureen, Michael, Kay, Rose and Carmel. Our teacher, Theresa McGovern was another arrival and she married Jim Dolan. Their children were Mary, Michael and Patrick. Then there was May, Anna, Jerry, Patrick and Tommy Sheerin. Terry and Baby McGovern had six children, John Thomas, Noel, Phillip. Paschal, Jimmy and Veronica. Francie and May Ellen Maguire (Connor) had five children at home. Jamsie, Pat, Hughie, Jerry, Bridget and Michael. There were two Moffat's born in the 'Mountain' Leslie and Willie. Three of the Johnny Maguire's children were still at home; Rose, Julia and John Joe. According to my calculations there were at least 57 people who departed from the 'Mountain' between 1946 and 1956. In that same period 32 people were born, or came to live in the 'Mountain'. All this means that in

1956 there were at least 25 people less living in the 'Mountain' than there were in 1946.. The postman, Willie Brown had retired, and the new postman, Reggie Johnson did his round in the 'Mountain' on a bicycle.

To stand on George's rock on the odd, unhurried moment, and survey the activity of the 'Mountain' hardly ever gave away any clue of what went on there; how people did their work. There was always a deadness; an awesome stillness that seemed to be inappropriate to the magnitude of the valley and the number of souls that resided in it. The houses that were peacefully and comfortably dotted about the landscape gave no clue that the occupants of each had any contact with, or anything, whatsoever to do with the occupants of any other house in the 'Mountain'. This had a lot to do with the peculiar contours of the area. For instance, from our house in Killykeeghan we could not see any other house in the 'Mountain' or what was going on there. Packie Dolan was able to do his harvesting completely screened from all the other inhabitants of the 'Mountain' and Hugh Maguire, the nearest neighbour was in a similar position. The only farms where there was a significant exposure of what each was doing was Francie Maguire, whose farm was visible to Ellie Mac and her sisters, and vice-versa. Nevertheless, it was the case that every house and farm in the 'Mountain' was, to some extent invisible from every other house that was there.

In the winter night time, total darkness was added to the deadness and stillness, creating in strangers and lonely travellers feelings of agonising despair and tormenting melancholy, enfeebling them and laying them open to the most fearsome and terrifying imaginations. These fears were only repulsed by a continual experience of walking about the 'Mountain' and the acquisition of a couldn't care less attitude. The reassurance that the lights in houses on dark nights might give of peacefulness and security were liable to fill the wandering stranger with a false and dangerous confidence of his ability to roam about the region at night with complete safety. He might think to himself, looking at a light in the distance, 'I'll make for that house.' He would find many surprises on the way, and would be extremely lucky to ever reach the house. Places like the evil-looking Lough Gola, bordered on one side by a two hundred foot cliff, and the rest of it sinking abruptly at the field's edge. The Hanging Rock is 655 feet above sea level, which means that it is at least a 400 feet high almost perpendicular face. Aghanran is a canyon-like chasm, with at least a 100 foot drop down to a river in the bottom. There is The Marble Arches, with their terrifying concealed holes in the footpaths, like booby traps, waiting to lure the unwary to a 40 foot fall unto the vicious looking boulders resting in the rushing river below. Then there is Nulty's Rocks which are nearly 2000 feet above sea-level, Reeds Rock, Cullentragh Rocks and Cuilcagh itself. There are countless dangerous entrances to a cave system that runs for miles underground, and James Nolan's well is an insignificant hole in the ground at least 50 feet deep. Another phenomenon that can imperil the heedless is treacherous instantaneous floods caused by sudden storms or squalls forcing deluges of water down the rivers from Cuilcagh. So this was what was on the menu for those who were prepared to wander about the 'Mountain' of a dark winter's night. Of course the excitement engendered in the wayfarer by circumventing these formidable hazards often more than made up for the danger encountered. But we have only to think back to Paddy Pat Oiney and our 'drain' to see how danger lurked in even the most dismal and uninteresting places.

The Bicycle

Early in 1957 I had to take a day off from George to help my father and Tommie McManus gather sheep on Jimmity's. Even the short time I had been away from the 'mountain' and not after the sheep, made a big difference. There was now an awkwardness about me, and I wasn't really in tune with the demands of the mountain terrain. Eventually I got a tremendous fall on Jimmity's and badly twisted my knee. A few weeks later I was after cattle on the Cullentragh Rocks in the late evening, while George and Jimmy Frazer chatted on the road below. Suddenly, I went tumbling down the rocks, seriously twisting and injuring my knee in the process. Even thinking of that event now brings me out in a sweat. Somehow I got myself down to the level ground at the bottom of the rocks. George and Jimmy didn't realise the seriousness of the injury, so they went off home after ascertaining that I would be able to make my own way home to George's. When at last I reached George's my knee was looked at and seen to be swelled to three times its normal size. I couldn't sleep.

It so happened that George was expecting his new car a few days after I fell down the rocks. When it arrived Roisin brought Mrs Sheridan out to sit at the front of the house to observe proceedings. I dragged myself out as well, to see this 'newcomer'. It was a stately Ford Popular, a sleek machine if ever there was one. George already had a garage, where the cart and horses things used to be kept, and these had been cleared out to make way for the garage's new resident. Of course George didn't know how to drive yet, and the car-deliverer set about instructing him. 'Look' says he to George, 'at the front wheels' as he whirled the steering wheel around. 'That's what gets you 'round the turns'.' 'Well, I'll be blowed' says George, 'is that all there's to it?' The car man went on, 'This is the choke. Pull it out when the engine is cold. Here's the throttle, the clutch, the brakes, and this is the handbrake, for when you're stopped . . . Now for the gears 1 . . . 2 . . . 3 . . . 4, and look where reverse is . . . over here. Now come on and I'll show you how it works,' and off they went with the car man driving down the rough lane. When they returned George was in control, arriving on the street in a series of erratic jerks, and bringing the machine to a halt with help from the car man. 'I'm danged if I'll ever be able to drive her Mother,' says George, 'blow me but there's far too many gadgets on her.' The car man told George that hob-nail boots were wrong for driving and that he would have to use light shoes, in order that he could curl up his toes like an elf to reach the pedals. Mrs Sheridan thought this was great fun. 'George dear' says she, 'I've heard you called many strange things, but I've never heard anyone referring to you as an elf before.' 'By jingo Mother, you can be very amusing,' says George, as he ordered Roisin and the car man to push the car about so that he could turn it around and push it backways into the garage.

Next day, as my knee had not improved, George asked me whether I wanted to stay with them or go home until my knee got better, and I opted for home. George got Roisin to help him push the car out of the garage and then he got the starting handle and started it. I hobbled out and we headed for home. It wasn't a very nice homecoming, with me on one of Mrs Sheridan's crutches, and George left saying that he would call back in a week to see if I was better. George came back quite a few times and I was getting no better, so it was decided to take me to the hospital in Enniskillen for an X-ray. Nothing was found wrong with my knee, and when it was no better after another couple of months, George took me back to the hospital once more. This time the doctors found serious injuries in my knee, so serious in fact that they could do nothing for me. They advised me rest to see if it would improve, and that, if I could manage it, to take up some sport to strengthen it, and the only suitable sport would be cycling.

Petie left school in 1957. He then had to help Dad with the sheep, going to Jimmity's every other day. I would hear him leaving about seven in the morning, as he headed off through the 'secret' pass that was made through the forestry, to meet Tommie McManus at the Barr Chapel. He used to complain to us at home that Dad didn't give him enough money to buy food and that Tommie used to have to subsidise him. He hated going to Jimmity's and was delighted when he got a job with Jack Wallace, a farmer in Moneen. However, Jack and Petie did not get on well. The tales he used to tell when he came home the odd time really frightened me. It seemed that life at Wallace's was a continuous daylong battle between the two of them, culminating in a climax as they were milking the cows in the evening, when they would fling iron bars, buckets of milk, stools and shovels at each other, up and down the byre around the cows, creating chaos as they ricocheted off walls and floors. My father, who had also worked for Jack Wallace, would ridicule these stories, saying he never worked for anyone better.

After spending many months on crutches, I eventually decided to return to George in November 1957. As I walked to George's, a reckless, wearying journey, for I was still hardly able to walk, and did so with an awful limp. I was a confused, bewildered and useless human being, completely different from the wide-awake, exuberant cub who had set off to work at George's on that first morning in 1956. A few days after I went back to George, my father broke his leg in a pub in Dowra.

My knee slowly improved, and I had to wear a bandage permanently. The bandage would cut great ridges in the back of my leg, and every so often I would have to remove it and replace it differently, where it would cut new ridges. At last I was able to buy a bicycle from Paddy Mooney, Blacklion, a racing bike with ram's horns handlebars, and three speed gears. This was the first acquisition that I had ever bought and paid for with my own money. Bit by bit I progressed on the bicycle, using the evenings after the cows were milked to go on trips about the country roads. The exercise on the bike caused tremendous pains in my knee, and often it would lock up and I would have to rest for an hour or so until it allowed me to continue.

In January 1958 George took me to the hospital in Enniskillen to have a new bandage put on my knee. As I would have to wait quite a while, George went home, and I would get a taxi back. When I left the hospital it was a bad day, very cold, with sleet, rain and snow. As I walked up through Enniskillen, I came to the Regal Cinema, and I decided to venture in. I got my ticket, and an usherette directed me through the darkness, along a wonderfully soft carpet, to my seat. Everything about that cinema was regal. The seats were soft and cushioned, with the tiers sloping gently towards the screen at the front, and there was lots of place to stretch out your legs. All the walls and ceiling were decorated with soft picturesque images, which were illuminated and seemingly warmed, by lighting in the shape of Olympic torches. The size of the Regal was immense, with two ice cream sellers based in the stalls, where I was, and two more in the 'balcony' overhead. Of course I didn't know what these people with their little illuminated trays were there for, and it never really bothered me. It was enough to take in the splendour of the warm cavernous theatre. The main film was 'China Gate', a romantic war film set in the jungle of Malayasia, with Gene Barry, Angie Dickinson and Nat King Cole. I was in total wonderment at the realism and magnitude of the film, on the panoramic screen. I sat through two showings of the film, and even then only reluctantly left the Regal to find a taxi to bring me back to George's. I have never forgotten that day at the Regal however, and have had a great interest in films ever since. The Regal also showed me the importance of architecture in buildings, and how the architectural ambience of the Regal's interior, even though stationary, combined with the technology of the motion picture, to move an audience on to a very special level of participation and satisfaction.

There was another tremendous snow in the middle of January 1958. One day as I was carrying a large load of hay, I slipped in the snow and tumbled over a wall and down onto George's Street, and twisted my other knee. I could do no work and so I traipsed home to Killykeegan once more.

The weather at home in January and early February 1958 was very dreary, with driving sleet, rain and snow. On February the 6th, there was about two inches of snow on the ground, and the floor of the house and the scullery was in a bad state with dirty, melting snow carried in on people's feet. The unpleasant state of the house seemed, while insignificant, in some sense deferring to, the terrible tragedy that occurred at Munich Airport on that day. The Radio Eireann news told of how the plane carrying the Manchester United football team from Belgrade to England had crashed in atrocious conditions while trying to take off at Munich Airport. The plane had crashed in the ice and snow, resulting in eight players being killed, and ten other people. The manager Matt Busby was gravely ill. We were all stunned, because all of us, especially Mammy had a keen interest in football.

The 'Busby Babes' was the name of a phenomenon that made Manchester United one of the favourite, and most famous teams in the world. The 'Busby Babes' was the brainchild of Matt Busby, the 'United' Manager, who, disregarding the proven success of teams of experienced and mature players, filled his team with 'babies'. These 'babies' were players who had only left school in most instances, and had little football experience. But Busby welded the genius and enthusiasm of these players into one of the most feared teams in the world. Then, it seemed, he had the temerity to contaminate and dilute the purity of his players, British and Irish players, by unleashing them into the cauldrons of European football. The accident at Munich, in this light, was seen by many as an inevitable disaster, as a result of getting entangled with the tricky Europeans. The accident finished the 'Busby Babes' but Matt Busby recovered and rebuilt the team of Manchester United, and under him the team went on to even greater glory. However, the Munich disaster has never been forgotten by those interested in football. From the day it happened, Harry Gregg, the Northern Ireland goalkeeper, has felt a sense of terrible guilt that he was saved, and he has never been able to summon up the courage to face the relatives of those who died. Bobby Charlton has said that a day has never went by when he does not think of that terrible day at Munich.

This was a time when the workings of fate contributed greatly to the bringing about of radical changes in my lifestyle. Because the doctors in Enniskillen advised me to strengthen my knees through taking on a sporting activity, ie cycling. George decided that in order that I should have more time to myself in the evening, we would from then on milk the cows about six. This was a great help to me as I now had a longer period to do 'my own thing'. Another radical change, which probably provided greater social benefit, was the one that occurred in myself. I have said earlier that when we were young we only wore wellingtons. For instance, I had never seen Daddy with anything on his feet only wellingtons. Everywhere he went he wore wellingtons. The rest of us were the same. We didn't know any different. And if we had socks, we didn't change them often. When Daddy and a few of us would travel along together, we would be accompanied by a perfume that was certainly not romantic. And if the lot of us went into an unfortunate house, the combined quantity of our emanations, when contained within the rooms of the house would be enough to drive the unlucky occupants away forever. I continued to wear wellingtons until I got the bicycle. I have to put my hand over my face in mortification even now, when I think of poor George marching up and down through the clinically clean corridors of Enniskillen Hospital guiding me here and there in those big smelly wellingtons. Another legacy from our younger days was our ability to hold on to whatever we perceived to be our clothes. For instance, while I was with George it looked as if my jacket was glued on. It never came off. No one ever saw it off. Even when the sun was splitting the stones, the jacket stayed determinedly where it was. And even when I knew I should take it off, and wanted to take it off, some psychological force would prevent me from doing so. This all changed soon after I got the bike. I found that my wellingtons were too light, and that the soles tended to curl themselves around the pedals, and when I pushed hard, the pedals pressed too much into my feet. As well as that, when it rained the water ran down my clothes and into my wellingtons saturating my socks, the whole lot turning into a totally obnoxious mixture, which then went on to produce curious squelching and disgusting obscene noises as I pedalled about my business. When the case for the jacket came to judgement it lost out through similar circumstances. When I got familiar with my bike I began to examine it more closely. I could see that it was designed to arrange its rider in such a way as to get the maximum strength and leverage to force around the pedals. With continuing investigations I found that the jacket was limiting my ability to stretch out my arms and shoulders to their full extent, and consequently reducing my effectiveness to pedal. As well as that I soon found out that the jacket had an extraordinary and thoroughly disgusting habit when there was a following wind, in that the back flap of it would fly up over my head preventing me seeing where I was going. No sooner had I pushed it down into its pace than HUP, up it would come again. One day I got sick of this, so I shouted to the jacket, well there was no one else there. I said, 'jasus chhrrissht of almighty . . . do that once more.' And I carried on peacefully for a few minutes until HUP, up it went again. 'Fuck off . . . to hell.' And I launched the jacket over the hedge and our paths separated for ever. I couldn't believe it was so easy to get rid of the bloody jacket. I sneaked a look down between my arms at the wellingtons pedalling furiously below.

CHAPTER 6

SOCIAL ACTIVITY

There was something magnetic about a bicycle where I was concerned. As soon as I sat up on it there was something driving me on. Go on . . . go on . . . go on . . . I would see the brow of a hill in the distance. I had to get to it. Go on . . . go on . . . go on . . . Or a bend ahead; go on . . . go on . . . go on . . . A person walking; I had to reach them quickly; go on . . . go on . . . go on . . . A car would pass me; I had to try to catch up with it; go on . . . go on . . . go on . . Sometimes when I returned to George's at night, it wasn't my knee that bothered me, it was my heart, as if it was going to give up because it wasn't able to take any more.

The bicycle allowed me to travel great distances, as well as allowing me to make new friends from all over the place. As well as that, my school friends, like John James McNulty, Paddy Maguire and Noel McGovern had bicycles as well. Petie had changed his job and was working with Robert Elliott of Gortatole, and he also had a bike. Sometimes we would all meet up and head for the pictures in Blacklion or Belcoo. If the pictures weren't ready to start, I would jump on the bike for a quick spin to Glenfarne or Dowra, and be back again before the pictures started. On our way home about midnight we would stop at Rossa to chat, before going off in our different directions. These chats used to be continually interrupted by Petie, who was always complaining that he had to be up at six. The rest of us had little sympathy for him. John James would say to him, 'Jasus Petie, we all have to get up sometime. There yare, working with big farmers, taking big wages off them every week; if I was in your shoes I could hardly wait to get up in the morning . . . Now take me and Noel here . . . we get up when we're ready to rise and rummage about through the leftovers in the pot, and not before.' And then we'd happily head off to our places of abode. When there was no pictures, we had a sort of an unofficial meeting place at John Maguire's (Besies) in Blacklion where hordes of cubs and cutties would gather.

Now that I had the bike I was able to go around the different houses in the 'Mountain', sometimes learning to play '25, learning to pull Tug O War at Terry's, or playing football at Terry's or 'Connor's'. Francie 'Connor' loved football, and wherever we were playing about the 'Mountain' he would be sure to be there. He would entertain us with imaginary football commentaries, as if he was Michael O'hehir, and through the great knowledge of football that he had, he gave us all a tremendous interest and infatuation with Gaelic Football, and the up and coming counties in Ulster, as well as their star players. Francie would line us up in the little sloping rocky field in front of his house, put out two jackets or wellingtons for each goal, and order us to our positions. Sometimes there would be fifteen volunteers, so eight would play on one side and seven on the other, and Francie told us to imagine that one team was Down and the other one Kerry, or Cavan. John Thomas would be in one goal and Hughie 'Connor' would usually be in the other goal, representing Down. Pat 'Connor' was one of the star players, his tricky switches and darting runs proving a serious handful. John Joe Maguire too was a dangerous player, and in more ways than one. John Joe persisted in wearing hob-nail boots when playing, and a kick from one of them would be like a kick from a horse. Even though he was small and young then, he was very strong, and could dart in and out through players like a cricket. Petie was a very good player, subtle and an accurate free-taker. Phillip and Paschal 'Terry' were also strong and determined, as was Thomas Moffatt and Jerry 'Connor'. 'Matches' would be played in a great spirit of sportsmanship and manly endeavour, for the first ten or fifteen minutes, and then a period of depressing bickering would set in. 'That's a free.' 'Goway ta hell with ya, how wid it be a free?' 'That's a fuckin free . . . give me that bastard of a ball.' Or 'That ball went over the line . . . that's a goal for us.' 'It's not a goal for 'us' for it never crossed that goal line.' 'That ball certainly did cross the line, and I saw you with your big fucking claws scraping it back across the hoor of a line.' 'Isn't that a goal for us Francie?' Oh dear, if Mrs Gilmurray heard us. Cubs cursing as if they were men already - and them 'receiving' only a couple of hours ago. The 'game' would then deteriorate into a battle of wills between Jerry 'Connor' and

Phillip 'Terry' when they would argue about every little detail, including the fact that there seemed to be more grass on one side of the field than the other. I don't know why I used to play, because I was both uncoordinated and dangerous. When I would compete for a dangerous ball, I would be laughing loudly at the fun of it. I had no comprehension of what a good position was, or that I might get my head knocked off. I was also a real danger in that no one knew what I was going to do next, and that included myself. The ball might be in a rough scrimmage where I could get a chance to kick it. Of course I wouldn't kick it; I'd fist it, and miss it and hit someone into the gob. Nevertheless, I used to think that we had a good team, and that if they got a break would startle any opposition, especially if I stayed on the sideline. That thinking all changed after I saw a Gaelic Football match in Blacklion one evening. I couldn't believe how civilised and disciplined they were, and how they were able to weave silky patterns around the field, making the ball do the work. From then on I decided that the only way that I'd be getting involved in Gaelic Football or any other sort of football was to be watching it.

We also played football at 'Terry's', and while we all had a tremendous interest in Gaelic Football, our 'matches' progressed in a similar depressing sequence to the way they did at 'Connor's'. However, when the football at 'Terry's' deteriorated into a fracas there was the saving grace that the 'Terry's' had in place all the elements to turn our interests in a completely different direction.

Everyone at 'Terry's' was a Tug O War afficionada, and that included Tommy and John Gilmurray who spent a lot of their time there. Them, and Tommy and Terry McGovern would enthrall us cubs with their reminiscences about great Tug O War contests, and great teams they had met when they used to pull in competitions. This was meat and drink to us all of course, and bit by bit we got a fierce interest and craving to pull Tug O War like the great teams from Marlbank that had gone before us. The 'Terry's had a proper Tug O War rope, and that was attached to a barrel of concrete. The barrel was dropped into a deep hole and the rope hooked around an overhanging branch, and here we would practice for hours, pulling the barrel up and checking it as it was let down again. John or Tommy Gilmurray instructed us in this training, and with advice from Tommy and Terry McGovern, it soon became clear that pulling Tug O War was not a simple matter of trying to pull another team of a similar weight a certain distance. First, the two teams would take the strain on the rope. Tommy Gilmurray said that when the order is given to pull, the other team will, naturally suddenly chuck the rope and try to pull us off our feet. He said to let them have a couple of feet of the rope. This will put them off balance. Then, suddenly, pull on the rope with all your might. This action will shift them, but probably not the whole distance. Because the other team have now been hauled back to your side of the centre line, they will be outraged, and determined to rectify the damage. They will have madmen's strength. You must not move. If you are properly positioned they will be unable to move you no matter what they do. With their efforts, the other team will destroy the ground underneath them, and you will find that there are periods when they are almost imperceptibly, adjusting themselves on the rope. During one of these periods when they are repositioning themselves on the rope, I will give the signal to suddenly chuck the rope as if your whole lives depended on it. If you don't pull them straight across the field, said Tommy, I know nothing about Tug O War. 'Now if you all do your training, and do what I tell you, we'll put this Marlbank Tug O War team on the map.'

'25

Then there was '25, which nearly every man, woman and child in the 'Mountain' played. All the 'Terry's' loved '25, but most especially Mrs 'Terry' and those of us who had reached a reasonable standard would go and play around the houses of the 'Mountain' and especially at 'Terry's' where '25 was a continuous nightly pastime. There are of course inherent dangers in playing '25', and one of them is that after a long night of playing, one is imbued with a remarkable ability, where the imagination takes one totally over and the most vile, wicked and terrifying monsters are encountered on the journey home. When these lonesome and woeful spectres fail to appear, other happenings just as gruesome entertain the lonely, homeward bound wayfarer.

When Farrell, Rose, Bride, Frank or Mammy were on their way home from one of these 'games', because their imagination's were so receptive, their journey was nearly always enlivened by the presence of a forbidding and macabre masquerade. These would sometimes come in the shape of great chains being dragged after them or some unearthly being 'doing' a performance in front of them.

In one such incident, Mammy, Rose, Farrell, Bridie and Frank were coming from a game of '25 and heading for home in the early hours of the morning. The night was fairly bright and cold, with dark clouds running across the full moon. As they walked briskly along the road near the school, they were all immersed in their own private thoughts of the night's events, and had little to say to each other. A strange morbid foreboding seemed to come over each of them. As they went past the school a flock of crows suddenly appeared over them. The crows were agitated, snapping at each other and darting about so close to our one's heads that several times they were hit by the birds wings and feet. At the beginning of 'Connor's Quarry' the crows disappeared suddenly and our one's who were by now very anxious and fearful, walked through the quarry silently except for the noise of their footwear, which now seemed loud enough to waken the dead. When they came out of the quarry, and into the fitful light of the moon, they were nearly paralysed with fear when they realised there was a stranger walking with them. They all knew there was someone there, but they could not distinguish between who it was and they themselves.

As they walked on in terror, an ass that had been grazing along the roadside suddenly took off in a frenzy, jumped across the stone wall and galloped away across the rocks into the wood. It was then that these people who were walking home, realised they were now also accompanied by a large black cat. The cat soon began the perplexing behaviour of darting out in front of the walkers and dive-bombing into the stone wall with ferocious, bloodcurdling screams. Then it would slink back to the walkers and brush itself up against one of them, curling itself around their legs, purring, leaving that unfortunate in dread and preventing them from keeping up with the others. Then it would leave that person and spring towards the stone wall with the bloodcurdling screams once more.

Suddenly the black cat disappeared, and Mammy, petrified with fear, whispered to the others, 'Thank God the bitch is gone.' Then a heavy, dragging sound was heard, and it was noticed that one of the walkers had a heavy chain clamped to his leg, and some of the others were trying to drag it along after the person who was clamped to it. Everyone felt an indescribable compulsion to drag the heavy chain, and they all began to pull the, seemingly endless, great chain after them with all their might. On past Big Phil's, and over the stile into Cassidy's land they went, dragging the terrible chain behind them for all they were worth. Sometimes the chain got caught in rock crevices or tree stumps, but no one ever went back to see what was wrong. They just kept savagely pulling the chain until it moved once more. When they approached an area in Cassidy's land called 'The Big Stone' which is a place where large stones protrude up from the ground at strange angles, the black cat was positioned watchfully on one of the large stones observing the progress of the travellers. As they got nearer to her, she slowly got up, arched her back stretched out each back leg behind her, flexing them. At the same time her tail was stretched upwards and the point was weaving with a snakelike viciousness, and the rest of her tail was oscillating threateningly and ominously. When our ones were only a few feet from the black cat she began to spit viciously and scream with the most terrible bloodcurdling and fearsome caterwauling.

As this harangue was going on, the brightness of the moon seemed to concentrate on one of the strangely angled stones which then disappeared into a brilliant area of light. The person who was anchored to the chain began to struggle, trying to pull the great chain along on his own. Everyone else seemed to be paralysed with fear and were unable to move. The black cat then let out a ferocious, ear piercing squeal and bounded off the stone. She then walked slowly and deliberately along the chain, flexing and switching her upright tail as she did so, as the person tried their best to move the chain. The cat then stopped and focused her eyes on a specific area of the chain. She began to examine this area minutely, pawing at it and sniffing at it. She then clamped her teeth around a link of the chain, and the cat, and the person who was clamped to the chain, went creeping slowly forward with the chain to disappear into the brilliant light. A terrible brawl was heard underground, the light instantaneously went out and all was silence, and pitch darkness. When they were able, Mammy and the rest began to move again, fearfully proceeding in the dark towards Dolan's. They came to Dolan's and found the pass to our house, much to their relief. Then the silence of the earth was shattered by a cock crowing loud enough to waken the dead, and he continued his hysterical crowing until the travellers went through the mearne gate into our land. Then there was silence.

Strangely, these late night scares never seemed to diminish the hunger of the 'Mountain' people for playing '25, and nearly every night a crowd of expectant players would arrive at 'Terry's' hoping to get a game. Often there would be a big game, where thirty or more players would play for a turkey, a lamb, or a sum of money. The less skilful of us would stand aside and watch these accomplished players in action, and hope we could learn tricks from them. When a game was going on you daren't open your mouth or it was a red card, and you were banished to the kitchen or some other apartment. This was because any comment or action could be construed as being a pre-arranged signal to a player. Eventually, players like myself, Farrell, John Thomas, Phillip and Paschal 'Terry', and others graduated to a level where we would be allowed to play with these 'experts'. This was not as great a concession as it might seem, because we would be still unlikely to win a game in this company. Initiation into these card-playing confraternities was accompanied by vicious and instantaneous sanctions for unruly and undisciplined behaviour. For instance, a newcomer, overwhelmed by acceptance into such rare and talented company, was liable to suffer from nervousness. And then to study your fellow players was enough to give anyone the willies. Men, who were always laughing and joking, and otherwise jolly good company, returned your look with a steely, glint-eyed stare. Your own father, who you would have talked and joked with a short time ago, now looked back at you with a withering look like a dangerous stranger who dared you to look him in the eye. The venom in his gaze would send a cold shiver of fear up your spine, and that was before the game even started. By the time the game began, the atmosphere would have risen to such a level of tension that the slightest twitch of an eyelid, or the squeaking of the chair you sat on, would be answered with an avalanche of the most venomous wrath and animosity, aimed by all in your direction, leaving you in such a state of trepidation you could be either expecting a terrifying thunderstorm or imminent execution.

Partners were selected by dealing out two aces, two kings, two knaves, etc, and the game began. Deal. Cut the cards. Give everyone a hand. Silence. 5, 5, 10, 5. Deal. 10, 15, 10, 5, 5, 5. Deal. 10. 15, 15, 10, 5, 10, 5, 5. Deal. 20, 20, 20, 15, 5, 10, 5, 5. Deal. 20, 20, 20, 25! **Game.** The cards are dealt again. By this time the expert players can deduce to a large extent, what cards each player has, and the weaker players are quickly eliminated. Every time players are relegated, new sets of partners are selected from the remaining players. At this stage of the 'game' the players that are left become increasingly voluble and excited. 'Deal' 'good trick Patrick - good boy ya - we're 10 - with nothing.' 'Play one tonight . . . play one and ate one . . . play one like a good man, if you're goin' to play at all.' Deal. 'What am I?' 'A right bloody bollocks, if ya don't mind me saying so.' 'I meant, what's the count now?' 'Up with your trumph Tommy . . . good boy yourself . . . that's the way to do it . . . clean out all the big ones . . . stuff a few more like that and we're laughin.' 'For God's sake Michael, have you no eyes?' 'Ah begod I have now Farrell.' 'Well it wouldn't do us any harm if you could manage to use them now and again.' Deal. *Stop!* 'Mrs Terry' says you's are taking you're tay now. Leave the cards where they are for a while.' Then Mrs 'Terry' would give everyone a big mug of tea and great chunks of ham sandwiches and sweetcakes, and everyone would forget about the cards, with the excited talking, stories, yarns and debates, with everyone animatedly joining in, all in a remote little world of their own. 'Deal.' Eventually the best players get to the quarter finals, and then the semi-finals. There is another interval, and Mrs 'Terry' reinforces all presents with more tea and sandwiches, and then the semi-finals begin. 'Deal again.' The cards are dealt out to select partners. Deal the cards, cut them. Slowly and precisely the dealer gives each player three cards and himself two. Then two to each player and three, for luck to himself. The cards in each hand are minutely examined, adjusted in degrees of importance, and cupped furtively and secretly in each players hand as if he was hiding jewels. The denominations and values of their cards are calculated, to the accompaniment of grins, snorts, giggles, winks, smirks and shuffles, and sometimes with faces full of wonder and amazement. A period of silence, terrible concentration, then an amiable voice says 'throw out one!' The person to play first, scrutinises the stern faces intently watching him, debates with himself whether to play a weak card, and allow his partner to gain the initiative, or chance the wrath of all by playing the most potent card in his hand.

At last the final commences. By then it is not just a turkey, money, or whatever that is at stake. The pride and reputations of the players is now on the line, and they will all do their utmost to defend it. Four players usually played in the finals, playing single hands; the winner, the first one to win three games. The cards are dealt to determine the first dealer. Then the cards are dealt out, examined, accounted, adjusted, secluded. This is the time when the players are best able to demonstrate, and activate, their full compendium of conniving, sneaky, low-down tricks of their well rehearsed trade. No quarter was given or expected, and as the contrasting styles of the players clashed and jarred against each other, the slightest hesitation or mistake was punished with an awesome and clinical cynicism. The players seemed to all take on different individual artificial personna or countenances, for the very purpose of protecting themselves, their pride, and their reputations for the duration of the game. Some of them would pore over their cards for incredibly long periods, as if they were considering which one to play, when in fact they would be testing the nerves of the other players to the very limit. Others would hold a card high up as if waiting to play, when the play had still not got near them. This served into unconsciously spur players to hurry up, and at the same time ensured that they lost concentration for vital seconds, giving the person holding his card up a definite advantage. As the pressure increased, players would begin to do silly things, like whacking down a card unto the table in elation, having made the fatal mistake that his card was best, and then suddenly realising that a better one has just been played. A devastating depression would then set in upon him, and he would be as good as finished for the rest of the game. Another would go straight to disaster by momentarily forgetting the count. His split second loss of concentration, coupled with a sense of fear would lead him to beat someone who was 15 allowing someone who was already 20 to get out, and win the game.

To the onlookers, who became immersed in these battles between players, their favourite players took on a God-like reverence as they battled with every ounce of energy and experience in their mind to try and emerge victorious. The fluctuating fortunes of their heroes were greeted silently with a range of frayed feelings from despair to ecstasy. As the game would be nearing the end, the players would put on a facade of false happiness, a childish joy, though you could see them wince every time they lost a trick, and you knew that inside, they felt as if an arrow had pierced their heart. With an air of rumbustious artificial humour, the game would come to an end. The winner, elated and deserving, with all the other players wishing him all the best. But the losers, for all their dignity in defeat, would go through a long period of melancholy and depression, minutely examining their part in the game. After a time of meditation and reflection, one by one they would eventually overcome their trauma and venture out to play the game of '25 once more.

The Railway

On the 30th of September 1957 the Sligo Leitrim and Northern Counties Railway was closed down. The line linked Sligo with Enniskillen, and ran through Ballisodare, Collooney, Ballygawley, Ballintogher, Dromahaire, Lisgorman, Manorhamiliton, Kilmakerill, Glenfarne, Belcoo and Blacklion, Abohill and Florencecourt to Enniskillen. This was the last private railway in Ireland, always struggling to survive. It was run with the most meagre economy, and suffered seriously from only getting from Government's, the most insignificant grants and attention of any other railway system in Ireland. Nevertheless, it was a reliable railway, made personal and humane by a dedicated, ingenious and proud staff, who done everything in their power to keep the line going, on a shoestring budget. It was not to be. How many times had I watched the little trains, huffing and puffing, sending clouds of steam into the sky as they struggled up the little incline near Granny's? Sometimes, when a train would be packed, she couldn't quite make it over the incline, and the passengers would have to disembark to allow it to get over the brow. Then the passengers would rejoin the train to continue their journey. Uncle Francie and I would often stand at Kellegher's around midnight to wait for Granny, who would be coming back from Knock. The train would come to a stop beside us and allow Granny to get off. Often, when I would be standing near the line as the train went past, the driver would lean out of his window and say something like, 'Good morning . . . how's she cuttin' . . .How's Francie . . . or how's your Granny?'

The SL and NCR linked the Midland and Great Western Railway with the Great Northern Railway at Enniskillen. The trains carried, as well as people, eggs, porter, cement, coal and all the other provisions that were needed to supply the towns along, and near the route. T F Pollexfen had a big flour mill in Ballisodare, from where flour was sent by rail all over the country. Probably the greatest trade was in hauling cattle. Loads would be brought from the south and west onto the Midland and Great Western, and from there they would be transferred to the SL and NCR, which would link up with the Great Northern, from where the cattle would be taken to Belfast, Derry or Glasgow.

The trains gave a feeling of constancy, reliability, dependence. They were always there, and you could take your breakfast, dinner and tea according to the times they ran. They brought you places. They brought people from other parts, and news from other places. They brought the newspapers. You could depend on them. Then they were wiped off the map of Ireland. Over 100 people were left without jobs when the SL and NCR closed down. Gatehouses, like the ones near Granny's, Keaneys, Francie Kelly's, Pegnium's, Quinn's and Keaney's at Brockagh, all suddenly became forlorn and desolate places, as most of their occupants were forced to flee to other places for their survival.

At the end of April 1959, the railway was shut down. Sleepers and rails were lifted, and some sections were levelled by farmers, and returned to fields. A railcar was left abandoned along the road at Manorhamilton, and sat there for years, rusting and deteriorating away. The 'iron Bridge' across Lough Macrean at Blacklion was eventually blown up by the British Army, to deter so-called terrorists from invading the 'North'. The jagged remains of the crazily angled wreck of the bridge were visible in the water for years, a pathetic reminder of a great little railway, until rust and the elements combined to lower the wreck into the water.

A new road now follows, and obliterates the route of the railway, from Blacklion to Loughan Quarry. For those who saw the railway in action, all this is a disaster, with the deadly saturating fumes of madly rushing cars, lorries and buses, destroying the clean and clear air along the route. There is only one section now, as far as I know, of the railway, that remains, more or less intact. That is the section that was near where Granny used to live. It serves to remind me that it was along the same line in 1941, that I came with my mother and Aunt Annie, on our way from Waterford to Blacklion when I was only a few months old.

The following is a lament about the passing of the SL and NCR by Maurice E Ferguson, (RIP) Belcoo.

> Farewell all to our train that's gone,
> Will I ever see you more.
> There is sorrow at Fermanagh
> And around Lough Erne's shore.
> Your loss is felt severely,
> No matter what they say,
> Your span of life was shortened,
> By the northern UTA.

For 75 long years or more,
You always kept good time,
In carrying cattle, horses, sheep,
And sometimes loads of swine.
The staff at Belcoo station,
Were most courteous and quick,
Good Freddie, Paddy, Kevin, Willie,
Not forgetting Dick.

With a great Cread Mile Failte,
They would view you up and down,
And banish all your cares away,
When you took the train to town.
Lough Gill and dear Lough Melvin,
I often times did view,
You were a stately sight to see,
When passing through Belcoo.

Your engines now are silent,
As the graves of Rossnaree.
For your task was taken over,
By the Dublin CIE.
Your whistle often thrilled us,
When sitting in our home.
From you left Glenfarne station,
Till you ploughed your way through Toam.

Farewell old mode of transport,
To you we bid adieu.
If you ever come back again,
We will surely welcome you.
Our little railway, they agreed,
To close, alas too soon,
For now I hear they'll make us travel,
On the shining Russian moon.

Maurice E Ferguson

Working Alone

Sometimes, when George had hay down, or wanted to set his potatoes, he would ask my father to come for a day or two to help. I always looked forward to the days when my father would come. He and I were alike in so many ways, and always got on so well together, and we had similar ideas about doing work. But maybe I was a child yet. The idea of this great, strong man, my father, being around, comforted me in some way. He made the work we done, so simple, whereas, George tended to make even the most mundane tasks complicated.

George bought a second hand Ferguson TVO tractor, and that made life a lot easier. From then on, the ass was made redundant, and whiled away the days until he died, hidden away on the upper slopes of George's land. In Autumn 1958 my father took pleurisy. He probably got run down from overwork and bad feeding. When I would come home sometimes, and hear him coughing, and retching uncontrollably in the 'Upper room', I would be fearfully hurt and dejected. Daddy was in bed for about two months, and when he eventually did recover, he never was as strong again.

Roisin left George's, and that meant George had now to take care of his mother. George loved his mother dearly, and took great care of her. He done everything in his power to look after her. To do that as well as look after the farm, was too much, and when Mrs Sheridan became ill, it was decided it would be better for her to live with her daughter Annie, who was married at Skea Hall. George missed his mother very much. With Roisin and his mother gone, and his relations, the Bertie Sheridan's and the Frank Sheridan's gone from the 'Mountain' to the lowlands, and now only me to keep him company, he decided to go and help to look after his mother, whose health was deteriorating rapidly.

I was on my own. The work was a non-stop round of milking cows, taking the milk to the road, cleaning byres, foddering cattle, feeding calves, pumping water. I didn't have time to cook proper meals. I became erratic in my work. Sometimes I would sleep in, and wouldn't have time to milk the cows, so I could only take last night's milk to the road. Often I wouldn't have time to clean out the byres, and would have to do a couple of days at once. Sometimes I would go tumbling with a load of hay and injure my knees once more, but by bandaging them again I was always able to carry on.

George would come every five weeks or so to pay me. One day he returned and told me his mother had passed away. I was very sorry. Mrs Sheridan had always treated me well. George told me he couldn't face coming back yet. George eventually returned to Gortaree after about eleven months, just in time to prevent me turning his farm into rack and ruin. He then employed Rose McManus from Gorvagh, at Gowlan, and she helped to bring both George and I back to the straight and narrow, by cooking us proper meals, washing our clothes, and looking after the house in general.

Our interest in the 'football' we played in the 'Mountain' and Francie 'Connor's' yearning for teams in Northern Ireland to do well, may have had something to do with the upsurge of Gaelic Football in the 'North' at this time. In 1959 Fermanagh were going great guns with the Fermanagh Juniors winning the All Ireland against Kerry at Croke Park. Then they went to London and beat them as well. Down too, produced a good team, which got to the All Ireland semi-final. They were beaten by Galway, 1-11 to 1-4. However press reports like, 'Down's flashing opening was short-lived', or 'Northern Chargers lose to Galway', may have hinted at things to come.

This interest in football led to Petie and I meeting in Belcoo one Sunday to travel to a match. Francie 'Connor', who was also going to the match arrived and told us it was cancelled. As a bus came up the street, 'Connor' said 'why don't we go to Bundoran for the day.' I griped about being parted from my bike, but Petie, 'Connor' and I left our bikes up against the wall and headed off to Bundoran on the bus. As we made our way towards Bundoran, I had only one thing on my mind; Bumping Cars.

Francie Maguire, (Connor) was such a grand man to be out with. He didn't smoke or drink, and he joined in all the amusements of Bundoran with the same childish glee and enthusiasm as we did ourselves. At last we got to the 'Bumping Cars' and this time there would be no hesitating. First Petie and 'Connor' went out in the same car. Then Petie and I. Then 'Connor' and I went out, and after that we all had separate cars. Eventually Petie and 'Connor' had enough of 'Bumping Cars' and wanted to go off somewhere else. I wouldn't leave When they got tired waiting for me they went off and left me there. They came back at 6-30 saying the bus was leaving at 7. Still I could not be got to leave. They came back from the bus at 7 and said it was leaving now. Still I would not budge and they left me there. I stayed on the 'Bumping Cars' until they closed for the night. I then set off for home walking. A man on a powerful motorcycle gave me a lift to Belleek. I walked on, to Garison, then Cashel. At Cashel the 'B men' had the road blocked, and they began to hustle and interrogate me. 'Who are you? From where? Where are you coming from? A likely story! How did you get here from Bundoran then? What'll we do with him then? Throw him into the river! If it was up to me I'd hurl him into the quarry! Why don't we string him up to a tree?' They said, 'you can go now and the next time you want to go to Bundoran, take the bus.'

After another few miles I was worn out. I decided to knock at house in Tullyrosmearn and ask them for the lend of a bicycle. They gave me a good, strong Rudge bike that took me to Belcoo. I was delighted. I left the bicycle propped against the wall as arranged, and jumped on my own. I was so glad to be back on my own bicycle that it seemed to give me great strength. For the first time ever, I cycled straight up the Marlbank Hills without stopping. This was something that had been attempted by many but accomplished by few people in the 'Mountain'.

Athletic Competition

On Mayday 1959, both Petie and I had the day off work, and we met up in Blacklion. My increasing confidence on the bike led me to suggest 'why don't we go to the cycle races at Florencecourt Sports.' First we went to Enniskillen and bought rolls of different coloured tapes, which we then used to 'doll up' our bikes, and if we were going bicycle racing, at least we would look the part. Of course the Florencecourt Sports was a Protestant affair, where the best fife and drum, and flute bands would be on parade. For Petie and I, innocent and wholesome Catholics, going to Florencecourt Sports was like walking straight into the lions den, or at least that was what it was presumed to be like. We went to the sports, held in front of Flrencecourt Castle, in lovely, scenic, wooded surroundings. Everything about the sports was enjoyable, and there wasn't a hint of animosity the whole day long, although many people there knew who we were. We all lined up for the cycle race, at least fifty of us. I couldn't believe how well I started and I was going so well, and with such speed, that I was going to pass the whole tumult of cyclists and get to the front as I rounded the first corner. Alas! I gauged the corner too finely, caught the newly decorated handlebar in the corner post and came tumbling off. Not to worry. As the cyclists came round again, amazingly Petie was way out in the lead. Without thinking, or as much as to say, what are you doing there, I put Petie off his bicycle and jumped on it myself. I thought to myself, I'll show them. Soon I was flying on the bike, and about to pass the whole lot on the next corner, when I gauged my space too finely and caught the newly decorated handlebar of Petie's bike on the corner post, and came tumbling off once more. John Ford won the race, as he had done for many years before. Petie and I retreated home in shame.

For the people of the 'Mountain' the 'big' day was the 15th of August, that was the day the sports were held in Belcoo. It was the one day in the year when the people could dress up in their finery and go down to the village and enjoy themselves, listening to wonderful marching bands like 'The Mountain Road Pipe Band,' visiting the shops, pubs and restaurants, and being entertained by the sports. For months beforehand people in the 'Mountain' would be saying to each other 'What are you going to do at the sports?' meaning were they going to climb the greasy pole, wrastle a pig, run in the egg and spoon race, or what. This is where I intended to make my mark. I'd make people sit up and take notice all right, and how was I going to do that? By winning the bicycle race of course. On the day of the sports, 15h August 1958, I was prepared and ready, and when the cycle race was announced I put down my name and lined up with about fifteen more contenders. But I soon noticed that many of these racers were of a completely different calibre and class to the bunch of cyclists that raced at Florencecourt Sports. They had an array of glittering and complicated machinery that flashed frighteningly, and they kept chopping and changing the lightest and most delicate looking wheels, as they fine-tuned and readied their machines. Many of them were attired in brightly coloured, flimsy vests and shorts, with their rough hairy legs scaring everyone near them. I sniggered to myself. 'A fine lot of good all that regalia I'll do ye,' a man blew a whistle and the race was on. Most of the cyclists were half-way around the course before I had even started. As I eventually got going at a reasonable pace, I could see and hear waves of the crowd willing me on. I hadn't a hope. I was totally obliterated, and the winner was Brian Curtis, with Patrick Reid second, both from Ederney.

In 1959 I went on my own to Florencecourt Sports, where I had another great day. But there was really only one thing in my mind, and that was the cycle race. I won it easily, with John Ford, who congratulated me, coming second. The prize was ten shillings. It is so pathetic, and can have such a far-reaching effect, when those with some sort of authority, demean themselves for the sake of bigotry. What else could I feel but sadness, a sadness that inflicts me to this day, that this distributor of prizes was prepared to belittle himself for the sole purpose of promoting sectarian bitterness, by substituting my proper prize of ten shillings with the laughable prize of a biro pen. I have never forgotten the shadow that was cast on that day, a day when we were all ordinary people enjoying ourselves, and yet this 'official' had to implement his own personal segratory sanction when and where it mattered.

On the 15th of August at Belcoo Sports, I was again left far behind in the cycle race, but this time I recovered and came second. However, these excursions into cycle racing made one thing crystal clear. I just did not possess the required strength to go from a standing start, to the end of a short race, and win against any reasonable opposition.

Even though I was now, more or less, a man (or boy) of the world, I still used to get a terrible yearning from time to time to go home and be with my family for a short time. I began to realise how hard a life my mother had, trying to bring us all up, far away from everything. It would have been a similar story for the Terry

McGovern's, the Johnny Maguires, the Francie Maguires and the Sheerins. But at least in these houses the men were at home, whereas my father was hardly ever at home.

Everytime I came home it seemed that my mother had grown smaller. This impression may have resulted from my own increasing stature, but there was no doubting that my mother did seem to be looking increasingly fragile and vulnerable as I grew up. From our childhood she had always been able to enthrall us with her fiddle playing, and as we all grew up we were better able to appreciate the enormous talent she had, and so we were always on to her to play. Sometimes, when she broke a string in the bow, we had to do without her playing as she went through the long process of getting a new string from Dublin or Glasgow.

Often when I would go home, Rose would be away in James Nolan's, Bridie would be visiting 'Connor's' and with Petie away working, and Daddy on Jimmity's, the house began to exhibit a terrible feeling of sparseness and space, and I would be filled with feelings of dejection, disappointment and disbelief, as I saw the integral pieces and composition of the family being scattered in all directions. Even so, on Christmas Day 1959, we were all together once more to fill ourselves with Mammy's Christmas dinner, play our games and look forward to the 1960s.

CHAPTER 7

ENTERTAINMENT

In 1960 there were forty people under twenty in the 'Mountain'. Harold Macmillan, the British Prime Minister, made a speech about, 'the wind of change is blowing through this continent'. He was talking about South Africa, and the growth of 'national consciousness'. But in many ways these winds of change seemed to be sweeping all over the world. In America, Martin Luther King was leading the blacks in a movement of passive resistance against the authority of the whites. In Africa there was mass protests by the black population against apartheid laws. As well as this, the world's teenagers took on a strange new influence and importance, fuelled by a new independence of spirit, and their own spectacular brand of noisy electrifying music. In the book 'Absolute Beginners' by Colin McInnes, the teenage narrator says 'no one could sit on our faces no more, because we'd loot to spend and our world was to be our world, the one we wanted.' To compound all this, John F Kennedy was elected President of the United States, the youngest ever president, the first ever Roman Catholic, and to cap all that, he was of Irish extraction.

In case this rebellion, and breakdown in authority, would get to us in the 'Mountain', Pope Paul XXIII presided over a synod that decreed what Catholics should watch on films or television. Women mustn't be bare-armed or trousered when they intended to 'receive' and priests were banned from going to the cinema or the theatre. All this authoritarian and revolutionary activity, transformed itself in the 'Mountain' to the people I had went to school with, now going off to dances or places like St Ninnidhs Hall Derrylin, or 'The Ballroom of Romance' in Glenfarne, where the foremost showbands of Ireland like 'The Melody Aces' would entertain the dancers.

The young people of the 'Mountain' would go off walking, or on bicycles, to Blacklion or Belcoo on a Sunday night, to meet a bus, or get a lift to a dance. John James McNulty, John Thomas McGovern, or Petie, would be constantly urging me to go with them, to hear the great bands. I never thought many of them had all that great of an interest in music, except for John James, and I knew that what they were really going 'dancing' for was to 'click' with a suitable companion of the opposite sex. The girls of the 'Mountain', like Anna and May Sheerin, Rose and Julia Maguire, Ann Moffatt, Bridgie and Eileen Maguire (Connor), and our Rose, also showed a remarkable single-mindedness in their efforts to get to these dances, for the very same reason.

Petie, and the other lads from the 'Mountain' would try to induce me to go to these dances. However my introvert nature, and my terrible shyness prevented me from going. I knew in my own mind that I would rather face execution by firing squad than ask any girl out to dance; and since the whole point of the exercise seemed to be to get acquainted with a girl through dancing with her around a crowded floor, and as I realised that I possessed no attractive qualities that would entice her to engage in such an act, I knew that the whole business would be a waste of time.

Anyway, I may not have been ready for romance, because I would far rather wander abroad on my bike, admiring the mountains, lakes, rivers and valleys in ever widening circles, than go to any dance. Often I would call at the dance-hall to meet Petie and my other friends from the 'Mountain' when the dance was over. I used to be amazed to find that they were nearly always womanless, and I used to think that it was an awful lot of effort to expend for no reward. On our way home, full of themselves after the dance, they would relate the most outrageous tales of romance and debauchery, and enlighten and instruct me in the art of conquering a desirable, agreeable and voluptuous companion, and making her my own.

One Sunday afternoon I left George's and headed for Sligo on the bike. I took the 'back road' from Manorhamiliton to Sligo. This road passes a little lake, and meanders through the most wonderful woods, mountains and valleys. I already had a sore throat, but five miles out of Sligo I grew very weak and became seriously ill. Soon I was unable to force around the pedals and had to walk with the bike until I eventually came to Sligo. The hustle and bustle of people and traffic, seemed to be in another world. At last I found a wooden seat on the main street, outside a hotel and I collapsed helplessly into it. Immediately, someone from the hotel bounded out, shouting at me to get out of there at once. I could barely lift myself up out of the seat, as I decided I must try and go home. Propped against the bike, I managed to struggle through Sligo and leave it behind. When I came to a down-hill part of the road I managed to sit on the bar of the bike and coast to the bottom. After many hours I had dragged myself to Granny's at Roo. Dr Hawkins was brought next day. I had acute tonsillitis, and other complications. I didn't eat anything for ten days, and neither George or my family knew where I was. Granny, Paddy and Annie nursed me, and after two weeks I arrived back to George once more.

Fermanagh's success in Gaelic Football in 1959 gave people an increased interest and awareness of the Gaelic Football situation in 'The North'. Everyone was hoping that Fermanagh would go on to new heights in 1960, maybe even getting their senior team into the All Ireland semi-final. Our attention was diverted however, by, in one sense Fermanagh producing a mediocre team, and on the other hand, Down producing an increasingly skilful and competitive team. This considerable interest in football, combined with the attraction of dance-halls, and the dispersion of people to work in far-off areas, had a devastating effect on our Tug O War training, and eventually it was abandoned altogether. This meant that, except for the diversion of dance-halls, the Gaelic football of the Down team became a major attraction for everyone, not only in the 'Mountain' but in the whole 'North'.

I decided to acquire a new bike. I went to John James Mc Hugh in Barran (the writer of 'A Tale of Generations') and ordered a brand new Raleigh 'Tour de France' racing bike. This bike had a 26 inch frame, seven Derallier gears, two water bottle container holders, and pedal shoes. The bike cost thirty-five pounds, a tremendous amount of money, and I had to wait six weeks for it. When at last I got my hands on the bike it was magnificent, a beauty, and no one else around had one like it. When I found out how useful the pedal-clips, or shoes were, I wondered why I hadn't thought of them before. Now, not only could I force the pedals downwards, I could pull them up as well.

Fermanagh County Council decided to construct a new bridge over the Shru Croppa river at 'Terry's', replacing the old bridge that Phillip McGovern and his brothers had crossed so fearfully with the stone crusher. Packie Tracey, of Tracey Brothers, was the bridge builder, and with his men constructed a bridge of steel girders set on concrete plinths, which were then covered with pre-cast concrete sections.

When I would be delivering the milk to the road, shortly after 8am, Tracey's lorry, with the men huddled in a little hut on the back, would be making its way up the Marlbank road towards the bridge. The weather would be freezing, and I used to wonder how they managed not to freeze to death on the back of that lorry. When the bridge was finished, the last mile of the road was built by JJ Scallon from Irvinestown. In the short space of time since the McGovern's made the road through Legnabrocky, construction machinery had modernised at a tremendous rate, and consequently, Scallon's finished their section in a very short time. When the whole road was complete, signposts announced it as 'Marlbank Scenic Route'.

The completion of this road meant that the milk lorry, grocery lorry, bread van etc. could continue on out to the Wheathill Road, and not have to turn around at 'Terry's'. For everybody farther on than Hughe's Gate, the road was a real boon. The James Nolan's, Big Phil's, 'Connor's' and all other families east of them could now go out the new road to mass, to the doctor, or if they had to go to Enniskillen on business such as selling cattle or sheep. Probably the family to benefit most from this road was the McNulty's of Gortmaconnell. Every morning they used to bring the milk out to the Wheathill Road at Sally's Grove, in two ten or eight gallon creamery cans, hooked on to the straddle of an ass. Then they had to bring the shopping from the road, and feeding stuff for the cows and calves, all on the ass and cart, and over very rough terrain for a distance of about two miles. In the winter, when it snowed, or froze, the trip to the road could turn out to be a very precarious and formidable journey. But the new road meant that their journey with the milk was not even half as far. The new road was also a Godsend to Mrs Gilmurray and her husband John because they used to sing in the choir in Wheathill Chapel. Mrs Gilmurray also played the organ, and now, instead of having to drive all around the 'Mountain' they were able to go straight down the new 'Marlbank Scenic Route' to Wheathill Chapel.

Still, new road and all, there was a nightly ritual that used to go on in the 'Mountain' that the creation of the 'Marlbank Scenic Route' in no way diminished. Every evening or night, a variety of 'Mountain' people could be seen jumping on their bikes and making their way towards Blacklion (The Black). In a way this activity regulated and purified their lives, because it forced people to 'do themselves up' and look presentable before they joined and infiltrated the company and culture of 'The Black'. Tommy 'Terry' would make his way down about six, for the paper, and fags and groceries for the family. Everyone knew Tommy because he sold the Sunday papers at Wheathill Chapel, and he also collected the dues for the priest. Indeed, many was the time that he paid our dues himself, because we wouldn't have the money. He was a quiet, gentle person, his only vice being the odd fag. He had a tremendous thirst for knowledge, to know things, how a ship worked, how a government worked. If anyone in the 'Mountain' or farther afield, wanted the answer to some obscure question, they would go and ask Tommy, and if he didn't know the answer straight away he would consult his treasured Encyclopaedia Britannica. Terry, his brother, who owned the farm, would also go for groceries and to meet people on business. Then there would be Con Boylan, Ernie Moffatt, Dennis and Hughie Curran, Francie 'Connor', Phillip 'Big Phil', James and John Nolan (of the bogs, nickname) Pakie Dolan, Jim Dolan, Tommy Sheerin, Phil and Charlie Cha (Maguire) and Jimmy and Tommy Nolan. My father rarely went from home to 'The Black' because he was nearly always away, and if he wanted to go to 'The Black' he would come home that way. Some of these lads would be coming home as others were going. Often, neighbours wouldn't be talking, after some minor tiff, and they would have to adopt a range of strategies in order to avoid direct confrontation on the journey. The most likely place for these cyclists to meet each other was on the Marlbank Hills, because it took such a long time for anyone with a bicycle to walk up them. A man would come flying down the

'Hills' on the bike, and see the light of a bike away below at Boles's. The person going down would be able to deduce who it was that was walking up the 'Hills' with the bike, and maybe it was someone he wasn't on good terms with at that time. He would bring the bike to a screeching halt, and then steal in along Barney McCaffrey's lane until the danger had passed. It also often happened that the person coming up the 'Hills' would also retreat stealthily into Barney's lane as he would be expecting someone coming down the road he didn't want to meet. The first person who went in the lane would be trapped until the second cyclist decided to continue his journey, and God only knows how long he would wait while monitoring all who came down the 'Hills'. At other times, when someone walking up the 'Hills' with his bicycle, saw a light coming down the 'Hills' he would vanish into a clump of bushes at Boles's house, where there was a well. Then he would stretch out on the ground, on his belly and drink for all he was worth out of the well, even though he didn't need a drink at all, until the danger had vanished into the distance. Another stunt, when you didn't want to meet someone directly, was to stand close into the hedge, looking through it, and pretend you were talking to someone in the field. 'A bugger of a night Tom'. When anyone overhearing would know that there wasn't a Tom anywhere within three miles. 'Horrid drockey weather for this time of year . . . Begod the rabbits have given that field a good skinning ... I suppose your cows are all calved . . . I might call in tomorrow for a haircut . . . No thanks all the same but I'm full up to the gills . . . Someone was telling me . . . ' and off he'd go again to continue his journey.

The women, who had to go to places like the dispensary in Blacklion for medicine, or to see the doctor in Belcoo, usually went in the daytime, and they didn't care who they met on the way, and would talk to everyone.

Calor Gas

The increased access from the 'Mountain' to the outside world, and vice versa, enlightened the people in the way other communities and districts were progressing and modernising, with services like mains water, electricity, sewerage systems, telephones etc. It could be seen how this had in turn led to radical changes in the workings of the household, with flush toilets, bathrooms, with hot water, light and power to drive all sorts of equipment. Naturally, the people of the 'Mountain' began to yearn for these things too, and periodically made representations to government offices, and their local MP to provide these services so as to improve life in the 'Mountain'.

The government done little, and slowly, the Calor Gas drum became a familiar sight outside houses in the 'Mountain' as the residents progressed from the oil lamp and the Tilley to brilliant light from the gaslamp. Eventually Mammy saved up some money and got our friend Jim Dolan to install pipework and fittings for a gaslamp, and I got a big surprise when I went home one night and saw this new contraption sending forth a modified and perfect light. Mammy had also managed to elevate another picture in her place of honour on the shelf-throne. Squeezing their way in between Pope John XXIII and Prince Phillip and the Queen, was none other than Jacqueline Bouvier and her husband John Fitgerald Kennedy, the President of the United States.

George used to take great delight in telling the story of my haircut. When there was no one around me like Mammy, who would order me sit on a stool while she clipped my hair off with a pair of sheep shears, I tended to let it grow until I could hardly see where I was going, before getting it cut. One night I walked over to 'Jimmy's' in Skeagh in the Barrs, so that Hugh Jimmy (Maguire) would cut it. There was only Tom and Hugh at home when I got there. Hugh started to cut my locks, but Tom wanted the oil lamp near him so that he could read the paper. When I got back to George's he began to laugh hysterically, and asked me who it was that gave me a haircut. I looked in the mirror and saw that on one side my head was nearly shaven, while the other side had hardly been touched. Even the cows seemed to be scared of me as I went to do the milking. I told George that Tom had the oil lamp for reading the paper, and that Hugh hadn't near enough light to see my head. George thought it was funny, and said that if he was in my shoes he'd seriously consider changing his barber.

Like everyone else in the 'Mountain' George cut his turf in our bog. I would look forward to this time, as it meant I could see the ones at home. George, like he always did, treated my mother and everyone at our house with great respect. Mammy would make the tea for George, Phillip Nolan and I, and we would eat our meals in the house, while Mammy would play the fiddle for George, as he loved music. The bog would be crowded. Bertie Sheridan still came, the Sheerin's, Reid's, Mick Maguire's, Dolan's, Nolan's, and many people from farther off. They all had their own allocated areas for cutting, which they used every year. Everyone worked at a tremendous rate until waves of midges drove them home in the evening. Often, when these boisterous workers converged in the evening, fearful clod fighting mock battles would break out, with fusillades of sods flying in all directions. When the unbeatable warriors, the midges, got too much for them, they would at last retreat homeward.

Every so often the tranquil regularity of a large area around Blacklion would be jolted out of normality by the strange and interesting phenomenon of 'road shows'. These 'road shows' brought their own arena, which they erected at the fairgreen Blacklion, and for a week or two they provided an exciting diversion for the local community. One of the best known was the 'Courtney Brothers Roadshow'. Every night they would have a programme of singing, dancing, magic or playing instruments. Their main activity however was performing great plays such as 'The Croppy Boy', 'Kevin Barry', 'The Red Barn Murder', 'Captain Boycott', or others, which the whole local population would look forward to eagerly. As well as all the older people who would attend, the young bucks and lassies from the 'Mountain' myself included, would be there. The sight and sound of people being shot, guillotined, butchered, buried in blood or chained up for ever more, would traumatise our senses nightly.

There were also other attractions. Outside the arena or theatre there would be bazaar-like attractions for the younger people, such as swing-boats, a shooting gallery, or throwing rings. Happy squealing and laughing voices would announce the children enjoying themselves in the throes of pandemonium. Inside the smoke-filled confines of the hall, me and others like me would be galvanised into a pathetic adoration of the beautiful ladies performing on the stage. These dolled up, scantily dressed, fabulously attributed young women, took on goddess-like qualities. Adorable, but out of reach, to vulnerable souls like myself. During the interval there would be a raffle and these girls would go around selling tickets. Slowly, lingering as she sold her tickets, a favourite would advance in my general direction. Excited, nervous, apprehensive, I would sneak furtive glances to monitor her advance, while trying to maintain a cool, couldn't care less, detached demeanour. Then the ticket seller would be beside me; a youthful dream of heavenly perfection. Like a radiant princess, her golden hair held in place by a glittering silver tiara. Her beautiful, perfect smiling face addressing me, 'tickets Sir' and I knew that if I looked into her eyes I would never be able to look away again. Her long bare legs would be almost brushing my shoulder, the sight of her flawless white flesh sending whirling shafts of uneasy temptation into my brain. I'd stammer 'Twenty please' and I could feel the heat from her beautiful, throbbing, pulsating body, and then she'd be gone, so near and yet so far.

I am sure that every man that went to these shows, fell in love with the women who were on the stage. Hierkegaard, the Dane, has said that the image is often more satisfying than the real thing, but there is no doubt that for a long time after these 'road shows' left the district, the hearts and minds of the males of the area were preoccupied with visions of love and romance which dominated and enhanced their dreams. The women as well, would go through a period of similar disturbing emotions, as they fawned and cried irreverently, over the immaculately attired, handsome, evil looking men. However, the women always seemed to bear the pain of separation with a much more stoic, silent disposition.

All Ireland For Down

Down's flashy football of 1959 transformed itself into them winning games of a tremendous rate in 1960. They had become a most formidable team, and nearly everyone in the northern part of Ireland became an enthusiastic follower. They went all the way to the All

Ireland Final, and on the 25th of September 1960 they met the mighty Kerry, the absolute masters of Gaelic football at Croke Park, Dublin. The whole 'North' was in pandemonium as the big day approached. Everyone wanted a ticket for Croke Park. One County Tyrone farmer offered to swap his farm for tickets to see the match. There were no takers, reinforcing the proposition that most people would rather go to a football match than go farming any day. I decided to go to the match. I told George, and as Petie didn't have to work on Sundays he would replace me at George's. For the first time since 1947, my father also decided to go, especially since he was sceptical of all new upstarts, and knew in his head that when Kerry got to Croke Park they were unbeatable. We all stayed at home on the Saturday night, discussing the outcome of the match into the early hours of the morning. We had our breakfast in the morning, and Daddy took off across the bog to meet the car in the Barrs that was taking him to the match. When I didn't go off with Daddy, my mother said, 'I thought you were going.' I told her I was. 'And how are you going then?' she said, and I answered 'on the bike.' Mammy said, 'Jaysus Christ you must be raving,' and she thought for a while before continuing, 'you've turned out to be a complete omidan altogether . . . a fierce gaumshite. Are you paralytic or what?' Petie and I began to walk with our bikes out towards the Marlbank Road. I knew that Petie was struggling with himself to be able to say the right thing to make me change my mind. But we just walked on, peaceful in each other's company and at 8am at Hughe's Gate, we said goodbye on a lovely sunny Sunday morning and went off in our different directions.

I commenced my journey fairly leisurely, passing over the new bridge at 'Terry's', then Nulty's Rock, soon coming out on the better, Wheathill or Florencecourt Road. The Orangemen were marching at Florencecourt, four or five abreast on the road, all dressed up with colourful banners and body trappings. They did not hinder me, and I passed on through Killesher, Kinawley, Derrylin, Teemore and on to Aghalane Border Post. The Custom Men quizzed me for a few minutes and then I carried on to Belturbet. I began to feel the hunger. I bought sweets, biscuits and minerals in Belturbet and had a snack while I rested on a street seat. The roads steadily became much busier, and soon I left Cavan town behind. The road got much better and I was fairly motoring. I felt exhilarated, free, going like the wind. With cars, lorries and buses, it seemed as if it had become integrated into a moving column of red and black. Passengers from vehicles shouted encouragement at me. A coachload of supporters passed me and I decided to up my speed, and stayed with the coach for about thirty miles, amidst continual encouragement from its passengers.

I stopped for a rest in Navan, and something to eat, not a proper meal, which would have been so much better, but more sweets and biscuits. On my way again; And then there seemed to have taken place an almost imperceptible change in the exuberance of the travelling contingents of red and black, more restrained encouragement, a dulling of enthusiasm, less rush of traffic. I supposed the long drive was having its effect on the supporters. Or maybe it was that after passing Navan, they suddenly realised that they were now at the point of no return, at the first bell of a boxing match, and was their brave team going to be wiped away by the mighty men of Kerry.

Unbelievably, somewhere outside Navan I took a wrong turn and became unaccountably lost. I carried on for many miles, because even though I knew I was lost I believed I was still going in the general direction of Dublin. Eventually I got back on a main Dublin road, and as I headed for the city, I felt sickened by the extent of my detour, and fatigue and weariness seemed to be creeping in on me.

I had never been anywhere near Dublin before, and as I got closer to it, from time to time I would sit upright on the bike to gain a better look. The planes landing at Dublin Airport were a wonder, as we hardly ever even heard a plane in Fermanagh. Factories, houses, so many buildings; I pedalled like hell through the traffic which now guided me, and when I saw a fruitseller, I dismounted to buy some of his wares. By a strange coincidence, since this was the first place I had stopped in Dublin, who should also be buying fruit but our own Parish Priest, Father John McGrail. He told me I had no hope of getting into the match, when I hadn't got a ticket. He said that Croke Park was already packed like a sardine can, and that thousands had been locked out.

'After coming so far' I thought to myself. I felt let down. I could hear the throaty, growling roar of the crowd, rising and subsiding, pounding like the mighty, pounding, agitating sea, as the waves collided with the rocks and land. The noise was just over the rooftops of the houses near me. So near. Still, my disappointment was tempered by the sudden realisation that I was very tired, and so I decided that discretion should be the better part of valour, and that I should begin my return journey.

Starting for home again must have been a bit like falling from a high mountain when you've almost reached the top. Defeat, dejection, shock even. This match was definitely a historic occasion, and I wanted to be able to say, 'I was there.' The exhilaration, exuberance and energy of the earlier day had long since gone. I began to fall into a sort of moronic trances, as long straights became endlessly longer. Alternating with these trances, I had reflective calm periods, during which I pondered the day's proceedings. Did my father manage to get to the match. What was Father McGrail doing there. I never knew he had any interest in football, but there you are, it takes all sorts; a wonder no one was with him; how come he wasn't inside at the match, if he had a ticket, that is. One thing that puzzled me about Dublin was them lights changing colours; now why on earth would they be doing that; ah well, we won't worry about it now. I was glad to leave Dublin. The buildings radiated an oppressive, confined, claustrophobic feeling which I wanted to leave behind. Wearily, after some damnable long straights, I got to Navan, which I passed by without any acknowledgement.

Strangely, it was not my legs or knees that were getting tired after all that pedalling, no, it was my head, and upper back, and when I got to Kells I could hardly hold up my head. I decided to have a break, and something to eat in Kells. I knew that my constitution was near breaking point, and that I was becoming dehydrated. To move again was almost unbearable, as I raised myself up on the bike and carried on. The deserted roads became alive again with traffic. The people were coming from the match; cars, lorries, buses, passing me out without an effort. The road was filled with a fantastic emblazonment of red and black. An awesome excitement was being played out about me. Passing heads shouted at me, *'Down won! Down won!'* I was not able to raise myself on the bike to respond. Anyway, I thought to hell with them; what the hell do I care who won.

I managed to reach Virginia, and through some sort of a terrible and lonesome nightmare came upon Cavan Town. All the stragglers from the match had long since gone and the road was deserted once more. I wanted a drink of water, but I was afraid that drinking might finish me off altogether. It started to get dark outside of Cavan. At Butlersbridge I spotted a water pump on the corner of the street. Oh for a drink of that lovely water. I began to become obsessed with an adjusting nut on the centre of the handlebars, thinking that if my head hits it it will knock me out. If only I could get a cushion or a board to put over it, so that I could rest my head on it. I wonder how Petie is getting on with the milking; this could be quite an awkward chore, even for me who's used to it. It was performed in a byre with twelve cows, in pitch darkness; the grey cow is here; then there's the old one George got in Manorhamilton; take the milk to the strainer; isn't it dark. My reactions became so slow that when I tried to avoid a pothole I would end up in the hedge. I got to Belturbet; its streets an arrangement of potholes; like a draught board; black ones here, white there. When I got to the bottom of the steep hill in Belturbet, I realised the one piece of good luck I'd had so far; I didn't get a puncture.

Outside Belturbet, I turned left for Ballyconnell, instead of going straight on; I just couldn't face any more long straights. I thought, I'll soon have to do something about water; maybe I'll ask someone to make a cup of tea; yes, that would be nice, with sugar; more acceptable than water; yes, the next house I see, I'll ask them to make me a cup of tea. When I saw a house, I went to the door, but there was no answer. I felt myself becoming cold, and this was a real fear. I didn't have the energy left to keep myself warm. Another fear I realised coming down a steep hill into Ballyconnell, was how easy it would be to just go asleep on the bicycle going downhill. My head had now become a massive weight, and I just wanted to lay it down anywhere and go to sleep. Pitch darkness had come long before, but

I thought to myself that travelling in the dark didn't matter that much because I was long past caring where I was going. I came to Bawnboy at last. I didn't have to worry about straights after passing Bawnboy, because the road was as twisted and deceptive as a wriggling snake. My sweated and matted hair had gone hard and frozen. I tried to rest my elbow on the handlebars, using my hand to rest my head on. This didn't work because I became completely unbalanced on the bike, and anyway, my arm wasn't able to take the weight of my head for any extended period.

I went into a pothole and hit my nose on the centre nut on the handlebars. The blood from my nose was dropping on the nut on the handlebars, and running down, twisting around the frame, and trickling down to the pedals. I was scared of blood. Like the day Petie and John Thomas and me and a few more, went fishing in the Shru Croppa River. I had never fished before. I flicked my line into the river, but it didn't go into the river; the hook went into my finger, and everyone was afraid to take it out; they were afraid of blood. We all walked to The Black for Dr Hawkins to remove it. He wasn't there. We waited all day. I was taken to Manorhamilton Hospital, no one there could take it out. Then I had to go to Sligo Hospital. Everyone afraid of a drop of blood. All over trying to catch a fish. Still, a fish would be all right now; a lot of bones, though; especially herrings; mind the bloody bones will you'se.

A muffled golden haze appeared in the distance. Slowly, my fettered feet propelled me towards Swanlinbar. That was a triumph of a sort. The last town before home. It was a cold, abandoned, eerie place. There was no one about to witness the traumas and pain I was going through. On the opposite side of the road to the Garda barracks, there was a green water pump. I decided to have a drink whatever happens. The ice cold water definitely revived me. The trip to Florencecourt was a blur of disorientated, wobbling meandering. For the first time that day I was forced to dismount because I was not able to pedal up a little hill at Florenceourt Cross. Half-way up this hill there was a spa well and I decided I had to have another drink, although I was reacting badly from the pump water, with retching and stomach-turning. At the top of the hill I didn't have the energy to get on the bike, and had to wait for an incline so that I could free-wheel off.

The next hill was Churchill, a steep 300 metre hill. I didn't even try to cycle up it. I would push the bike forward while I stayed stationary, then hold the brakes on the bike while I dragged myself forward, and so on. At last I reached the top. Then I had to go through a similar performance at Nulty's Rock. I could smell Cuilcagh. There was a light in 'Terry's'. 'School, how are you?' 'Connors', 'Big Phil's'. 'Hughe's Gate'. Someone left it open; that's nice. Bit by bit I dragged myself home, reaching there at five minutes to midnight. A few minutes later Dad returned, at twelve o'clock exactly.

Mammy was disbelieving about my journey to Dublin. When my father came home he said, 'that's a sight' so I knew he was impressed. He told us about the match. Down were so fast, mighty fielders, such accurate free takers, that they were in a different league to Kerry. They were playing a new kind of Gaelic that was so blindingly fast it was almost impossible to follow it. For the next week or so the pages of the newspapers were full of the match and how Down overwhelmed Kerry. 2-10 to 8 points. This was the first time that the Sam Maguire Cup had come to Northern Ireland. Players on the Down team were treated like Gods. Here is some of what *'The Fermanagh Herald'* said about the match. *Down triumph in great game.* Mourne men's team-work crushed Kerry. Country rejoices as Sam Maguire comes North. On Sunday last a thrilling,. pulsating historic hour of football, witnessed by almost 88,000 people, saw the All Ireland Senior title cross the border for the first time. The victors were Down and the vanquished Kerry, and the scores were emphatic-2-10 to 0-8- reflecting in sufficient measure the superiority of the Mourne kingdom to that of Kerry on this memorable day at Croke Park.

The Down cup of happiness was surely flowing over on this occasion, for to win an All Ireland at any time and against any opposition is truly a wonderful achievement, but to win it against indomitable Kerry adds much to the victory. James McCartan struck the match with his goal and Paddy Doherty set it to the bomb with his penalty, and up in the air in smithereens went that Kerry myth.

Up in the air, too, went a mighty roar that could be heard at the farthest ends of Dublin city - a roar from the throats of approximately 50,000 supporters of Down at the game, the roar that sounded the death-knell of Kerry hopes of a twentieth All Ireland crown that day and trumpeted forth to the world the fact that at long last the coveted title had been brought across the border by one of our sundered counties.

That moment in Croke Park on Sunday when Paddy Doherty sent the ball crashing to the Kerry net from a penalty to clinch the issue was one that struck forcibly at the heart of every Down man in that vast arena, and many an involuntary tear burst from eyes that saw this wonderful historic event - a great day for Down, a great day for Ulster, a great day for the Irish nation.

How the crowd thrilled to the Down team after the deciding goal, and how those Down players hammered home their advantage against a now bewildered Kerry fifteen. They jumped higher than ever before, safe hands held the ball and sure-footed deliveries smashed again and again into the Kerry defence, where some of the game's best defenders floundered in the face of this whirlwind from the North . . .

The great stands in Croke Park shook in their concrete foundations as Kevin Mussen appeared on the stand to receive the Sam Maguire Cup and hold it aloft for all to see and to the mighty roar of the crowd. This time not only from Down throats, but from almost every soul in the stadium, wave upon wave of cheering rolled over Dublin and any there who did not know the result before then must have realised that something new had happened in Croke Park, for never was enthusiasm at the end of a game so great.

President De Valera was there to shake the hand of the Down captain and deep down in that great Irish heart there must have been a silent prayer of thanksgiving that he had lived to see such a great day of joy for his people cut off by a barrier the removal of which he had devoted much of his active life.

And out in that vast crowd the hearts of the men from Armagh, Antrim, Derry, Tyrone and Fermanagh must have throbbed with a new hope, a new declaration of determination to emulate the feat of Down that day . . .

On Monday evening at the colossal reception in Newry for the team, Rev H Esier Adm Newry said, 'These young players have brought honour to Down and to Ulster, and I am confident they carry that honour worthily.' We echo that statement with confidence, for never was the county represented by a more exemplary band of athletes as on this occasion; and never was the honour of Down entrusted to move worthy custodians. (*Fermanagh Herald*).

CHAPTER 8

DISGRACE AT DOWRA

Down winning the All Ireland made everyone in the 'North' feel special. It also demonstrated that though the Six Counties had been severed from the rest of Ireland, the spirit of gealdom still survived, flourished and inspired the people, despite a bigoted attitude from many quarters. The people of the 'Mountain' felt as strongly as any Down man or woman about the great win, and 'Connor' was delighted, ecstatic. 'What did I tell you'se; by God I told you'se they'd win, and by God, win they did.' 'Where is Johnny Culloty and his men today?' 'I'll tell you something now for nothing, it'll be a long time before you see Kerry at Croke Park again, after that beating; they're finished for a very long time.'

We were soon brought back to earth however with an account of a spectacular performance my father put on in Dowra on a wet day at a wool sale. Two weeks after Down's great win, Papers like the *Fermanagh Herald* announced:

> '*Wild Scenes at Dowra Wool Sales.*
> Fermanagh farmer prosecuted.'

The reports went on to say that Farrell McGourty, farmer of Florencecourt Co Fermanagh was charged with escaping from the custody of the Gardai and occasioning a breach of the peace by using violent words and behaviour. The Superintendent stated that he was using vile and aggressive language, and standing up on a cart while inciting a large crowd of about 200 people to violence. My father explained that he was doing the exact opposite, urging the crowd to have a 'bit of wit' and let the buyers buy the wool. What had happened was that people like my father were there at the proper time of 10am to sell their wool. It was a very wet day. The wool buyers were late and I didn't begin buying wool until 2pm. The people who came last were trying to sell their wool before the people who came early, and that was what started the rumpus, which resulted in the buyers refusing to buy any wool. My father therefore maintained that he was trying to make the people see sense so that the buyers could buy their wool. Case dismissed.

Everyone was at home for Christmas dinner 1960, and now, Petie and I, as well as Rose, were able to buy little presents for the others, and we all had a very happy Christmas Day. Pat was eight years in 1960. Farrell was ten and Frank and Bridie were twelve. Frank, who had always been sick and delicate, was getting visibly stronger. For some reason the older ones of us had always seemed to lump Farrell, Frank and Bridie together, calling them by the nickname's, 'The Wee Lad', 'The Big Lad', and 'The Lassie'. After Christmas, those of us who were working returned to our jobs, and so 1960 came to an end.

Even though George and I always got on well, in March 1961 we had a major disagreement. Before I had left to bring the milk out to the road one morning I had lit a fire in a field to burn rubbish. While I was out with the milk, George came to the fire, and as he did so something exploded in it. He wasn't hurt or anything, but he accused me of deliberately putting something in the fire, and we had a blazing row about it. I got my things and went home. The next day George came to the house, inviting me to return to my job, but I didn't go back.

It was with a sad heart that I left George's, to embark on whatever my new phase of life was to be. George had always treated me so well; like a father even, putting up with my idiosyncrasies with a paternal like extravagance. Living at George's had made me aware of the fascinating world of books, as the walls of George's parlour were hidden by beautifully bound, hardback volumes, of books, stacked neatly on strong wooden shelves. George was always reading some book or other, and his knowledge of history and politics was immense. Every so often intellectuals and historians would visit him, and a crowd of them would discuss politics, religion, history and folk-lore around the table all day. The magnitude of his knowledge which I steadily became aware of as I worked there, had the effect of creating in me such a terrible yearning to know things, that I knew that I also would have to immerse myself in the world of books.

After I left George I used to look after the sheep at home, and go to Jimmity's with Tommy McManus, as before. The forestry at Michael Neddy's land looked like a massive high wall as one came towards it, eerie and impregnable. But there was a secret pass through it, which allowed us to make our way to Melanophy's. There was now a new road from Fee's to Melanophy's. Melanophy's house was beginning to look dilapidated, run down and repulsive. The long ago whitewash was gone, grey, streaky and mouldering into oldness. Hugh had taken to going on bouts of drinking to 'The Black'. Often times he would crash off the bike and suffer severe injuries. I found them very amiable. We would all sit on the wee stools around the fire, talking away for hours and looking out at the rain; not a worry about work, and outside, the grass gently growing lush and green all the while. The Melanophy's seemed to have settled into a sort of retirement, as if they had done enough. The forestry too, while it prevented our sheep from trespassing on their land, must have been debilitating for them, as it enclosed their farm in a semi circle. By its impenetrable nature, it also stopped Hughie and Francie from coming over to our house, or other houses in the 'mountain', like they used to do, or for that matter being even able to see over into Glenawley. Bruiser's (Maguires) new house was already beginning to look vulnerable, with cracks appearing in the pebble dashing, paint flaking off the windows, and the guttering sagging. Mick and John, the sons had departed, and now only Paddy, another son and the parents were left. Jimmy's also (a\so Maguire's) too, looked smitten with decay, and where once a fine family strode out to the chapel on a Sunday morning, now the house contained three weary looking old men. There was only one woman left in Fee's. The fine strong men from Curry's house were gone. You could now travel the whole way over to Tommy McManus's at Mullagboy and not meet a living soul. On the way home from Jimmity's at night, walking through the Barrs was now a lonesome, lifeless experience, where humanity, if it existed, was hidden, tired, expiring.

My separation from George also gave me the chance to go leisurely about the 'Mountain', contemplating and meeting my friends there. I would saunter out to Jim Dolan's house. Mrs Dolan would be away teaching, and Jim was more or less housebound looking after the children, until she returned after her work. The children were a handful, boisterous, noisy and frighteningly active. Mary was the oldest, then there was the twins Michael and Patrick, and Jacqueline came next. Jim would give me a job cleaning out a byre or foddering cattle. Often times I'd go out to James Nolan's house. Nolan's was still the same, thatched and surrounded by flowers, as when Mammy and I first went there. James and Lizzie were older of course, but Lizzie still limped about, doing her work, laughing and joking, a lovely woman; and still making those lovely buns that I could die for. James wasn't as well as he used to be, and now their son John done all the farmwork.

It was the case in all the houses in the 'Mountain' that when you went visiting you would just lift the latch and walk in. However, it was good manners to 'announce' your coming by whistling or singing a tune, scraping your shoes on the street, or prompting a dog to bark if there was one. You would hardly have sat down in any house before tea and something to eat was presented. You weren't asked if you'd like a cup of tea or any of that crack; it was made for you as a matter of respect and hospitality; you would be told by your host, 'ah sure it's only a drop in your hand., and it would be bad manners to leave anything behind you, as if your neighbour's fare wasn't good enough. And even if you visited every house in the 'Mountain' after each other, you would get tea and something to eat in every one of them.

I would mosey over to 'Connor's' or 'Terry's' of an evening. In 'Connor's' house, the children would all be arranged in a semi-circle, facing the fire, sitting on little three legged stools. Francie and Mary Ellen would be on two chairs at the hob, at each end of the semi-circle. When I arrived the stools would all be adjusted so that I could fit into the semi-circle. Every so often, the regularity and companionship of the semi-circle would be broken as someone got up to put turf on the fire, made tea, or went out into the night on private business.

Everyone would be involved and immersed in a great gabble of conversation that flowed spontaneously and automatically through a great range of subjects. All our conversations in

'Connor's' were conducted with a wonderful democracy, and even the youngest person able to speak was given a fair hearing and freedom of speech.

'Terry's' was a bit like our own house, in that whatever age a young person in the 'Mountain' was, there was someone of a similar age in 'Terry's'. 'Terry's' new house had a large kitchen extended out from it, and that was where visitors first deposited themselves, to get warm, chat to the family, and await Mrs 'Terry's' big mugs of tea and large chunky sandwiches. When the atmosphere was nice and convivial, we would all vacate the kitchen and move to the dining room, which overlooked the Shru Croppa River, so that we could all listen to the radio, hear the news and so forth. Often times we would go to play '25, but sometimes, because Tommy and Terry would embark on some discussion about politics or what not, we would forsake '25 and instead, listen to their debate intently. Terry and Tommy never argued about things by shouting and spurting fire. Instead, they discussed events great and small in a low, amiable, measured way, promoting their side of the discussion with great accuracy and conviction. I would always be enthralled by their discussions and often wondered would it ever be possible for anyone else to know half as much as them.

Petie and the Motorbike

One night Daddy arrived home with big news. He said, 'What de ya think that omidhaun Petie is after doing?' We were all guessing, keeping in mind Petie's coolheaded and stable, if somewhat religious nature. 'He fell off the bike I suppose,' said one. 'I'll bet you he is getting married,' another ventured. 'Is he going to be a priest Daddy?' It wasn't any of them. Daddy said, 'He's after going and buying a frigging motorbike, the cluuson.' Mammy exploded, and really it was no wonder, because there had been a lot of motorcycle deaths in Fermanagh recently, and most people thought that motorcycles were a fearful danger. My mother didn't want anything happening to Petie, her favourite, so she walked down to Jack Wallace's and collared Petie, giving him a good talking to. Petie had to return the bike to the seller, and then he gave up his job at Wallace's as well, returning home, like me, resolute but redundant.

Robert Elliott asked me to go and work for them for a while, and so I was employed once more. Simultaneously, Petie started with George Sheridan. Robert's father, Robert Elliott, of Gortatole, was a very wealthy man when he died, leaving a widow, four daughters, Carol, Charlotte, Jean and Ruth, and three sons Robert, William and Richard. The Elliott sons were known far and wide because they were so adventurous and wild. They would fill their tractors with fuel and race around the field until the fuel ran out, which might be a day later. They would balance the tractor on two side wheels and drive two or three hundred yards down the road with some unfortunate soul like Jack Wallace clinging on to the back in fear of their lives. They used to drive the tractor towards a river at speed, put the front wheels over the edge, and reverse out before the front wheels had time to descend into the water. One day Tommy McGovern was working with them, and Richard told him to get on the seat of the tractor. Then he started the tractor and off it went with Tommy, who knew nothing about a tractor, in the driving seat. Tommy managed to steer the tractor and trailer along the road and into the long steep avenue that led down to the house. The tractor speeded up going down the hill, and to get into the yard there was a sharp double bend between buildings. Tommy managed to get through the first bend, but as bales of hay went in all directions, he was unable to make the second bend and crashed into the wall knocking the wall down and shearing the front wheel and axle clean off the tractor. Richard thought it was great fun and could hardly wait for a chance to try the same again. Another day Richard and Jack Wallace were loading bales of hay in the same field, with Jack building the bales on the trailer and Richard handing them up. When the load of bales was good and high, Richard jumped on the tractor and set off with the load, leaving Jack stranded on top of the load of bales. Straightaway, Jack knew what was about to happen, and as Richard came to various bends along the route, Jack would have climbed some distance down the side of the bales, on the same side as the bend, to lessen his danger in case the whole load of bales tumbled off. At every bend Richard tried his best to topple the load of bales, but Jack had built them so well they were difficult to move. Richard flew up the road and fairly hurtled into the long avenue down to the house. Still the bales stayed put. Jack was down one side for the double bend at the house. He didn't have time to get back up for the second part of the bend and the load of bales went over, Jack in the middle of them, breaking windows and doors in the kitchen, and Jack landing in beside Mrs Elliott where she was cooking the dinner in the kitchen. Robert and Willie, who were the two oldest, were complete genius's at driving cars. My father, who didn't like speed would go anywhere with Robert, and his greatest pleasure was for Robert and him to go up to Drumkeerin to buy sheep when there was a good fall of snow. Robert would delight both my father and the natives as he shot through snow covered lanes and boreens, slithering in all directions but nevertheless in full control. So when I started work at Elliotts I began a particularly crazy period of my life.

Life at Elliotts was completely different to what went on at George's. At Sheridan's we got up in the morning at the reasonable hour of 7am. Charlotte Elliott would now call me at 5.30 am, and I would go straight out to do the milking. Everything was done running. Milking cows, cutting silage with a knife, loading silage on trailers for feeding indoors and outlying cattle, and then cleaning byres and washing milking machines. All this stuff had to be finished before we had our breakfast at 9am, after which work commenced on the land, cleaning and making drains, cutting hedges, clearing and burning trees and shrubbery, levelling the fields, spreading manure, cutting the grass twice for silage, bringing cattle and sheep to the market in Enniskillen, and helping on the milk lorry. The Elliott's owned two milk lorries and took all the milk from the 'Mountain' and Florencecourt to the Creamery in Enniskillen.

When Richard, Robert and I came in for our dinner or tea, if I didn't hurry up I would get hardly any food, because they both ate so quick they would have everything cleared and be standing up waiting to go again before I had rightly started. I would be so tired I used to wonder why I wasn't able to travel very far on the bicycle any more. However, I always got on tremendously well with all the Elliott's, and when Robert and Richard would go off in the car in the evening they would often bring me with them. They would go flying around Enniskillen, meeting up with their friends and racing them around the town. Then they would ogle some foolish car driver into racing them, and when they had completely beaten and humiliated him, they would go home happy. sometimes they would prowl about the back streets of Enniskillen until they would meet some brazen young fellow, and then they would challenge him that, pointing to me, 'This cub will bate the shite out a ya.' I certainly didn't intend beating anything out of anybody, but they would keep on at the youth, picking at him until he threw off his jacket and took on a Jack Johnston pose, ready to flatten anything. Then we would all drive off, thinking what a hilarious finale to a very exciting night, making plans to do something similar very soon again. Whenever Richard or Robert left Enniskillen in the car, they always timed the journey, trying to do it that bit faster every time.

Richard thought I needed a haircut, so one night he decided to cut my hair. He got the electric clippers and shaved one width of the clippers from my neck, up over the back of my head, coming out on the middle of my forehead. I told him that he was cutting it far too short, and he said, to wait a minute, and he went off and hid the clippers. No one could find the clippers, so I had to go around with my head covered for a month until the swathe of hair grew and I was able to get a more normal haircut.

One wet day we were silorating, which meant that a forage harvester was cutting grass and blowing it into a trailer towed by a tractor. I was driving one of these tractors, an International Harvester B275, and each time we had a full load of grass we would take it away to the silage pit. I set off with a full load, and then reversed the trailer up the steep ramp to the silage pit, and tipped up the trailer to remove the grass. When the trailer was tipped, the wet grass jammed in the back of the trailer. This load on the back of the trailer lifted the wheels of the tractor off the ground, which meant that now I had no brakes, and the tractor and trailer ran down the ramp towards Lough McNean, which was only a few yards from the front of the silage pit. I automatically turned the steering to the left, away from the lake, and immediately both tractor and trailer went tumbling over. The tractor went completely upside down, its four wheels in the air, and was completely hidden by black smoke from the now unrestricted fuel supply. The back wheels were still spinning furiously, the grips of the tyres skidding off my head. I thought of all the things I should have done for my mother and father, all the things they told me to do which I didn't. I thought of all my brothers and sisters that I'd never see no more. I asked God to not be too hard on me. Charlotte heard the commotion as she was getting the dinner in the kitchen, saw the accident, and ran for the men in the field. Richard, Robert and Jack Wallace arrived, and couldn't see where I was because of all the smoke. Along with Charlotte, they managed to lift the tractor on its side, and the engine stopped. I was curled around the seat and jammed in between the hydraulic arms and the mudguard. Since then I have always had a special regard for the International B275 tractor, because I doubt I would be here now if I had been driving any other tractor that day. As it was, I escaped with hardly a scratch.

One Saturday night I was in bed and I could hear great commotion through the house, but as my room was far away from the centre of the house, I stayed where I was, wondering. I thought it strange when Mrs Elliott instead of Charlotte, called me on Sunday morning. I went out and began doing the chores. Richard and Robert came to help. Silence. We ate our breakfast through silence. Then, when we went outside, Richard asked me did I know about the accident last night. No, I knew nothing about any accident. He led me out through the massive walls of the yard and into the lovely garden at the front of the house, at the end of the avenue. The place was carnage. The lovely flowers, shrubs and trees were flattened and destroyed. The pedestal water fountains, and the total population of statues and gnomes was shattered into smithereens and scattered across the remains of the garden. Buried among the rare fish, in what had been the pretty and peaceful ornamental pond, was the shattered remains of a Morris Traveller. Then Richard brought me to a shed where another car was lying ripped to pieces. There had been a terrific accident in the avenue leading to the house, and Jean had been very badly injured and in a coma. Elliott's was a wonderful alive, adventurous place, where a constant excitement abounded with the threat of ever present danger. A couple of months later I decided that if I was to have any chance of staying on this earth for a reasonable period of time, the quicker I left for more sedate surroundings, the better. When I eventually left, Jean had still not recovered consciousness. After about seven months, Jean came out of the coma, and thankfully she made a full recovery.

New Job

Home again; But I was only a few days at home when Jack Wallace arrived and asked me to come and work for him. He wanted me to start right away, and I began to think of Petie's gruelling, and the constant battles they used to have. I said I wanted time to think, and told him to come back in two days. But Jack seemed to be such a quiet and amiable man that when he came back two days later, I happily headed off with him, though as I came to his house I was in a state of some trepidation.

Jack lived with his mother, and his nephew Gordon worked on the farm intermittently. I had my own room, which was on an annex of the house. We started in the mornings at 7am and finished at 6pm. In the mornings at George Sheridan's, George used to shout and bawl at me to get up, then go out and milk two cows, come back in and shout some more, before I would decide to get out of bed. All Jack ever had to do was stand at the foot of the stairs, and say in a normal voice, 'John, time to get up' and I would rise immediately. As my father had often said, Wallace's was one of the best houses he was ever in. I could only say the same, because for all the time I worked there, I was treated tremendously well. We would have breakfast at 9, then 'elevenses'. Dinner at 1, tea at 3, and our main tea when we finished at 6. Then we would have a final small meal between 8 and 9pm, and we would always have fish on a Friday. Jack had a massive conurbation of buildings near the house. He had thousands of battery hens in one, temperature adjusted shed. He had sheds for fuel, machinery sheds, haysheds, a byre, dairy, two silage pits, a massive cattle fattening shed, an engine shed, with a massive engine for generating power, and a shed for sawing timber on a large circular saw. The engine powered the saw and the water pump, and generated electricity for the milking machines and the house.

One of the first ideas I had when I went to Wallace's was, that I was going to get my hands on that motorbike that Mammy prevented Petie from having. When I had saved up the price of it I went down to Brady's house on the banks of the Arney River, and asked the owner to sell me the machine. He himmed and hawed, because he didn't want my mother coming after him, but he sold me the bike. The motorbike was a 350cc Royal Enfield. He showed me how to work it, balanced me on it, and off I went, wobbling. I sprawled across the great wide seat, trembling with fear and anticipation, the road in front of me, my hands gripping the handlebars, in control. Jaysus but it was glorious, a profound combination of excitements. The great, wonderful engine of the machine, thumping steadily beneath me. The gentlest twist of my right hand sending showers of dust and stones from beneath the wheels. When I got to the main road I had to take a chance, because I had no driving licence, until I got safely into Jack Wallace's avenue and roared up to the house. As I parked the machine in the fuel shed I had a great feeling of pride and achievement, because the motorbike was now mine.

The regularity and stability of working at Wallace's allowed me time to go about on the bicycle once more. I seemed to become physically stronger at Wallace's, and as well as going on long spins, I still went up to 'Connor's' and 'Terry's' to play football, and I went home at least once a week. The sports of Clabby were coming up, and there was a gruelling cycle race there in the summer. The Elliott's and Wallace's and many other people urged me to enter for this race, and as there was a crowd of relations at home in Wallace's, they took myself and the bike to the 'Clabby Donkey Derby'. This seems to have been an ironic and appropriate name for what happened that day. I readied my bike; there was one competitor from Letterbreen, and most of the rest were from England and Scotland. There were qualifying heats to get to the final, which I reached. The venue looked like a real stadium, with a steep hill covered with the largest crowd of people I have ever seen. The final began; I was already weakened from progressing through the heats. At the start I was left way behind; I steadied up, and slowly I caught up on all the other racers. I went in front, and then left them all far behind as I reached the finish. Unbelievingly I was consigned to third place. Everyone there knew I had won. The Elliot's were there watching the race; they told my father what happened. He told me that everyone he met, who was at the race, told him I had won the race by miles. I didn't care. I knew myself that I had won the race, that was enough for me.

My time at Wallace's saw a radical improvement in some farm machinery, especially machinery for drainage. Part of Jack Wallace's farm was low lying, with a number of deep drains. I found out how deep one day when I saw someone coming down the road that I didn't want to meet because he'd be asking me too many questions. I jumped into the drain to hide until he passed. I sank into a couple of feet of glaar (soft wet mud) and the sides of the drain were so slippery, I just could not get out. I began to think of the story my father used to tell me when I was a child. He was working at Wallace's one day, cleaning a drain with a long handled drag, when a big rat ran up the leg of his trousers. He trapped the rat up at the top of his trousers with his two hands. He daren't let go of the rat, so someone had to cut out a hole in his trousers, where he was holding the rat. After an hour or so, when I still couldn't escape, I realised that I would have to dig steps out of the hard bank with my hands, and after about three hours I was able to extricate myself, minus my wellingtons. But now there was new machinery coming on the market that would eliminate many of these dangerous drains by making them underground, and making the open drains safer by changing the angle of the banks.

One new machine was the 'mole'. This machine could make a drain underground, and insert a pipe into it without interfering with the top of the ground. There was a machine called 'The McConnell Arm'. This was hitched onto the back of the tractor, and hydraulically driven by the tractor PTO. The farmer could drive along the drain and use the 'arm' to clean the mud out of it. Then a much heavier machine called the 'Dinkum' came on the scene. It was also attached to the back of the tractor and could be used to make deep drains, dig large holes and foundations for buildings. It was an unwieldy machine, far too heavy for the back of a tractor, and was almost useless in wet ground. After that the JCB came along. The JCB was designed and built by Joe Charles Bamford. It was specially designed for digging, and was a compact, balanced unit with a front shovel and a backactor. They were immensely powerful, and could travel over the most treacherous surfaces, digging drains, foundations, levelling ground or knocking down trees. These machines were amazing. They could travel over hedges and ditches, swamps and rivers, with the greatest of ease. It was fascinating to watch the tremendous work, or the combination of tricks the driver could accomplish by the gentlest manoeuvring of a few levers.

I bought another motorcycle, a BSA army bike, because I thought that if I couldn't go on the road at least I could race around the fields. I began to spend hours at night slithering around the fields, perfecting my balance and improving my ability. Jack then started Brian Crawford, and he also bought a motorbike.

On the 16th of September 1961, after our breakfast, Brian and I took the tractor up to the Wheathill Road to cut a whitethorn hedge around one of Jack's fields. It was very windy in the morning, and when we began to cut the top of the hedge with the billhook, each time we cut a branch it was whipped away with the force of the wind. As we went about cutting the hedge, Jack Wilson, whom I knew well, a man who was adored by everyone, stood on the road and talked to us. He was accompanied by Jack Crozier, and George Frazer. As they were going away, Jack Wilson said for us to watch out that the wind didn't blow us away. Soon we were hardly able to stay erect with the force of the wind, and as the air all around was filled with a mixture of branches, plastic sheets, corrugated iron sheets, and other stuff, a gradual, fearful roaring sound enveloped the place as if it came from the heavens.

Suddenly, we saw George Frazer waving violently on the road. When I got to him he said that Jack Wilson had been seriously injured and to go and get Jack Wallace to call the Doctor, Police and Ambulance. I jumped on the tractor as Brian begged me not to leave him there. I flew down the road on the tractor, and Jack Crozier ran across the road in front of the tractor I was driving, and fell on the other side of the road. At the same time I met a car, and the people in it thought I had hit Jack Crozier with the tractor. I realised that Jack

Crozier was probably coming with the same message that George Frazer had brought earlier, and so I kept going for Wallace's like the hammers of hell. When I got to Wallace's slates were coming from all directiors and shattering on the street, and corrugated iron and wooden missiles were flying across the yard. Jack was away at the market, and neither Mrs Wallace or I were able to open the door. The phone wires were down, I shouted at her what I had been told, and then started for George Latimers. George was at the market and his phone wires were also down. I decided to go on to Robert Elliott's.

On the way from Latimers to Elliott's I went along the Wheathill Road, past Bowles's Cottage, and then past the sheep dipping tank on the left. All the time branches, logs and pieces of steel were flying across me, and filling up the road. At the sheep dipping tank a tree fell and I just managed to drive through the branches before it came completely down. Then I passed the Junction for the Brockagh Bridge road, and from there on, up the hill towards 'The Hanging Rock' there was a line of large larch trees on each side of the road. The roaring noise was absolutely frightening, and as I went up the road between the trees the noise became so tremendous that I knew the trees were going to fall, and I only hoped I would be able to get through before that happened. A massive tree fell way up the hill in front of me. I began to reverse the tractor, when another giant tree fell across the road just behind me. On my right, between the two fallen trees, there was a gate leading into the field, and this gate was attached to two large stone built pillars. I jumped off the tractor, opened the gate, and jumped back on the tractor to drive it through the gate into the field. As I went between the two pillars a tree on that side fell, broke on the left pillar, and then came crashing down, on the right, eventually resting across both pillars. I was jammed down in the seat, entangled in telephone wires and branches, but amazingly, uninjured. I extricated myself from the tractor, all the time thinking about Jack Wilson, and the complete haimes of a job I was making of trying to get help for him. I began to run across the fields towards Elliott's. The fields were covered with water that had been forced out of Lough McNean. The roofs of

Elliott's silage pits, byres and haysheds were gone, some of them in pieces out in the lough.

I found Charlotte and Richard. Richard and I made our way by car up the 'Mountain Road' and eventually back to where the accident happened to Jack Wilson. The three men had been working with cattle, and some of them saw the roof of the shed coming and shouted, but Jack Wilson was unable to get out of the way, and was fatally injured. Richard and I helped to carry him to the road.

The early morning, reddened sky, looked brooding and in
pain.
The muffled, bloodied, austere clouds, repelling with
disdain,
Our troubled, suffering angry world, in chaos and in flame.

The mighty flaming, austere world, soon blew with all its
might
The broken oak and sally screamed, and living things took
flight,
And many were the joyous hearts, destroyed before the
night.

But the whistling, cursed, searing wind, hammered our
hearts in vain,
Torn, bereaved and anguished, still our hearts rose up again,
And fondly remembered the unfortunate ones, those who
were loved and slain.

The unfortunate ones who were loved and slain, still guide
us through our day,
The thought of their temperate, gentle smile, enough to
light our way.
And encourage us all with the hope that soon, together we
all can pray.

When I got back to Wallace's, Brian Crawford had still not returned. The wind had died down, and then I met him coming down through the fields. What happened to him was that, every time he got to his feet he was blown down again, and all he could do was to lie behind a wall until the furious wind of 'Hurricane Debbie' blew itself out.

Football in Sligo

One Sunday I went up to the 'Black' on the bicycle after mass, and got a surprise to see Mammy and Granny waiting on the street outside Phillip Dolan's pub. 'Good women' says I, 'I can see you'se are go'an someplace.' 'Aw, we're go'an to'da match . . . We're waitin' for a bus,' they said. 'What match?' I said, 'where's da match?' They said, 'Did ya not know that Cavan and Mayo are playin' in Sligo? . . . We're waitin' for da bus ta bring us . . . it'll be a grate game . . . throw the bloody bike there and come on with us.' Well I thought it wasn't such a bad idea at all to go to the match, and so I said, 'jaysus I might go to it alright,' and then they wanted me to go with them on the bus, so I said that I'd go on the bike and meet them in the football grounds. The bus came and they set off, and then I headed for Sligo as well.

When I got to the football ground there was no trace of them to be found. I looked everywhere, and when the match started I gave up looking and took my seat amongst the crowd to watch the match. Like the football matches at 'Terry's' and 'Connor's', this match started off with a wonderful glow of exciting sportsmanship and noble endeavour, but quickly deteriorated into a shameful free-for-all, with football taking second place to the very necessary retribution 'players' judged should be meted out to their opponents. The antics on the pitch in this shambles of a match soon transferred themselves to the spectators, with opposing sections of the crowd becoming increasingly voluble and aggressive. 'Ref! . . .ref! . . .*Rrreeeffff!* Go home ya blind fucker of a referee ya!' There were Mayo supporters behind me and Cavan ones in the seats in front of me. Mayo people behind me were shouting 'as blatant a fucking foul as ever was committed on a field of play. Animals! *Animals!* . . . with an ass for a referee!' . . . Someone near my ear shouted, 'I can certainly see now for myself what I always knew, Cavan' and he spat out between myself and someone else, 'animals, cheats and thieves!' A Cavan supporter in front of me could take no more of this and he stood up and lashed out at his tormentor with a flailing right cross. He missed his intended target and caught me flush on the side of the head with a fierce wallop. I thought it was hilarious and laughed out at the fun of it. Some time later I saw my assailant gingerly feeling his knuckles and I laughed out loudly. Luckily he didn't attack again, and when we were all thoroughly fed up, the referee blew the final whistle.

As I was weaving about in the heaving crowd that was leaving, I saw Mammy and Granny in the distance. When we met up they pounced on me as if I was a cool, clear spring well in the desert, or their own personal saint, sent down from heaven to save them. 'Oh John, what a madman!' what a journey! I'm damned if we're going home again with that eejit!' Granny said, 'be japers the omidhauan is completely dulally. Jay pee what took me here at all? will we ever get home again Bridget?' They wanted me to tell them of another way home, but anyway it turned out that they had no option but return home on the bus.

On Monday night I went home to find out how Mammy and Granny got on with their bus journey. On the way to the match the driver began travelling at fearful speeds up towards Manorhamilton throwing his passengers all over the bus. Some of the passengers asked him to slow down and he became even more reckless. When the passengers demanded him to stop the bus, the driver walked back through the bus until he came to a male passenger, and he said to him,' if you don't shut your fuckin' mouth I'll flatten you on the fuckin' floor.' The driver then went back to the front of the bus and continued as before, while the passengers in the back prayed and held on for dear life. As the bus careered through the mountains of Sligo, the driver turned into a narrow lane and travelled along it for miles, eventually stopped the bus in a bog on the top of a mountain. Then he got out of the bus and walked off.

When time went on and there was no sign of him returning, some of the people on the bus went off to look for him. They found him, stretched out on a flat rock, snoring, an empty spirit bottle beside him. They woke him up and persuaded him to continue the journey, arriving in Sligo as the match finished.

On the way home with the bus, he continued his antics, eventually driving the bus into a field near the school at Doon Lough. The bus bogged down to the axles in the field, and the driver got out, threw his coat over his shoulder and nonchalantly walked off towards Manorhamilton as if he hadn't a care in the world. The passengers went to a house to explain their predicament, and someone from one of the houses went away to find a telephone and summon another bus. Granny and Mammy arrived back at Granny's house in Roo at 1am on Monday morning, far more experienced travellers than they were before, but nevertheless none the worse for wear. Daddy said that it was amazing the destruction they were able to cause going such a short distance in a big bloody bus, when he had went all over Ireland in a pair of wellingtons and no one ever heard a mum out of him.

Uncle Francie

I had always spent a lot of my spare time at Granny's at Roo. It was so quiet and peaceful, and I could come there any time of the day or night. As well as that, my good friends Charlie and Michael Dolan lived up the lane, just past John and James Murray's house. I would always help Francie to win the turf and bring them to the house, and Aunt Annie always bought me a new shirt for doing that. Granny's house was always like a second home to me, and then disaster struck. Uncle Francie decided to clean up the land. He gathered up all the stones and boulders, and stubbed all the blackthorn bushes. Soon, every wayward bush and boulder had been cleared, except for the clumps of bushes that were growing in forths around the land. Francie was determined to cut down these bushes, but when neighbours heard what he was about to do they reminded him of the terrible consequences of such an act. Francie waited and considered. Granny maintained that the house they lived in was accidentally built on a fairy pass. She said that the fairies lived in the forths on the land and to leave them alone. They came out at night and went along their 'passes' about their business, and as long as they were left alone they left you alone. She said that earlier residents of the house had come to an agreement with the fairies that they could walk around the house until they could get back on their own 'pass'. Francie said that this was only balderdash, nothing but pisherogues to keep the simple in their place. But Granny went on to remind him about all the strange happenings about the place; all the times her and Annie had been frightened out of their wits travelling up or down the lane to Dolans; the times when they woke up in the middle of the night to find three or four other strange people in the room talking among themselves. And it was true. I always found Granny's the scariest place I had ever been. There always seemed to be some evil presence about. Even though it was like a second home to me, and even though I am not easily scared, I always had a tremendous fear when moving about the house; my brothers and sisters stayed there with the same trepidation.

Anyway, Francie began to cut the bushes out of the forths. After a few days he arrived back to the house one day completely deranged. The Gardai had to be got, and they took him away to the mental hospital in Omagh. He went from that to Monaghan Mental Hospital. After a time he was alright, but he would not return home. Eventually he went to St Phelim's Hospital in Cavan, a home, and he was able to get a job there as a gardener. Mammy and I often went to see him. Granny, Annie and Paddy went to see him too. His sisters came from America. Everyone tried to persuade him to return home but he wouldn't come. He never came back. He saw something, or something happened to him in that field at the forth. And whatever it was, it was something that fearful that it drove him out of his wits, something so terrifying that nothing would ever entice him to set foot in Roo again.

The Motorbike

Life went on leisurely at Wallace's. I got a driving licence for the motorbike. This allowed me to take it up into the 'Mountain' and show it to all my friends. I was always aware how dangerous motorcycles were, and so I went about the roads and lanes with well intentioned doses of care and caution. I would arrive home in excitement and exhilaration, swelling out with pride as the younger ones examined my wonderful machine. While Mammy seemed to accept my motorbike as an inevitable consequence of growing up, my father more or less ignored it, his only concession to its presence, a distant and vacant glare.

One day Mammy asked me to take her to the dentist in Manorhamiliton. 'No bother,' says I, and we straddled the machine and set off. Halfway to Manorhamilton a dog ran out in front of us and got stuck between the two wheels. My feet were jammed against the dog as we went down the road, and weaving out of control. I got my feet out, and the back wheel then ran over the dog as we still wobbled and swerved down the road. Mammy and I continued on to the dentist, but she maintained that she would never again get on a motorcycle. Granny used to be mad to get on as a passenger, but she wasn't able to lift her long voluminous skirts high enough to be able to get on. One night I caught up with my father walking home from the 'Black' and stopped to give him a lift. He himmed and wondered, and eventually decided to get on behind me. 'Go aisey, for God's sake.' 'Of course I will,' I said. 'I'll crawl along, you'll hardly know I'm moving.' As I went along I could hear him scolding to himself behind me. After a while I thought that he would be more confident, so I went a little faster. Dad shouted, 'that's a sight.' 'What's a sight?' says I. 'That's horrid speed! that's horrid frigging speed,' he said. I told him I wasn't doing 10 miles an hour. He then said 'Oh, that's a fret . . . a terror . . . a holy terror . . . I'd rather walk. Let me off! Let me off for God's sake! *Will you let me off!*' I had to stop and let him off and he walked on home.

There was a tremendous frost before Christmas 1961, which seemed to abate before the year ended, but then became very severe indeed as the new year went on. Temperatures were so low that 19 degrees of frost were recorded at Aldergrove. Lough McNean froze over and Richard and Robert Elliott used to race their cars over it from shore to shore. Francis Ferris, who used to work with us at Wallace's occasionally, was spreading manure at Cloonacleena, on Monday January 1st when the tractor and trailer he was driving accidentally went into the Arney River and Francis was drowned.

In another poignant tragedy on Lough Erne three days earlier, on the 29th December 1961, William Rooney and his brother

James both lost their lives. William Rooney was a married man, a postman, and his older brother James was a farmer, and both lived on Inishturk Island, in Lough Erne. When William didn't return from his job as a postman in the evening, his brother James got his boat and set out to look for him at about 6pm. Mrs Rooney, who had two children, one aged three and the other just over one, could hear the two men breaking the ice as she waited through the night on the shore. There was no phone on the island for her to call for help for the two men. At 10pm she heard William and James shouting to each other away across the frozen lough. All through the night she could hear the men breaking the ice, until twenty minutes to 3am when there was silence. The two brothers were found by the police next day, their boats locked together in the ice, which was nine inches thick. The brothers had indeed reached each other. One had laid down his life to save his brother and sorrowfully they had both perished. The whole country was shocked by all these deaths, and once again it highlighted the terrible cost the people of rural Fermanagh had to pay every time there was a bad winter.

I bought a proper, dirt-track, second-hand motorbike, and every spare second I had was spent on this machine. I had no interest in jumping drains or barrels, or any of that crack. My sole ambition was to gain perfect balance, and to do that I would continually go flat out towards mucky corners so that I could slither around the bend without my feet touching the ground. Then I bought a brand new Royal Enfield Crusader, a beautiful, gentle bike, all equipped with a streamlined, protective fairing. This motorcycle was so clean and refined that if I had good clothes I could wear them on a journey and they would be as good as when I left. But the 'Crusader' only lasted three months. Although never crashed, it was worn out. I sold my 350 Royal Enfield, then I left the 'Crusader' into Paddy McNulty's of Enniskillen and bought instead a Honda 425. This was one of the first biggish Honda's around, and as Honda were winning nearly all championship motorcycle races, I thought that now I had a good motorcycle at last. The Honda was a dull red, with silver panels on the petrol tank, and finished off with white sidewall tyres. It also had a push-button starter.

The white tyres were very slippery, and initially the Honda seemed completely treacherous in comparison to my beloved and dependable 'Crusader'. It also seemed sluggish and slow and nothing like what I expected it to be. Even though I now had three motorbikes, I still used to go about on the bicycle. There was something raw and beautiful about flying through remote places, like Glan Gap at night, totally propelled by one's own effort, through the pouring rain or snow, and only wearing a light vest, and knowing that at the end of the journey, the clothes would be dry from the heat radiating from one's body. Bit by bit however, it seemed that the bicycle was losing its attraction for me, and that day to day I was becoming increasingly more fascinated by motorcycles.

One Sunday after mass, I was going up the long straight that went past Wallace's, on the Honda, when suddenly it took off as if I had just connected another engine to it. There had been some blockage in the carburettor which suddenly rectified itself, and now the speed of the machine was absolutely lethal, with a correspondingly awesome roar from the exhausts to match. Motorcycles have always been considered dangerous, and something that young people should be kept well away from. In that sense it is difficult to explain to those who have never ridden a motorcycle, what the great attraction for motorcycles is.

There were many people with motorbikes close by to Wallace's. Pat and Owen Carrigan had two bikes. Dessie Howe owned a Norton, and Sammy Thompson, who lived down the road from Wallace's had a few motorbikes, and Eddie Bracken, who lived a mile down the road had a lethal 750 Triumph. There were also plenty of people in Florencecourt with powerful motorbikes. Because the road past Wallace's was about four miles of a straight, motorcyclists used to race up and down it testing the speed of their machines. I could listen at Wallace's in the evening, and hear Dessie Howe or the Carrigan's starting up their machines across the lough, and heading off, with their machines roaring as they went along the roads. Likewise, when I started up in the evening, the people across the lough as well as those nearer hand, could hear me and listen to the changing note of my machine as I accelerated and throttled off, when I went about the roads. I had a particular circuit that I constantly used. That was, turn right at Wallace's gate, via Brockagh Bridge, Letterbreen, Belcoo/Blacklion, Glenfarne, Manorhamilton, Sligo. From Sligo I would either go to Bundoran, or to Carrick-on-Shannon and then return to Wallace's. Sometimes when I returned to Wallace's around eleven, I would feel an incredible yearning to continue on the bike for another while. I would take off again, maybe going as far as Strabane or Dungannon before deciding to return.

My sole objective, whenever I left Wallace's, was to go as fast as it was possible to go. Every bend and corner on the route was a separate challenge. I would go as fast as it was possible to go, towards every corner and bend so that I would have to do everything in my power to get around it quicker than the last time. Up through Glenfarne and Kilmakerril, there would be crowds of people lined around the bends every evening, because they knew I'd be coming, and often I was able to look into someone's eyes as I went around a bend and I could see they were afraid. Often men with far more powerful machines would appear in my mirror. I could see straightaway that they were racing me, and I would slow down ever so slightly so that they could pass me. But that nearly always proved to be a mistake for them. The truth was that while I could be passed easily on a straight road by a more powerful machine, I believed that no one could get around bends quicker. Once I did pass a challenger he usually decided discretion was the better part of valour and kept well out of my mirror for the rest of the journey.

One day a man who used to bully us when he was a pupil at the Marble Arches School, asked me to leave him in Glenfarne on the motorbike. He had spent years in England, and now he was back on holidays or something, and he 'urgently needed to go to Glenfarne.' He adjusted himself on the bike behind me, in Blacklion, had a big laugh with his pals from the pub who had come out to see him off, and away we went. I began gingerly enough to sort of get him acquainted with the machine, but gradually and evilly I began to put on the pressure. When his head passed within a few inches of Rosaleen McLoughlin's porch, while part of the machine was airborne, he screamed at me to slow down. I pretended not to hear him, and anyway my mind was on the road way ahead, where the railway crossed it, and where the road had a vicious double bend. At Killnagh cemetery I blessed myself and prayed for those departed, and almost immediately we were at Killinagh Chapel where I blessed myself once more and asked for God's safekeeping. As soon as we passed the chapel we were at the bends leading to the double bend at Keany's Gatehouse. When a motorcyclist conveys a passenger behind him or her, it is important that the passenger or pillion rider leans the same way as the driver when going around bends, and an experienced pillion rider will automatically do this. On the other hand a less experienced passenger, or someone who is afraid, will try to counteract the downward force of the leaning motorcycle by leaning out in the opposite direction. My passenger seemed to have circumvented all this thinking however, because his head was buried into my back, as if he was hiding, and he was clutching me in a vice-like grip as if he was holding on for dear life.

When we got to the house he wanted, he told me to go on home and the people he was visiting would give him a lift home. They told him they would not leave him home, and said what sort of a man was he, having transport with him and him wanting a lift home. He then wanted them to ask some of the neighbours if they'd leave him in the 'Black' and they laughed at him, and so he had no option but mount the motorbike once more. We carried on back towards Blacklion in a similar crazy fashion until we approached the double bend at Keany's Gatehouse once more. As we were slithering around the double bends we met another motorcycle with a pillion passenger. As they were going past they may have thought I didn't give them enough room, and the passenger directed a mouthful of serious language at me. We were at the Chapel before I was able to get turned around, and then me and my mate set off in hot pursuit of the unfortunate motorcyclists. As we went down the hill at Forhill Post Office we caught up with them. This was one of the best parts of the road between Blacklion and Manorhamilton, and as they opened up their machine, trying to get away, my passenger and I motored on beside, and only inches from, the reluctant desperados, and their passenger started to shout out that he was sorry. Then we were at Keany's Gatehouse, at Brockagh, where there was another double bend, and as the other motorbike came out of the corner, my motorbike was in front of him and cutting off his road, leaving him no other option but drive into a drain at the side. Not forgetting my passenger, I turned around and delivered him back to where he had come from, Blacklion, and considered that I had filled him with enough excitement and knowledge to last him for a very long time.

So what is it in a motorcycle that has such an attraction. With a motorbike you are attached to a powerful, wonderful machine, but exposed to the elements. The wind, rain, or whatever, rushes at your face, and your vision is the same as if you were walking, unobstructed. With you and the machine alone, to face the elements, you become a part of each other, united; bonded. Very soon it feels as if you and your machine are one whole being. The machine can't get around corners without you, and you can't get around corners at such a speed without the machine. The fact that now you and the machine have the ability to go as close to destruction as it is possible to go, and survive, unravels in your mind such combinations of excitements and mind-boggling exhilaration's and sensations, that you begin to feel a very special and privileged individual indeed. Running parallel with these emotions, or at least that's the way it was with me, is the clear realisation of the fact that, but for the will and benevolence of the Almighty, one could never have went so near the brink of annihilation and continued to exist. I was very lucky in that I never had a bad accident, though I did come tumbling off a few times. I have always considered myself very privileged to have ridden a motorcycle and I believe that if I hadn't done so I would have only half lived.

Sometimes I would go up home on Sunday, and then walk to the top of Cuilcagh. When I would eventually get to the top, the sensation of the chill wind on my sweaty face made the tough climb worth the effort. Then there was the added bonus that the most beautiful part of Ireland could be seen from the summit. A visit to Cuilcagh also provided a useful antidote to the increasingly clamorous tenor of life now being produced by noisy machinery, busy roads, and rushing people, as they whirled towards modernisation. On Cuilcagh one could appreciate the mesmerising simplicity of the gurgling beginnings of rivers; experience the awesome loneliness present on the summit of this immense citadel that had been carved out by the Almighty's Hand, and realise there were other aspects of life far more important than rushing around the roads on a motorbike.

Other times I would go scorching around the Marlbank Road in the evening, on my way home, and I would become aware of the gradually accumulating, changing features of an area, the contours and landscape of which had already been indelibly and irremovably imprinted on my brain. Brilliant bright lights began to appear around Jim Dolan's house and about the farmyard, because he was the first person in the 'Mountain' to get a 'Startomatic' electric generator. This machine started up automatically at pre-determined times, and needed no other attention than to be supplied with sufficient oil and fuel. Other families like the Sheerin's, 'Terry's', Dolan's and Nolan's got 'Startomatic' engines as well and soon large areas of the 'Mountain' were awash with light and illumination. On calm, peaceful evenings, the distinct beat of the delayed thumping of the engines in the distance could be heard all over the 'Mountain'. The appearance of the 'Startomatic' in the 'Mountain' generated a momentum that prompted other things to happen. Jim Dolan had a huge steel contraption erected on the chimney of his house, with a brown cable leading from it to a black and white television set that sat in the corner of the sitting room. George Sheridan already had a television. Soon nearly every house in the 'Mountain' had both a 'Startomatic' and a TV set. In the stillness of the night time, symphonies of engines played their automatic compositions to all the living things that resided about the hills and valleys of the 'Mountain'.

From Easter 1963, a new face began to appear regularly about the 'Mountain'. Sixteen year old Nigel Haggan was a city boy from Malone Road in Belfast. He was being educated in Enniskillen at Portora Royal School, one of the top schools in Ireland or Britain, where such illustrious characters as Oscar Wilde and Samuel Beckett had been educated before him. Nigel visited the 'Mountain' and its caves and rivers a few times, and he liked the place so well that he adopted the area, especially 'Terry's' as his second home. Nigel now works with the Indians in British Columbia, in Canada, and when I asked him about his time in the 'Mountain' this is what he said:

****

Letter From Nigel Haggan

I was about sixteen when I first met the 'Terry's'. I was in Portora, and our chemistry teacher, Duncan Miller, I think his name was, took us caving. I loved it and pestered him to take me again. Around this time I got friendly with Bruce Rodgers; he was interested in caving, but rock climbing was his real game. To cut a long story short, we went camping in Monastyir Gorge one Easter. The first night was cold, but we woke up and loosened our joints a bit, and took a walk to get some drinking water.

Well, we walked past Carr's, and met Terry on the bridge. Some of us asked him where we could get drinking water. Terry said, 'The water in the river is the best we have; why don't you go down to the house and get a cup of tay?' So we went and knocked on the door. Mrs Terry looks us up and down, and said, 'What do yiz want?' I said, 'The man on the bridge said you'd make us a cup of tea.' Mrs Terry said, 'I'll make no tay for you'se bastards till you's sing us a song.' So we sang, 'The Jug of Punch' for the first of many times.

From that day I spent as much or more time in 'Terry's' than in Belfast. I learned a great deal that I would otherwise would have missed growing up on the Malone Road. Buying and selling cars, buildings - ask Mrs Terry or John T to tell you about the day Terry and I fell out when they were building the first hayshed. In the beginning I remember always grousing about having a flat battery - John T would use it on the TV. We had a string of old cars that JT (John Thomas) and I bought, some bad vehicles, tho' nothing to compare with Nulty (John James) for automotive disasters.

In the beginning Bruce and I camped in the 'Mountain' just below 'Terry's'. Then I was in Duffy's (Aghnahoo) for a while, and Tommy Gilmurray's place in Cohen. Mostly I stayed in 'Terry's'.

My first impression of the 'wilderness' (of the 'Mountain') was one of pure delight at escaping from incarceration in Portora to a place which was both beautiful and fascinating in the way rivers and streams disappeared and reappeared from the ground at a whim. My initial impression of the people was also very favourable for the reasons stated. This evolved into an abiding affection; I was a bit of a lonely cub, inclined to live in my head - create my own world as it were. Terry's, Nulty's, your house, all the others welcomed me into them. There was always something to talk about.

Mountain people are deep thinkers. There wasn't a lot of formal education in those days - no more is there today among many of the First Nation (ie British Columbian Indians) I work with today. But there are other educational traditions - other systems of knowledge. Above all, other values and ways of looking at the world. Terry, Uncle Tommy, all that generation were well worth talking to. Uncle Tommy always strikes me as an example of how little a man needs to be content with himself (if not always with everyone around him) a dog, a bicycle, a good radio to listen to the news and a suit of clothes for mass. Quite a bit different to the way most of us live now.

I'm inclined to believe that the mountain lifestyle lends itself to deep thinking and good talk. Unlike lowland farmers, mountain people, at least in those days, had time. There would be a bit of a flurry from time to time to make hay or gather sheep, but most of the year not much more to do than carry a load of hay to a handful of cattle. Long winter evenings to talk, wonder and speculate about the world.

Lots of fun too. Boxing the Tailor, I was good at that, except one night I couldn't get the last spud - Jimmy was lifting it every time I took a swipe. Wrestling the Connaughtman, pulling the stick, I remember one night there was a crowd of Yorkshire potholers I was knocking round with. We set to pulling, and to my enormous surprise, I was able to lift every one of them. Terry said 'You'll pull me now Nigel.' I thought it wouldn't be the thing to pull the man in his own house, so I decided to go easy. I needn't have worried, I think he could have lifted me with one hand.

My experience of living in the 'Mountain' - and, in particular, discovering the gap between the Protestant perception of Catholics as narrow and dominated by authority, and the reality that (even the very liberal) Protestant tradition that I grew up in, was far stricter. Not much chance of them setting off to a dance on a Sunday night! That perception that 'It ain't necessarily so' has coloured the rest of my life. The example that Terry set of honourable and fair dealing also reinforced my own upbringing. One thing I think I did learn from him was to have no time for pretence or bullshit, to put it North American terms. Example, Some lads beat up some of Terry's sons. Later, the father of the culprits tried to make up with Terry. Terry hit him 'Didn't have time for any of his 'oul sweetness,' he says.

I haven't written much if anything tho' I should. I remember sharing a pipe with James Nulty, your mother playing the violin, and Owen Nulty reciting 'The Ghost in Boho'. I have a knack for remembering things. I think I had it after the third or fourth time (The Ghost in Boho). Also the rhymes for the Mummers. I remember writing them down for Bruce's Mother, Mary Rogers for her book 'Prospect of Erne'.

From a letter written by Nigel Haggan

****

Dundrod

Jack Wallace had three sisters, two of whom, Edith and Irene lived in Belfast and were married to policemen. Whenever these two families had time off work they always came to Wallace's with their children, and we all looked forward to their coming. Edith was married to George McCauley, an elite police driver whose duties included driving VIPs like Lord Brookeborough around. When George was at Wallace's he immersed himself totally in farming, and him and I would have long discussions about many things. He used to explain some of the procedures used in high speed driving, and tricks to learn to eliminate accidents. He wasn't very impressed with me hurtling about on the motorbike and told me that if it came to a test between what he had learned through experience and my impetuosity, experience would succeed every time. He said that if I really wanted to see something that would open my eyes, I should go and see the motorcycle races at Dundrod circuit near Belfast.

Well I thought to myself. Right! And I made arrangements to go to Dundrod. I went with Richard Elliott, and Gordon Wallace and Dessie and Willie Reid came with us. Scores of other neighbours from around also went. We set off at 4am and arrived at a field at Dundrod long before dawn. We found a position where the car was facing about three-quarters of the circuit, and where we could easily reach the roadside once the races began. After many hours of waiting a murmur went through the crowd, and the microphones relayed to us that the first race was about to start. I wanted to give my total concentration to the races, so I picked a place away from the others, sticking my head out through the strands of wire with my face about a foot from the edge of the tarmac road. I could see more than a mile back towards the pits, and with rising excitement and a surge through the crowd, the call came. 'They're away.' I could hear the whine of finely tuned engines, then I could see a mass of differently coloured objects moving through the landscape away in the distance. In seconds they were upon us, inches from my nose. A buffeting rush of air, like an invisible boulder, tumbled past in their wake. An overpowering smell of high octane fumes permeated the air around us. They were travelling so fast I was unable to focus on them properly as they passed. The riders went around at least three times before I was actually able to see them from the blur of speed and wonderment. The greats of motorcycling were there. Jim Redman, Gary Hocking, a Robb man from Belfast, and one of my heroes, Mike Hailwood on his beloved MV Augusta. Right before my eyes Takahashi went into a terrifying skid, coming straight for where I sat. He recovered and carried on. My heart was nearly bursting with excitement. I have never forgotten that day at Dundrod, nor never will. One could just not comprehend that such anticipation and incredulous excitement could be created in oneself by seeing an event that one had no actual part in. The memory of a fallen motorcycle and rider in the middle of the road, with a following rider having no other place to go, taking off like an aeroplane over bike and rider. The incredible genius of Mark Hailwood, (who was tragically killed many years later as he drove with his children to a fish and chip shop) who could lower his motorcycle to such impossible angles when cornering that it often seemed as if he was lying on the road.

A rider was killed that day on a part of the circuit we could not see. Everyone was filled with a terrible sense of loss. I returned from the race chastened. I realised that I was a complete novice and really knew nothing about riding a motorcycle. If people with such skill could be killed during a race on a closed circuit, what chance had I on the public road, where there were no rules?

Millions of people all over the world still remember clearly where they were, or what they were doing, when they heard the news that President J F Kennedy was assassinated on 22 November 1963 in Dallas, Texas. Just five months earlier, on 26 June, President Kennedy had spent three days in Ireland, visiting his relations in Wexford, meeting huge crowds in the major cities and ensuring that the whole country fell in love with him. Now, on a dark November evening, as I was going to the 'Black' I met Petie coming on the bicycle to tell me that Kennedy had been shot dead. I went home to tell the news. They were all shocked, and Mammy went into mourning in disbelief.

The whole country was devastated over Kennedy's death, but it's strange in hindsight how it appears that when one great person is taken away, another similarly great one surfaces. In May and June 1963 farcical stories began to be produced in the media about Cassius Clay the American boxer who was to fight Henry Cooper of London on 18 June. No effort seemed to be spared to mock Clay, and his laughable claims as to what he would do to 'Our 'Enery' were paraded out with derision. Everyone about the area, including Jack Wallace thought he was a complete sham, a will-o-the-wisp maybe, but a sham nevertheless, and Cooper would soon stop him. All the locals became boxing experts. I would listen to Jack and George McCauley as they laid out the path that Cooper would pave for Clay's destruction.

Secretly, I never believed what was said about Clay. A picture appeared in the paper of Clay wearing a hooded cloak, and armed with a builder's pick, digging in London's Hyde Park. More ammunition for the sceptics; 'He's nothing more than a glorified labourer.' But I could see that it took a wonderful courage for him to leave himself open to criticism, and only a total belief in his ability would allow him to make what where thought to be outrageous predictions about the outcome of a fight. So even before he became the greatest boxer the world has ever seen, Cassius Clay, or Mohammed Ali was and remains one of my greatest heroes.

Petie Migrates

Petie bought a grey-green mini-van, but then decided to go to England in spring 1964, leaving me the mini-van. For me, Petie going away to England was an awful wrench. After all, we had spent more than twenty years more or less together, and as we were the two oldest boys we were especially close and depended a lot on each other. Mammy was heartbroken and begged him to stay. His little case was packed and Jack Wallace and I took him and the case to Enniskillen. He got the bus from there to Dublin, then the train to the boat at Dun Laoghaire. Michael McLoughlin met him at Euston Station in London. Petie left me his mini-van, but I didn't bother with it and parked it in one of Wallace's silage pits.

More people from the 'Mountain' began to go off to England and other places. John James McNulty went over when Petie got him a job in a paint factory. John James Sheerin went to work on the buses in Willesden. Jamsie and Hughie Maguire, and Tommy and Anna Sheerin went to England. May Sheerin went away to Belfast. Jimmy McGovern (Terry) went to England. His brother Noel went to the US. Mrs Hugh Maguire and her son Paddy went away to the lowlands. Julia McManus got married and went away.

With people moving away from the land and rural districts, to more urbanised areas, towns like Enniskillen began to expand rapidly, and these growing populations meant an ever increasing need for services like electricity, water, sewerage and other utilities. So, the Marble Arch Water Scheme came into being. The roads between Enniskillen and the Marble Arches were all dug up, and large steel water pipes laid in trenches. Tracey Brothers done the section from Brockagh Bridge to Killesher Graveyard. They used a 19 RB (Rustun Bucyrus) to dig the trench through the road. A major operation was carried out in the Marble Arch Glen and near Killesher Graveyard, to get water into these pipes. J J Scallon built a gravity fed reservoir beside Killesher Graveyard. A pumping station and a dwelling house for the water supervisor was also built there. Large pipes were laid from the reservoir, across to the Marble Arch River, and then all the way up through the river bed to within a few feet of the Marble Arches itself, where a large concrete water container was built to feed the pipes to the reservoir.

For a year or more, massive dumpers travelled non-stop between the work in the Marble Arch Glen and the reservoir in Killesher. When the work was done, the area looked completely desecrated. The whole beauty, atmosphere, and tranquillity of the peaceful glen was wiped out. The disgraceful destruction and wilful ravishing, of an ancient and irreplaceable domain. The bluebells that used to weave, and radiate serenity, obliterated, never to grow again. A swathe of an access route, tore through the trees. Branches were left hanging off the trees, like the broken arms of mutilated warriors. Huge boulders were indiscriminately dumped into the river, to lie beside original boulders like obscene aliens. And the most majestic part of the glen, the Marble Arch, where people come from all over the world to see and hear the wonders of an awesome natural construction, dotted and destroyed with man-made concrete aberrations.

One Sunday I was in Granny's, and Uncle Paddy asked me to go to Curran's shop at Killinagh Chapel to get fags for him. Usually I was very happy to go for messages, but this day for some reason I refused and went off in a huff. I wasn't going anywhere in particular, it was enough to be just moving, and I found myself travelling towards Blacklion intending to go on to Belcoo. There was no 30 mph speed limit then, and as I approached Blacklion I was fairly shifting. Before I got to Blacklion it began to barely rain, making the smooth road surface like a skating rink. To get through Blacklion in the direction I was travelling, you had to prepare the approach from the end of the 'Marian Crescent' cottages. From the 'Marian Crescent' there was a dip at the bottom of the hill at Flynn's, where the bike was aimed for the centre of the road in order to have place to counteract whatever forces might be applied by travelling through the dip. Where the 30mph sign is now I had to be as tight as possible to the left until a critical instant when I could see enough of the right-hand corner to get around it, while at the same time allowing only the minimum amount of space to the possibility of a vehicle coming towards me. These two criterions had to be accomplished in conjunction with the fearful speed I would be travelling at. After leaving that corner I would shave the end of Armstrong's shed, shoot from there to Hawkins's Chemist shop, where I would be completely in the right in order to get around the 'Diamond' and travel towards Belcoo.

I got a slight skid at Armstrong's shed and then just as I braked at Hawkins's shop the bike went into a terrifying skid. This was my third time to come off at the 'Diamond'. A car drove into me the first time, and a Gardai stepped out in front of me the second time. As the bike slithered along the road I had automatically managed to get most of myself on top of the sliding machine, and as we went along various aspects of life in Blacklion began to reveal themselves, as if in freeze- frame. A large dog, like a greyhound, was walking across the road. As the bike and I slithered towards him, he politely waited until we had passed and then continued his journey. Peter Fitzpatrick, who had played football with my father in the great Blacklion team of the 1930s-40s, was standing with another man at Phillip Dolan's petrol pump. I noticed how their flat caps moved in perfect unison, as they monitored the progress of my perilous procession. Johnny Green, the butcher, resting himself on the window sill of his house after a very good Sunday dinner, left his position quickly and began to run like hell down the street, as I came straight for the window where he sat. The bike slammed into the wall. Mrs Farrely, the woman who had given me the lovely dinner on the fair day many years earlier, was walking across to her house with two buckets of water; Ownie Rooney was standing in his doorway; Mrs Farrely shouted to Ownie, 'Jasus but that's the charity! not half enough for the bloody bastard.' The bike rebounded off Green's wall; I was flung around the curved wall between the wall and a telephone pole; the bike was spinning on the road, and the wheel gripped the road and flung the bike between the pole and the wall, on top of me. Amazingly I was uninjured, sore certainly but

OK. There was an interval of silence, doors silently closed; Then people began to come out of houses, and began to help me get up, and to access the damage to the bike. The bike was in a sorry state, with all the gear levers and pedals broken off. When I faced the wheels out towards Florencecourt, the handlebars looked as if they wanted to go to Belcoo. One side of the handlebars was bent towards the road. I began to push it towards Wallace's, but it was all jammed up. I left it at a house and later had it taken to Enniskillen to be repaired.

CHAPTER 9

DIGGER DRIVER

Loss of the motorbike was a severe blow, and I was more or less forced to use the mini-van if I wanted to get about. With Petie gone, and my friends from the 'Mountain' disappearing in all directions, I too decided to take stock of my position. I was getting £6 a week from Jack and there seemed to be little chance of any radical rise in wages in the near future. As well as that I was getting fed-up with farming. I wanted to drive a digger, and began to scour the pages of the Irish *Farmers Weekly* for a suitable job. Eventually, I saw an advertisement, 'Digger driver wanted. Contact N Halpin. Fore. Phone no' . . . When I eventually found Fore on the map, I travelled to Westmeath in the little van and spent all day trying to find the place. I got the job, starting a week later when I had worked out my notice with Jack.

Leaving my family and friends was heartbreaking, but on a Sunday afternoon, I set off for Fore, St Fechin, and 'the Seven Wonders' wondering what I had let myself in for. My new boss was supposed to have lodgings ready for me, but when I got to the pub he owned in Fore, his wife said he was away working. I found him outside of Castlepollard at about 10pm, driving a combine harvester in the middle of an otherwise dark field. I stayed with him and the other men until he finished, an hour later, and then he brought me to my lodgings nearby, where Mrs Maguire, who was to look after me like a mother for the next few yeas lived.

Next morning, my new boss, Nicholas Halpin, who was at least as wild as the Elliott's, took me to Major Thompson's farm at Athboy, County Meath, where I was to use the digger to make drains and install pipes in an 1800 acre swamp all on my own. Sometimes the boss would want me to go ploughing with his Fordson Major tractor, in fields so large they would dwarf Jack Wallace's complete farm.

I soon made friends of course, but I missed home, and the 'Mountain' terribly. I came home as often as I could, but it wasn't the same now. Bridie was away working, Frank had went to England and disappeared without trace, and Farrell was nearly always away. Now there was only Pat, Marian and Kevin left with my parents. Gerry Maguire was gone to the US and Pat and Hughie Maguire and Jerry Sheerin, Maureen and Kay Dolan had gone to England, Michael Dolan was also gone away. Of my school friends, there was now only Phillip and John Thomas McGovern left in the 'Mountain' and every time I came home they were preened and polished like princely Casanovas, and drove about sedately in their sleek sedans, while I nearly always resembled a rag-and-bone man, both in my personal appearance and in my vehicular transportation.

Of course Packie and Aggie Dolan had Martin, Rose and Carmel at home, and Jim and Tessie Dolan's family were all at home. Phillip and Mary Nolan also had a growing family, while Sheila and Phil Maguire's cubs, who were all under ten, never ceased to amuse me as they drove about on their father's tractor, smoking crooked pipes and explaining the merits of farming with a worldly wisdom. But some kind of an invisible vacuum seemed to steadily reveal itself, a definite space between our generation and this new generation of young people now growing up in the 'Mountain'.

For a few years my close association with home, and the people of the 'Mountain' was severely curtailed, because of a traumatic working and economic situation, where I often didn't have the money or the transport to make a trip home. I left Nicholas Halpin, and the 'wonders of Fore' and went to work for a man in Castlepollard who owned two John Deere diggers. But he was a drinker and a gambler and it wasn't long until both him and I ended up penniless. I decided to move on.

I saw a job in the paper, phoned and arranged to meet my prospective employer at the Gresham Hotel, O'Connell Street, Dublin. I got the Thames van that Patrick Corrigan had given me, and set off for Dublin. As I was passing the Gresham Hotel, a tall, whitehaired, distinguished looking man jumped into the passenger seat beside me. It was my new employer. He gave me directions to head north, and when there was no instructions to stop after about thirty miles, I demanded to know what was going on. He told me the digger had come from England, and had been delivered to the docks at Greenore. I didn't know where Greenore was, but we travelled on through Drogheda, and then through Dundalk until we came to Greenore on the Carlingford Lough, and just across the lough from Greencastle in County Down.

At Greenore we got through the paperwork, and found the machine. I was already used to all makes and types of tractors, but this machine was massive, and there was a crowd of dock workers waiting for me to drive it away like an experienced expert. Luckily, the dock area was large and empty, and I was able to get my bearings, but I was all but overwhelmed by the size of this monster of a machine. The machine was a JCB 4c, the only one I have ever seen. When its retractable outriggers were extended it was about twenty feet wide. It bore no comparison to the nifty, easily manoeuvrable machines so often seen on the road or building sites today.

My enigmatic-looking whitehaired employer ordered me to head for Dundalk with all speed, and that he would catch me up in my van. Off I set, with a growing feeling of excitement and exhilaration as my confidence of handling the machine grew. Very soon it started to rain, not enough to wash the road, but certainly enough to make it slippery. The bulk of the machine was taking up three-quarters of the road, and as I came around this right-hand bend a car came towards me travelling much too fast, and it skidded. The front bucket of the digger hit the drivers door at the hinge just ahead of the driver, taking the door with it, carried on taking the rear door post and door, emerging from the rear of the car nicely cutting the booth clean in half, the whole lot resting in the front bucket. As I am coming behind this destruction being wrought by the front bucket. I see two middle aged men sitting there helpless, the side of their lovely car cut clean off. The Gardai were called. Meanwhile my new 'boss' turned up and accused the two harmless men of being drunk. The outcome was that the Gardai told the car driver that if he didn't admit it was his fault he would be prosecuted for drunken and dangerous driving. He therefore admitted he was to blame and that was the end of it.

As so often happens, this accident was a godsend to my new employer in that the shock it had given me meant that the new 'shock' he now had in store for me was almost of no consequence. In fact he delivered the information to me in no different a way than if he was telling me to open a gate at the side of the road. 'Take the machine to Gort, in Galway, and meet me at Geoghan's Public House in the Main Street.' Well after causing such damage I could hardly refuse, so I cleared out the front bucket of doors, lamps and glass and proceeded on my way once more.

As I reached Dundalk, it was getting dark, and once I left the town it became pitch dark. I proceeded satisfactorily, without any drama and reached Ardee about 10.30pm. There were lots of people about, bound for dancehalls, leaving cinemas, and the street corners were well attended without anyone having the slightest interest in my progress. Leaving Ardee behind I carried on into the pitch darkness again, except for the lights of my machine. It almost seemed as if I was in a world of my own, the cavernous interior of the digger, insulated from all outside, powerful, dependable, the great noise of the engine carrying this world along; but you don't really hear this noise inside the cab of a digger, and are aware of the tiniest sound.

In this remote area I suddenly saw a girl thumbing a lift, and from my experience any sort of a lift was better than none at all, so I stopped. Without any hesitation the lady joined me in the cab, and we resumed our journey through the night. We were trundling amiably towards Kells, when, *Bang!* For a split second I didn't know what had happened, then I saw the railway bridge above me, and another smashing bang. What had happened was that we had met a low bridge concealed in the dark, and the high boom on the back of the digger collided with it. This in turn lifted up the front shovel of the machine which then smashed up into the bridge, leaving the front and back of the machine jammed up into the bridge. The girl was a bit shocked, but otherwise alright, as for myself I could well have done without this incident.

To release the machine was just a simple matter of lowering the hydraulics, and we were on our way once again. The occurrence put a damper on the rapport between us however, and soon after the girl disembarked at a house and I was alone in my own mechanical world once more. Because I didn't know the roads, it seemed to be instinct that brought me along the road through Kells and then on to Oldcastle, heading for Castlepollard where Mrs Maguire lived. As I went through the towns and villages the noise of the machine reverberated off the high walls of banks and churches, as slowly Mrs Maguire's got closer.

As dawn was breaking I parked the machine on the grass verge outside Mrs Maguire's house, and then rapped on the door. Soon she opened the door and welcomed me in, all concerned because of my haggard looking appearance. I was her only lodger and so had free reign of the house. It was like an Aladdin's cave of discovery, with carbide lamps, horse harness, and most precious of all, a gramophone with records. There were records by John McCormick, Percy French and the most unbelievably beautiful recording of 'The Rose of Tralee' by the boxer, Jack Doyle. There were also other wonderful recordings of 'The Holy City' 'The Prisoner's Song' and others by singers whose names I can't recall. Mrs Maguire was a widow woman, very religious, her benign appearance resembling Mother Theresa. I was rather taken aback when I first met her, because she had a hoarse, gravely voice that took a bit of getting used to. The folded tablecloth was put on the dining table to protect it from the ravages that she knew I would wreak upon it, and soon she placed a wonderful feed in front of me.

All sleepiness left me, and although Mrs Maguire could give me no information on how to get to Galway, I resumed my journey. Down through Castlepollard, and past Kennedy's Public House, where the Firehouse Five showband used to practise. I was becoming worried about getting diesel soon, but it was a lovely day as I passed by Lake Derravaragh and the trees of the Crooked Wood. The day wore slowly on. I went through Mullingar, all the time on the look out for a likely place to get diesel, and eventually I reached Clara in County Offaly, where I bought seventy gallons from a farmer for £2. The lush green fields of Westmeath deteriorated into marshy bogland, and the good day of earlier disintegrated into a fierce storm, with waves of rain rushing across the bare and barren bog. I became completely lost, and in the process of leaving the machine and asking for directions, I got soaking wet, the steam from this in turn covering up the windows of the machine. I became completely disorientated as to my bearings, not knowing which was North or South. Unless I went back the way I came, the directions I got could not possibly have pointed me in a worse direction.

It became pitch dark once more, with torrential rain carried along by gale force winds. Still I motored on until I found myself in the dim lit village of Shannonbridge. A tremendously steep hill led up on to the bridge, but when I dismounted to examine it, I found that this was no ordinary bridge. This bridge over the Shannon was constructed of two concrete approaches leaning out over the river, but not meeting. High above the river, the approaches were linked by wooden planking. Where the planking was installed, the roadway was dramatically narrower than the rest of the road, and not wide enough to take my machine. The noise of the raging river below was drowned out by the howling wind that was shaking the planking of the bridge about. As I stood there shivering with both cold and fear, the hair on the back of my neck froze as a result of the decision I had to make.

Even though the machine would not drive across if I lifted the front shovel about four feet I could drive the front wheels between the railings and proceed forward until the rear of the machine cane in contact with the railings. I done this; then I rested the back boom with its bucket on the concrete approach, and raised the back of the digger four feet in the air in order to clear the rails. This meant tremendous pressure on the planking where the front wheels rested. My position resembled that of an ice-skater. If a plank cracked, a sudden gust of wind came, a hydraulic pipe burst, or I lost concentration, it would be goodnight. The machine moved almost halfway across, and then I had to lower the machine on to the rails, hoping they'd hold until I got a new position for the bucket to push me on. Miraculously the rails held as bit by bit I inched my way over the bridge, and then continued my journey.

I got to Ballinasloe, and then the good road was signposted to Galway. It was already more than 36 hours since I had started from Mrs Maguire's house with the Thames van. The Guards stopped me in Loughrea and were amazed at my journey, they directed me to Gort, which was now only fifteen miles farther on. It was noticeable from the lights of the digger that this was a land of many stone walls. I negotiated my way around the 'Seven Eye Bridge' then through Peterswell. I passed a sign for 'Thoor Ballylee' Yeats's home and half an hour later I entered Gort. It was after 4am and the Guards pointed out the only lodgings that might keep me. I knocked on the door of the house, and sure enough the landlady let me in, landing me into a bed beside another lodger. It wasn't a time for fussiness, so I said my prayers and went to sleep. Next day my employer materialised, minus my van, which I never saw again. Needless to say, our partnership didn't last long.

Crane Driver

While I was working for this whitehaired man from Gort, I was getting good wages, £35 per week, and I was able to buy a comfortable car, and as soon as I could, I left him and his job and headed back home to apply for a job I had seen in the paper. This job was for driving heavy earthmoving equipment, and was with J J Scallon, Irvinestown. When I arrived at Scallon's yard in Irvinetown to enquire about the job, the workers were arranged around the yard having their lunch. I asked them to direct me to the Plant Manager's office. Complete silence. I thought they mightn't have heard me right and repeated my request. By this time the message was getting through to me. I returned their stares of animosity with a cheeky, humorous nonchalance, but never before or since have I seen such a fearful manifestation of collective hostility, aimed at God knows what. There is no doubt that at that time a lot of people in the Six Counties grew up with a superiority complex in relation to Southern Ireland, and so these workers may have become self-conscious when I, now with an obvious Southern accent, found them dining in what they may have suddenly perceived to be crude conditions. Or, their anger may have been directed at the fact that I arrived in a southern registered car to take one of their jobs. Whatever was bothering them, I left them to it. Despite foraging among the offices however I failed to find the plant manager, and on my way home I called into

Tracey Brothers in Enniskillen and got a job driving a JCB and a tower crane.

I was at home again and suddenly the 'Mountain' seemed to be a place without people. An evacuation took place every evening, and the young people went off to the pubs, dancing or to meet their friends in the lowlands. It became depressing visiting houses because there would be no people there. Our Pat was away at the time, working for people here and there, and staying in their houses. Marian was going to school in Kiltyclogher, and used to stay in Granny's. Now there was only Kevin at home, and he too would probably be soon gone. The mothers of the 'Mountain' and sometimes the fathers too, began to be manacled to a mighty depression. My mother took it worse than most, and increasingly she began to give the impression that she wanted to give up. She adored Kevin however, and despite illnesses and trouble with her teeth, she tried her best to be always there for him. To take their minds off their increasing isolation, many of the mothers of the 'Mountain' began to club together and go off to the Bingo that was played in the bright lights of faraway places. Meanwhile, a new generation was swiftly growing up in the 'Mountain'.

Electricity came to the 'Mountain' in 1968, poles dotting the landscape like the 'matchstick men' from one of Ls Lowry's paintings. No matter how much we encouraged my father however, he refused to make any concessions whatsoever to modernisation, and our conditions of existence at home remained the same in 1969 as they were in 1946, except that we had a road to the house. Another sign of the changing times, and a severe blow to the continuity of the 'Mountain' was that Marble Arches School closed forever at the summer holidays 1969 after serving the people of the 'Mountain' for 86 years. By this time my father had realised that none of his children had acquired any overwhelming interest in farming, and he more or less stopped going to Jimmity's himself, and got people from Collegrain to help Tommy McManus look after the sheep.

Romance

Tracey's worked five and a half days per week, and one Sunday when I was off, I decided to go to Bundoran. There, on a wet, stormy day, I saw the girl of my dreams in the distance, attending to a large mass of patrons in a busy, but appealingly low lit cafe. When our eyes met, a storm of shattering atoms exploded in my brain, stamping as on stone, a moment never to be forgotten. We did not make contact however, and the dreary bus soon came to drag me back to reality.

When the job with Tracey Brothers was complete, I was made redundant. I went to Dublin and got a job there. Then I was moved to Waterford, and then from Waterford to Sligo. One day while I was working in Sligo, I had to go on business to a house. I knocked on the door and who answered but the lady I was smitten with in Burdoran a year earlier. The girl was working there, and she only appeared fleetingly until the man who owned the house came out. After three more similarly fateful meetings, we eventually made contact and began to go out together, to be an item.

I was moved from Sligo back to Waterford. I left that job and started with Gerry Nash in Limerick, driving a mobile crane all over Ireland. Later on I left crane driving and got my own JCB. I began working in Peterswell, County Galway, carrying out drainage schemes for farmers under grants from the Department of Agriculture. I was only doing this work for about two months when the longest bank strike in the history of Ireland began. This meant that farmers weren't getting money, and in turn they couldn't give me any money. After struggling in Galway for a year with the digger, I eventually returned home with it, in a state of both physical and economic exhaustion.

I got lots of work around Marlbank and the surrounding areas, and there was never any trouble about paying. It was wonderful to be back home, and Marian was finished school, and now at home, and when I would be near hand, Kevin and her would come out and help me and often bring me my dinner. Frank however was still missing, and Mammy and the rest of us were becoming increasingly worried about him. The younger generation of the

'Mountain' were already testing their wings, visiting the houses around about, enlightening us about the latest fashion, or what was happening in the pop world. Kevin was learning to play the guitar. Many of those who had gone to England had now returned. John James McNulty, Hughie 'Connor', Tommy Sheerin had all returned. Jerry 'Connor' had come back from America, and Petie had returned, bought a farm at Roo, Blacklion, got married and built a house. Once again we practised for Tug O War and played football at 'Terry's'. These activities were now attended by hordes of people from the lowlands, and once again 'Terry's' became the focal point and meeting place for a multiplicity of people, looking for companionship, challenges and inspiration.

I was kept busy and worked for nearly every family in the 'Mountain'. I dug a long trench for Francie 'Connor' through the limestone rocks, to bring a water supply to the house. Then there was a land drainage grant job for Phil Maguire, open drains for Jim Dolan, and John Nolan, and then I made a road through the rocks of Legnabrocky for Harry Sheridan. But despite all this work there was a continual struggle to keep the machine going, because it was just worn out. Often, when I would be working in the wilderness of Crossmurrin, or up in Legnabrocky, and near no house, Mrs Terry would send a message for me to 'come on in for a drop of tay'. She'd say to the messenger, 'Tell him a drop of tay wouldn't kill the oul bastard,' joking, and when I was more or less on my last legs, as far a being able to carry on with the digger was concerned, these mugs of 'tay' and the meals that invariably came with them, were more important to me than the finest meals I have taken anywhere since. The important thing about the people of the 'Mountain' was that they knew how to share things, and just like the 'Terry's' they would share the last bite they had in the house with you.

Modernisation

The generosity and homeliness of the 'Mountain' people however did not hide the fact that the creation of modern concrete and iron monolith's was signalling the impending doom of traditional ways of life in the 'Mountain'. The people of the 'Mountain' discovered that they were unable to find the manpower to set arable subsistence crops like potatoes, turnips and cabbage any more, and suddenly, fields where there had always been tillage done, were now returned to grassland. Even Sheerins 'cabbage garden' which was so well known it became a landmark along the Marlbank Road, was now made redundant and could not furnish as much as a spring onion or a stick of rhubarb. People stopped making their own butter, baking bread, knitting and sewing. It became an increasing rarity for people to make their children's clothes, to make their own clothes, or to employ a tailor, even if they could find one, to make their suits. Francie and Hugh Melanophy threw away their 'last', because no one any longer wanted shoes made, and they didn't want them repaired because when these new 'technically advanced' 'machine-made' 'super vulcanised soles', shoes showed signs of wear, they were simply discarded for another new pair. People stopped keeping and killing their own pigs, which put an end to home-cured bacon, and the custom of passing around presents of giblets to your friends and neighbours. And the women of the 'Mountain' aquesised to the relentless march of modernism by foregoing the custom of having their babies at home, helped by a midwife, to having them in the impersonal, detached, ordered confines of a clinically clean county hospital.

So it was, that everything began to come from the shop; even if you had cows with milk, you daren't drink it for fear of contracting some disease. It had to be pasteurised and pulverised and come boxed from the shop. Consumerism had taken over, and maybe when all is said and done, it was a good thing. John James McNulty tells the story of how he came back from England for the first time at Christmas 1965. Him and his brother Tom decided to go to a dance at Glenfarne, at 'The Ballroom of Romance'. They got ready for the dance, washing and shaving in the basin, in water heated by the kettle. When they were ready, they had to put on wellingtons to walk a mile through the muck to get to the road, where Tom had a van, then they would change, leaving their wellingtons under a bush until they returned. On the way home from the dance it began to snow fiercely; the van began to slither about, and would go no farther than Sally's Wood, on the Wheathill Road, about three miles from home.

Tom and John James left the van and began to walk through the snow in their low shoes, with the blizzard blinding them. When they got to where they left their wellingtons, they had to rummage about in the snow and darkness to find them. The act of getting their soaking feet into the freezing wellingtons caused them huge discomfort, and John James thought of London, with its level, brightly lit footpaths. Bathrooms in every house, with hot and cold water, and he thought to himself momentarily 'for fuck sake . . . what the hell am I doing here?'

The rest of the people who went away from the 'Mountain' and then returned, were filled with similar feelings, and set about changing things to make life easier for themselves and their descendants than it had been for their parents and earlier ancestors. Great conurbation's of concrete and steel buildings began to rise around farmhouses, some to house cattle and sheep during the winter, with others nearby holding their feed, ensuring that farmers no longer needed to traipse through the land foddering cattle and sheep. Strong, reinforced concrete roads were constructed to even the most inaccessible areas, so that farmers could drive to every part of their land.

By 1971, nearly every farmer in the 'Mountain' except us, had a tractor, and the main work during the year was fattening livestock, looking after young lambs, winning the turf, making hay and silage, and reclaiming the land.

The scenery and sense of wilderness found in the 'Mountain' began to exert an ever increasing attraction for visitors and tourists, and at the weekends, especially Sunday's many cars would drive along the Marlbank Road, their occupants inspired and exhilarated by the magnitude and tranquillity of the 'Mountain'. They would stop their cars at beauty spots along the way, like at the top of the Marlbank Braes, to be captivated and enraptured by one of the most beautiful panoramic views in Ireland. There was also a constant stream of potholers who began to inhabit and explore the maze of caves that lie around the Marble Arches, Gortmaconnell, and Screg na Connell. As well as that, there were fishermen seeking to catch the silver trout that populated the mountain rivers, and there were other hardy folk who craved to climb to the top of Cuilcagh.

But even though these 'visitors' were enjoying many aspects of life in the 'Mountain' they were a separate and detached entity, and except for the potholers, never integrated or socialised with the local people, and passed through the life and culture of the 'Mountain' more or less like shadows. The potholers were somewhat different. They were mostly students from colleges and universities, and not yet financially independent, and many of them would stay in houses in the 'Mountain', especially 'Terry's'. When they came up out of the caves, they would often socialise with the local people, going to 'ceili' in their houses, and taking part in whatever was going on. They would also go to the pubs in Blacklion in great numbers, where them and the local people would get 'steamed up' together, and all would have a great time and enjoy each other's company.

Tug O War

We once more began to practice Tug O War with a resolute determination. The team then was John Thomas, Phillip, and Paschal McGovern, (Terry), Patrick, Tom and James Corrigan, from Wheathill, Peter and Tony Fitzpatrick, Willie and Dessie Reid, and myself. Our coach was still Tommy Gilmurray, and Terry McGovern helped with advice. On the 15 August 1971 we took part in our first Tug O War competition at Belcoo Sports. We got through all the preliminary heats to the final with Dromahaire, who beat us. Losing in the final made us far more determined to win something, and we began to practice and practice unceasingly.

As the digger got harder and harder, and more expensive to keep going, I began to realise that only drastic action, and wonderful luck, would save me from complete financial ruin. I decided to contact the regional development officers in Enniskillen, in the hope that they could offer me some help and encouragement to ease me out of my predicament. I had to fill in forms detailing all the work I had already carried out, accompanied by the appropriate drawings, and then I had to wait to hear the outcome from the development officers.

While this was going on, my girlfriend wanted to go to London for a holiday. I neither wanted to go, nor could I afford to go, but she had made up her mind she just had to go, and so I thought, after being told so many times what a great place it was, why not; let's see it. During a fortnight in London, which proved to be the most traumatic of my whole life, I was forced to change from being a happy go lucky, considerate human being, to a cynical selfish, uncaring sceptic. On the second week my girlfriend and I had a blazing row, and I returned home on my own. While I was in London, I tried a few places for jobs, and they said they'd write to me when they had work.

When I returned home to the 'Mountain' I carried on working with the digger as before, but I knew it was the end. If I ever was to recover again, I would have to go to England and find work. After working around home for two more weeks, I was shocked to come home one evening and find there was a letter from one of the firms I had contacted in England, offering me a job with the qualified command, 'please report to this office immediately.' Well of course I had to finish the work I was doing, which took two more days, and then I was ready. On the last day I finished what I was doing for Jim Dolan, down in Blunnick, and then I began the journey back to the 'Mountain' in the machine.

It was a lovely, sunny, September evening, and the clean, cleared fields showed that the farmers had gathered in all their hay and silage for the winter feeding. As I came through the cutting in Nulty's Hill, Cuilcagh slowly revealed itself, seated there in all its majesty, like an ancient god waiting inscrutably for a demanded sacrifice, the placid contours and landscape of Glenawley lying reverently and expectantly at its feet. As I travelled along, the retreating sun slowly sank into the west, and plumes of blue smoke started to rise from the chimneys of the 'Mountain' as people put on their fires to combat the chill of the coming evening.

When I came over the hill at where Kerr's house used to be, I saw the hills at 'Terry's' were covered with sheep, and when I came to the dipping tank, my father, Terry, and other men were busy dipping the sheep that were held in the pens. I passed them by, and then I parked up the machine on the very spot where Daddy had been cross-examined by the detectives all those years ago. I said goodbye to my machine, because a digger is one mechanical instrument that one becomes as attached to and dependant on, as if it was another human being. Then I made my way down to 'Terry's' house to get my car and headed off home.

When I arrived home, I got a tremendous shock, because there was a very important letter for me. This letter was from the regional development officers, and what it contained amazed me. It said that in accordance with the amount of work I had already done, and provided I employed two men, they would provide me with the finance to acquire two new JCBs and enter into an arrangement to help me pay off the balance on them. This was fabulous news, far better than I expected. However, I had got myself into a frame of mind for going to England, and even though I discussed my predicament with Mammy and other people who were visiting, I decided to carry on as intended, and head for London. I got myself ready and packed a flittered case. Daddy had still not returned, and I said goodbye to Marian, Kevin and Mammy, and left for Granny's at 9pm. I just couldn't face leaving the 'Mountain' in the clear light of day, when the humbling magnitude and awesome grandeur of the beloved valley would be tearing at my heartstrings, when I didn't know if I'd ever return; so I thought it was better to stay at Granny's for the night. Stealthily and steadily I stole away, like a thief in the night, not having the courage to say adieu either to the 'Mountain' or its people.

Next morning, I parked up my beloved Jaguar, and then set off from Granny's, taking the route that Francie and I had walked so many times, until I got to the shop at Frazer's of Gortahill. I boarded the bus for Enniskillen. As I went along in the bus, the lovely lakes and mountains began to reveal themselves, and I wondered whether Mammy, Marian and Kevin were up yet; or whether Daddy had came home. I knew that Patrick Corrigan would be driving the milk lorry around the 'Mountain' about now, collecting the milk from the few farmers that were sending milk any more. I suddenly gulped when I thought of our Tug O War team, and wished I could have said a last goodbye to them. The all-encompassing influence of the undeveloped scenery began to fade away gradually as the town of

Enniskillen came into view, and once I boarded the Belfast bus my demeanour resembled that of a statue as I steadfastly pointed my head in the direction of our travel.

CHAPTER 10

MIGRATION

And so I arrived in London. I didn't know anyone or have any friends there. I got a room in Ladbroke Grove, and then I reported for work. I worked in St Anne's Road in Tottenham for one day, and then the firm went bankrupt. I started with a firm in Croydon and the same thing happened. Gradually I sorted myself out, but by the time Christmas 1971 came, I couldn't bear London any longer and went home for Christmas. The Christmas break was all too short, and I had to return to England once more. My sister Bridie also left Ireland for Birmingham.

I became slowly immersed and integrated into the life of England, and the longing and homesickness I felt for my friends and family, and the green fields of Ireland gradually abated. Every time I went home I would be amazed at how friendly, warm and open-hearted the people were, in contrast to the ever present tensions and pressure of a massive urban city, and the worried looking faces of the people of London.

In 1972, as Christmas was getting near, I didn't intend to go to Ireland because I had just bought a great big Mark 10 Jaguar and couldn't afford to go. But as Christmas was getting closer and closer, I started getting more frantic, and when Christmas Eve came, I just headed towards Swansea and boarded the boat to Cork, not caring whether I ran out of money or not. I had to get home. I arrived home just as Mammy was about to put out the Christmas dinner, and I had a wonderful Christmas. Daddy would always cut down an ash tree whenever I was expected home, and this Christmas it was great to be home again, relaxing in our own company, in front of a great roaring fire. My father had also got new boots, the first ones I ever saw him with, which seemed to be a sign that he intended to take life easier. I would go around the 'Mountain' visiting 'Terry's', Melanophy's, 'Connor's', Nulty's, Sheerin's, Dolan's, Nolan's and seeing all my friends in the 'Mountain', but the short break would fly by, and reluctantly I would return to London.

Eventually, as the years passed, Farrell, Marian and then Kevin joined me in London. This led to my mother becoming utterly depressed, because all her children had now gone and left her, and because Daddy was away so much she was almost on her own. Mrs McNulty too ended up alone in Gortmaconnell, because her husband James died in 1965, and then Tom and John James got married and went off to live in their own homes. But Mrs McNulty was a far stronger and more stoic character than Mammy, and as well as that she did see John James daily. But that was the almost inevitable tragedy of life in the 'Mountain' then, that parents would spend a large part of their life bringing up their family in a beautiful, remote and peaceful community, but many of them would be likely to end their days alone.

After all the years of waiting, the training finally paid off, and the Marlbank Tug O War team won an Irish championship. I was proud of them, but unfortunately I wasn't there to see them do it. Afterwards, they all celebrated the event with a tremendous party in Blacklion. In 1972 Francie Melanophy died, Hugh died in 1973, and Alice died in 1976. James Nolan, Con Boylan, Hughie Curran, Mrs Hugh Maguire, and some of the Pat McManus's died. In 1973 our beloved teacher Mrs Christina Gilmurray died. After a few years in England, when I would be at home in the summer, I would go up on the Big Hill and I wouldn't see a human being moving anywhere about the 'Mountain'. The only sign of life would be cars; blue ones, green ones, every colour, moving like coloured caterpillars out on the Marlbank Road, which was now covered with a lovely smooth tarmac surface.

Fermanagh County Council decided that the Marble Arch caves could be utilised as a useful commercial and social enterprise, and began to develop the cave system. With the least possible interference with the integrity of the caves, access to a mile long section was made available to the public, and a conglomeration of buildings for eating and other facilities were constructed at the cave-head.

In the latter part of the nineteenth century, the Marble Arch Caves lay in part of a large domain owned by the Earl of Enniskillen, and in 1895 he invited Eduard Martel, a famous French speleotogist to explore the caves. Martel used a collapsible wooden boat to explore parts of the cave system. He discovered various caverns and chambers, some of them housing intricate and unique stalactite formations. Since then, other cavers have continued exploring the Marble Arch cave system, discovering new passageways and chambers, and proving that the total length of the different routes through the Marble Arch cave system is about four miles.

To visit the Marble Arch Caves, you turn off the 'Marlbank Scenic Loop' at Legnabrocky, and drive to the reception area at the cave public entrance. A guide will then take you and about twenty others through the part of the cave system which has been developed for public access. A descent of 160 steps brings you down into the caves. There is a surprising coldness in the caves, but the guides are friendly, commenting on various aspects of the cave with knowledge and a humorous sensitivity.

As the tour progresses, part of one's mind is filled with an ominous foreboding, as irregular drops of water from the dark, cavernous, unseen roof, splash on one's head, from where you think God knows what creature may be lurking. This feeling is balanced however by the excitements engendered by walking through the parted waters, like Moses did, and travelling on the boat, where there is barely place for your head to pass underneath the dripping, forbidding interior. Raging, roaring, foaming rivers, rush out of dark, distant caverns, turning away from our route at the last moment. The constant industrious roar of distant rushing water is ever present in the rarified air of the caves, until after travelling about a mile, one returns to the 160 steps an hour and a half later.

The opening of the caves prompted a serious increase in the flow of traffic along the Marlbank Road, and people like my father, who were used to the wide open spaces, would continually utter warnings like, 'It a woeful danger to be near that road now' or 'you'd be run over on that frigging road now.' Although the road was busy with traffic during the daytime, the cars vanished at night, and for Mrs McNulty, Mrs Mary Ellen Maguire, Mammy, George Sheridan, Dennis Curran, John Nolan, and John Gilmurray, it must have been an incredible lonely place at times.

Decline

It was heartbreaking to come home to the 'Mountain' and see the people who I used to know when they were young, become older, grey-haired, slow-moving, stooped. Even my father was showing signs of oldness, because he could no longer walk far, and his body had suffered so much from neglect, wettings, and sleeping in wet clothes, that he was now forced to use a chemical inhaler to allow him to breathe. My brother Farrell had to return to Ireland because my father was no longer able to look after the farm on his own; but Farrell did not live in the 'Mountain'. John Thomas McGovern (Terry) also returned from England to look after their farm when it became too much for his father Terry. But of everyone I went to school with, only Tommy and Patrick Sheerin, and Paschal McGovern (Terry) actually stayed on and lived in the 'Mountain'.

Twice each year, Marian and I would begin the long drive to Holyhead, Stranraer, Fishguard or Swansea on our way home to Ireland and the 'Mountain'. Every trip was a magical journey for me, and as we whipped along the roads towards home even the grass on the green road verges seemed precious. I could hardly wait to partake of my great vices; ice cream, Cidona, buttermilk and wheaten meal bread, which, no matter how hard they tried, they could not recreate in England. Every time Marian and I went home there would be a great welcome for us, not only at home, but in all the other houses in the 'Mountain'. There seemed to be a new phenomenon taking place in the 'Mountain' where large numbers of relatives, sons and daughters, brothers and sisters, and their families, would visit their home place during the summer or Christmas holidays, and the 'Mountain' would come to life once more with parties and get togethers. Even in our own house there would be other visitors like Bridie and Rose and their husbands and children, Pat and Farrell and their girlfriends, and other people that we didn't know at all. It sometimes seemed like the early days, when we were all at home, as we caroused about, singing, telling stories, and giving recitations, and when we all retired to bed the fun would continue with Daddy the ringleader, keeping us singing, telling outlandish stories or relating the most preposterous lies. But the time would quickly arrive when we, like all the other visitors, would have to leave the 'Mountain' for our own places, and when the time came to leave, we all had to go through a terrible trauma. But like myself, the visitors would vanish as if they had never been there, to leave the people of the 'Mountain' to struggle through the dreary and lonely nights of the winter mostly on their own.

My mother became so distressed and depressed with the remoteness and loneliness of the 'Mountain' that she eventually persuaded Marian and me to take her to Wembley. The boat trip from Belfast to Liverpool was the worst I have ever been on, taking fourteen hours to cross plus seven hours waiting to dock, so when we eventually got to Wembley we were fagged out. The journey was so bad that I thought Mammy wouldn't be in a hurry to contemplate a return journey. But she could just not make the adjustment to urban life. She would be looking for the bucket of water to make tea; she wanted a basin to wash in, and she would complain about no trees or grass. She couldn't sleep, or eat right, and she would be waiting out on the pavement at 5.30am as I went to work, saying to me, 'I want to go home,' and after a short time we had no option but to take her back to her home in the 'Mountain'.

After Christmas 1984 I suddenly decided to go home for a few days. There was only my parents there when I arrived, and even though Mammy was up and about, it was clear she was becoming increasingly weak and feeble. I wasn't worried however because my father was looking after her better than I had ever saw him do before. On the last evening of my holiday, I left my father to Blacklion and then returned home, where there was a great roaring fire on, and I made tea for myself and Mammy. It was a lovely, clear, starry night, and I walked out into the fields to experience the atmosphere before I left. The black hulk of Cuilcagh was outlined in the distance, and the contours of the hills and valleys were etched against the clear night sky. And the grey, scary, secretive bog was more or less invisible against the dark backing of Michael Neddy's forest. Periodically, a sheep would bleat plaintively, suddenly lonely as she found herself separated from the others. I could still make out the groove in the steep hill, where Rose, Petie and I used to hurtle down on the wooden wheelbarrow all those years ago. I thought of all the times we had argued with my father, and why he couldn't get the electric like everyone else, and did he not see the advantages of services like water, telephone sewerage, bathrooms, television, and him laughing at us as if we were aliens from outer space. Now I began to reflect; was he all that wrong. While it was very nice, and as Samuel Johnson would say 'commodious' to have a road outside your front door, a level footpath for walking on, and every other imaginable modern convenience, does that matter all that much. I have lived at places in London for ten years without knowing who was living next door, never mind talking to them. Where I live now, even if you had a powerful telescope, you could not see the end of the roofs of houses. And I thought right there, in the freshly frosted fields of our farm, that Mammy and Daddy were far better off than those of us who have opted to spend our days in a modern urban environment. If it was possible then, I would have gladly traded my house and all I possess for the friendliness, peace and solitude of the 'Mountain' and the privilege to live among its people.

Five days later, on January 11 1985, my mother died, with my father and our friend Jim Dolan attending to her last needs. Sadly, none of her children were able to be with her when she passed away, and sadder still she died without knowing what happened to her son Frank, or even her brother John.

Marian and her four year old son Sean and I changed our times of going to Ireland to Easter and summer, and our father would be looking forward eagerly to our coming, always making sure that he had a turkey or a goose cooked to time with our arrival. He would also get someone to cut an ash tree, so that there would be a roaring fire while we were there. He had tremendous interest in travel, and people and places, and he would question me minutely about this place and that, and he would also want to know about such and such a one in England. He had such a knowledge of people and places that God help you if you made a mistake, or tried to bamboozle him and got found out.

The knowledge he had about people around the border area was so great, and him and I spent so much time discussing the people and history of the place, that it fuelled in me a desire to know far more about the area and its people. I would go and see people like Packie Dolan, Jim Dolan, and George Sheridan, to find out more about the people of Glenawley, The Barrs and Glan, and how the history of the place evolved around them. I would talk to 'Terry' who could have been a historian, his knowledge was so vast and accurate, and he had such a way of explaining things from beginning to end, that everytime I went to talk to him I became sorrier and sorrier that I hadn't had such talks with him years earlier. All this knowledge, combined with the visible effect of migration from the 'Mountain' impelled in me a desire that since no one else seemed to be about to put down in writing what life was like in the 'Mountain' in our day, I must do it before it is too late.

Frank Surfaces

Mr Terence McGoven (Terry) died on the 12 of December 1989. I was devastated, and so were the people of the 'Mountain' and surrounding areas. Beth Midler singing 'The Rose' in the film about Janis Joplin, always reminds me of Terry. It is such a lonesome song, but so true, like the 'Mountain' is so much more lonesome without Terry.

Mrs Theresa Dolan, our school teacher, retired in 1991. It seems such a short time since she started on that cold and frosty October morning in the Marble Arches School. Mrs Dolan bore, and with her husband, Jim, brought up six children while in full time teaching. When the Marble Arches School closed in 1959, Mrs Dolan continued to teach in St Mary's School, Killesher, which was much farther away. While I was only taught for a short time by Mrs Dolan, and did not have the privilege of undergoing extended learning with her, all her past pupils speak of her with loyalty and devotion. On her retirement, past pupils from all over the world, myself included, attended a wonderful retirement party and ceremony, held in Vincent McGovern's 'Bush Bar' in Blacklion, in her honour. The regard and affection in which she was held, both by the people of the 'Mountain' and her past pupils, was reflected by the large and happy crowd that attended the function that night. John James McNulty, a past pupil, summed up her standing in the community with the following song.

A Tribute to Theresa Dolan

Good people, ladies and gentlemen all,
A small piece of history tonight we recall
As we give our best wishes that I know are well meant,
To our local school teacher on her retirement.

It is well I remember a long time ago,
When first to the Marlbank hills she did go,
A wee slip of a lassie, with a job to fulfil,
To take up her first post in our school on the hill.

I wonder what passed through her mind on that day
When she took her first look at her pupil display.
There were big ones and small ones, some young and some
old,
Some that were gentle, and a few that were bold.

I was there myself, just as bold as they come,
But I know she has forgiven the rash things I have done.
She settled in well and with life's great plan
Love blossomed for her with a Marlbank man.

And I know that it was a big day in her life
When Tessie and Jim became husband and wife.
In a few short years a dual role she did play,
A mother and teacher, and she did it her way.

She raised a fine family, two girls and four boys,
That brought her few sorrows but a great many joys.
I feel sure if she had to live life over again,
She would want nothing changed, everything the same.

Now that she has entered her new retired life,
No longer a teacher but still a mother and wife.
The hassle is over, from now on life can be fun,
God bless you dear teacher, your job was well done.

Marian, Sean and I still went home twice each year, and sometimes Kevin and his wife, and Rose and her family came too. When we went home in summer 1991 I had decided to investigate more about Frank's whereabouts, thinking he might have written to people he had known in Ireland before he left. Marian, Rose and I went up to Arigna where he had friends called Culls. There was no one there, so we went back the next day. They had heard from him all right, but it was twenty six years earlier.

On Thursday 28 November 1991, I was working on my own in Watford, and when teatime came I was looking at headlines in 'The Daily Mirror'. I was unable to read the small print because my sight had deteriorated, but a photograph on Page 19 electrified me, though strangely I couldn't tell the reason why. I ran a mile to the firm's workshop in Watford and asked someone there to read the article and tell me who was in the photo. It was a photo of Jeremy Beadle presenting Frank McGourty with a cheque for over £394,000 and the article said he lived in Draycott, Derbyshire. None of us where positive that this was Frank, and we waited to see if we would hear more, but when we sent a copy of the photo to Daddy, he said, 'Oh that's the omidan all right.'

None of us were still able to make any headway in finding Frank, and Marian and I decided that if he had not made contact before a certain date, we would go and try to find him. On Saturday 21st of December 1991 the whole of England was covered in a pea-souper of a fog. Marian and I debated for a couple of hours whether to go or not, and eventually we set off up the M1 towards Derbyshire. There were hundreds of cars and lorries involved in an accident at Luton, but we kept going until we came to Junction 25, where we turned off for Derby. We spent the next three hours driving about the narrow roads and lanes of Derbyshire in the fog, trying to find Draycott, which wasn't listed on any road map that we had. We went into shops, called at houses, and stopped policemen, asking if they knew where this man who won the 'pools' lived, but all to no avail. We eventually had to give up when night came, and Marian went across the road to a shop to get cigarettes before we returned to London. As she walked up the street in the fog and darkness she met a middle aged man in a long overcoat coming towards her. She stopped the man and asked him if he happened to know anything about the man who won all the money. He told her he didn't and asked her where she was from. She told him she was from the 'Mountain' in Wheathill, Florencecourt. He then told her he was Frank McGourty, and then wanted to know who she was. A few weeks later he came to live with us at Wembley.

In August 1992, Frank, Marian, Sean, Rose and I, and Kevin and his wife Kate and daughter Karina, all readied ourselves and headed for the boat at Holyhead and Ireland. As our two cars drove on from the Marlbank Road, we could see children from our house, on lookout duty on the Big Hill, running off to tell the people at home that we were approaching. When our house came into view, a long line of people, with the tall lanky figure of my father on the end, were stretched across the newly concreted street. Every one of our brothers and sisters, and their spouses and children were at the house that day, the first time since 1956, and it was sad that Mammy too couldn't have been there to see all her children together once more.

Frank stayed in Ireland, and so Marian, Sean and I still continued our twice yearly excursions home to the 'Mountain', and for me every new time I came, the place seemed more precious and unique than the last. Even though our father wasn't now able to do much himself, he would make sure that everything was ready for us, and Farrell and his wife Carmel would be kept busy in the weeks before our arrival, airing beds, painting and wallpapering. There would be an ash tree cut for firewood, and a fantastic feed would be ready for us as soon as we landed on the street.

The extent of our father's activity was now limited to walking about the street. He had such a tall and identifiable stature that you could recognise him from a tremendous distance. Whenever Marian, Sean and I returned from shopping, visiting or whatever, as soon as we came within sight of the house, we would see his tall frame draped across the yard wall, waiting for us. When we would return in the late evening, we would see this unmistakable figure walking about the yard, waiting for someone to come and keep him company as the evening turned to night.

On Sunday January 15th 1995, the latent danger that mostly remains dormant and concealed beneath the pleasant hills and valleys of the 'Mountain' exploded into life with terrifying and tragic consequences. On Friday 13th of January, a group of students from University College, Dublin, decided to go caving in the Marble Arch cave system, and arrived in the area. On the following Sunday morning ten of the students went to the Marble Arch caves, and some of them proceeded to enter the caves at the 'Cradle Hole'. Those who went into the caves were almost immediately engulfed in a flash flood, and tragically, three of the students lost their lives. The students were, Patrick Brian Kennedy (22) Aughrim, Co Wicklow, Phillip Marshall (20) Salters Green Road, Armagh and Conleth Cormican (21) Howth, Co Dublin. Who can ever understand what the families of the lost cavers must have went through. If there had been an innocence and harmless simplicity felt about the caves of the Marble Arch before then, that was now all gone. The 'Belfast Telegraph' of January 16th reported weather conditions at the rescue site as 'atrocious' as the search for the unfortunate cavers went on. In the same paper, Mrs Pamela Fogg, an experienced caver said 'the conditions where we are now, some hours after the incident are absolutely normal. It is dark, total darkness.' In the *Fermanagh Herald* 12th May 1995, Mr Tim Fogg, an experienced caver with a vast knowledge of the Marble Arch cave system, said about the tragedy of the cavers, 'That on this occasion, I feel they took one step too far.'

It is some relief to learn that this accident could not have happened in the area of the Marble Arch caves open to the public. This area of the caves is protected by early warning flood alarms, and river surge control measures, ensuring that members of the public are protected at all times.

In 1996, Marian, Sean and I went to Ireland, and stayed at home in the 'Mountain' as usual. Our father was physically a bit more feeble, but his vicious wit was unimpaired, and he travelled around to various places in the car with us, ordering us to drop him off at the most unlikely looking destinations, miles from the 'Mountain', but he always managed to get home early next morning.

I decided to walk to the Barr Chapel one day. I walked across the bog to the impenetrable looking Michael Neddy's forest, and managed to find a way through. I took the road through the forest and came out at Johnny John Dan's vacant house (John Melanophy). The house was low and squat, as if it was sinking into the ground with age. There were blinds still on the windows, which were all opaque and coagulated with the impenetrable film of time. One hundred yards away, there stood a house whose contrast with Johnny John Dan's abode would be almost impossible to imagine. This house was an architecturally elaborate, massively imposing two storey, ten roomed house. Except for the roof, the house was completely painted in pink, which would probably be all right in Hollywood, but clashed so aggressively with its surroundings that it discouraged one from long looking at it. And the number of persons populating this precocious looking citadel; one man.

I carried on along the nice tarred road towards Melanophy's. I remembered when Phillip McGovern (Michael Neddy) first made that road, paving it with large limestone and sandstone boulders. To see Melanophy's house was heartbreaking. All that was left were the fallen walls, which were fused into the ground around them. A massive ash tree grew up out of the fireplace. The flagged street, where Francie and Hugh used to create such riotous behaviour on a Sunday morning, shaving, was now obliterated with grass and sections of fallen stones from the walls of the house. Some of the machinery for making butter was still there, the steel cog wheels visible in the ground, and the little river still ran past the gable of the house as it had always done, unperturbed by the ravishes of time.

Bruiser's (Maguire's) house, that I had saw being built, was in ruins. Jimmy's (Maguire's) was the same. On the whole way out to the chapel there was only two houses occupied, and they contained only three people altogether; and at the chapel the water pump no longer worked and the little shop that used to be so busy, was long gone. I returned from the chapel by the route that Mammy and us used to travel to and from mass. The smooth tarred road led me past an array of abandoned houses. Terry Thomas of Oines (McCorry's), Con Kangs, Fitzpatrick's, Tommy Murray's (beside

Dev's) Betty Dev's, Poraghs, Cowan's, Michael Neddy's, Patrick Dolan's, Danny's, until I came to Phil McCaffrey's. Phil still lives near the border, with his wife and son Kieran, but the rest of his children have all gone away to other parts. When I was commenting to Phil on what a disaster it was for the people to be all gone, and houses shut and abandoned, he agreed and said, 'and you'd hardly believe it, but they're trying to bring back the corncrake and the moorhen.'

It was the same story in the 'Mountain'. I went down to Legolagh where Bertie Sheridan used to live, and where my father and I had tea with Bertie's mother all those years ago. There wasn't even a sign of where the house used to be. Frank Sheridan's was gone as well, with nothing there only a pen for sheep. Then I came to George Sheridan's. The smell of decay permeated the land as I walked about it. The farm was now sectioned into strips by dangerous high barb wire fences, while new concrete roads scarified and disfigured the place as they probed the most inaccessible parts of the land. The lovely spring well, that once spurted from the rocks, was unrecognisable from the dirt and filth that littered the area where it used to be. I then went on past the byre, where Roisin, George and I used to milk the cows, then came the diary, the haysheds, and lastly the house, all exhibiting an aura of inevitable doom, yet seemingly crying out to be rescued before it was too late.

I went home and looked for the 'drain', that we had worked so hard on when we were young. It was almost impossible to find it, from the maze of drains and other cuttings that now riddled the bog. The heather and scraws had been wiped off the top of the bog as a result of the turf being cut with a machine, and now the surface of the bog was covered in a layer of fine dust or turf mould. Sean was busy riding his modern motorcycle over this malleable, elastic surface, but when I tried to have a go, riding his motorcycle through the bog, I was actually afraid to do so, because the motorbike now seemed to be such a fearsome and dangerous machine. I went on over to the house, and later in the evening Daddy and us were talking, and I said to him, 'you don't seem to be half as fond of going to the chapel as you used to be! Why is that?' and he replied,

'Arragh quit will ye . . . is it any wonder . . . when a body sees the way the world is going today.'

Despair

On Friday 13th September 1998, Daddy called Marian, Sean and I at 4.30am in order for us to get ready for the journey to London. It was always incredibly harrowing and traumatic for both Daddy and us every time we were leaving for London, and this time it was equally traumatic with our father burying his head in the bedclothes saying that he would be gone next time we came back, and that he would never see us again. Later that day our father left the 'Mountain' for the last time, almost fifty years exactly since we came there in September 1946.

On the 9th of January 1997, a light went out in the 'Mountain' when our nearest neighbour Aggie Dolan passed on. Charlie Maguire, who had lived next to Dolan's died three months later. Marian, Sean, Rose and I went to Ireland at Easter 1997, and stayed next door to our father in Belcoo. Though he was as quickwitted as ever, he wasn't well. He yearned to go up to the 'Mountain' and would stand at the window looking up at it. But the weather was too bad to take him. On the last day of our holidays, he seemed a bit better, and decided this was his chance to get up to the 'Mountain'. But just as we were ready to go, he baulked. He just didn't have the strength, and looked at me forlornly and entreatingly, hoping I could wave a magic wand or do something else to make him better.

We said goodbye to him as he was sleeping, and stole away in the middle of the night to begin our trip back to London. One week later, on 12 April 1997 he passed away. His funeral was an astonishing event. Before we went back to London, Rose, Marian, Sean, Kevin and I went up to see our home for one last time. As we travelled up the road towards home, I was filled with a desire to review just where the 'Mountain' and its people were now. There were only twenty nine people left, and more than half of them were over fifty years of age. Nine were employed away from the 'Mountain' and ten more were either pensioners or retired. There was two children under ten. This highlighted the remarkable fact that there was only one person under the age of fifty residing in the 'Mountain' and occupied making his living there.

Large parts of the 'Mountain' like The Marble Arch Glen, Crossmurrin, or the Hanging Rock are now nature reserves or conservation areas, and Biddy McGrath's house is restored as a sort of museum of the 'Mountain' with various maps and 'Mountain' artefacts on display there. The 'Ulster Way' hikers trail also meanders through the 'Mountain' going up to the top of Cuilcagh from one direction and returning a different way. Cuilcagh and its adjacent surroundings are the scene of constant activity by students of outdoor pursuits, where the rough and remote terrain provides a welcome change for schoolchildren and adults who probably spend most of their life in an urban environment.

There is no school in the 'Mountain' or no communal meeting place, like Mick Maguire's, Sheerin's or 'Terry's' used to be, and even if there was a meeting place, there is no one to go there. Mrs McNulty moved down to Belcoo to live near her son, John James and his family. When Francie 'Connor' died seventeen years ago, his wife Mary Ellen had no option but to leave her home in the 'Mountain' because she was on her own, and there was no one living near her if she got into trouble. She moved to one of the nicest spots you could ask for, with her own little house near Blacklion, between Lough McNean and the hills of Marlbank and Cullentragh. But she wasn't happy. In fact she was heartbroken to leave the 'Mountain' and craved for years to get back there. But eventually her yearning subsided, and she lives contentedly at Blacklion now, close to other members of her family. And Mrs 'Terry' whose home had for many pears provided the heartbeat of the 'Mountain' moved down to Killesher to live with her son Phillip and his wife Mary.

And so I mused as we came to our own house. We all disembarked and dispersed around the fields in different directions, with our memories. The door was unlocked, as it always was. I walked in and passed through the large partition that I had put up twenty five years earlier to keep the draught of Mammy. The great fireplace was wide open, as if it was waiting expectantly to be filled with turf and split ash timber, and kindled. Pope John XXIII beamed down from the throne-shelf that Daddy had made with the hatchet so long ago, and beside the Pope the endearing picture of Jacqueline Bouvier and John Fitzgerald Kennedy, taken on the day he was inaugurated as 'The President of the United States of America'. The bull's head that Kevin stuffed was still in place above the fire, and the statue that Jim McCabe made in Portlaoise Prison was still eminently displayed in the window. But as I walked around, inside the house recalling memories of the times we had when we were growing up, I realised that there was something missing. There was something gone that I would not find no matter how much I looked. I gazed out of the window, and up at the hills to Cuilcagh. Cuilcagh sat there, solid, solemn and inscrutable. The crows, that used to create such a din in the ash trees at the 'Ould House' were gone. The ash trees that they used to rant and rave in had all disappeared. As I walked around I realised that our old home still stood sturdily, but nevertheless, its heart had gone.

Mountain

You were there, Mountain, when I was so young,
Benignly you shadowed my days.
As our valley expanded, grew rich and demanded,
Improvements with farming done much better ways.

I played with an army of children and youth,
And together we all went to school.
We became educated, grown up, cultivated,
And inspired by your presence, we accepted our rule.

But the world of our valley so soon became small,
Insignificant in 'the great plan',
Of man's evolution, and mass distribution,
And soon unfulfilled people were leaving the land.

But Mountain, is that not a tear I see creeping,
Along your escapment so hostile and cold.
Like the tears in my heart that are steadily weeping,
For a people gone forever, as you and I grow old.

I walked out of the house, and we all drove off. As we were driving down the Marlbank Road, slowly leaving the 'Mountain' behind us; a 'Mountain' that was now filled with fallen walls and vacant places, I was wondering whether it was finished, whether it too had lost its heart. In the distance, a dog sauntered leisurely across the road. A young child, accompanied by her mother, came from their house and followed the dog into the rocky field at the foot of Reid's Rock. The child bent down to pick daffodils from underneath a tree. I thought to myself then that the 'Mountain' was indeed severely wounded, but it had not lost it's heart. Not yet.